A BOOK OF WALES

[*R. Cecil Hughes*

SNOWDON

A Book of Wales

EDITED BY

D. M. and E. M. LLOYD

Collins

LONDON AND GLASGOW

GENERAL EDITOR G. F. MAINE

First Published, 1953
Reprinted, 1953
" 1954
" 1961
" 1964

To
RHIANNON

Printed in Great Britain by
COLLINS CLEAR-TYPE PRESS

ACKNOWLEDGMENTS

Cordial acknowledgments are here tendered to the following authors, owners of copyright, publishers and literary agents who have given permission for poems, prose passages and photographs to appear in these pages.

THE RICHARDS PRESS, LTD., for passage herein entitled *An Enchanted Land*, from *Autobiography* by Arthur Machen.

SAUNDERS LEWIS and J. D LEWIS & SONS LTD., for the poem, *The Eagles Depart* by Saunders Lewis; passage herein entitled, *A Vineyard Placed in My Care* from *Buchedd Garmon*, by Saunders Lewis and passage, *The Essence of Welsh Poetry* from the essay of the same name by Saunders Lewis.

THE HONOURABLE SOCIETY OF CYMMRODORION for extract from the poem *The Swan of Syfaddon Lake* by Dafydd ap Gwilym translated by Sir H. Idris Bell; passage, *Owain Myfyr* by R. T. Jenkins from *The History of the Honourable Society of Cymmrodorion*; extract from *The Hirlas Poem* by Prince Owain Cyfeiliog translated by T. Gwynn Jones.

JONATHAN CAPE LTD., MACMILLAN CO. and THE EXECUTORS OF THE COPYRIGHT OWNER of *Kilvert's Diary*, for extracts herein entitled *Oh Aberedw, Aberedw* and *A Hermit and his Haunts.*

IDRIS DAVIES and J. M. DENT & SONS LTD., for the poem *The Places of my Boyhood* from *Gwalia Deserta.*

IDRIS DAVIES and FABER & FABER LTD., for poems *Rhymney* and *In Gardens in the Rhondda* from *Tonypandy and Other Poems*; *Mrs. Evans, fach* and *Capel Hebron* from *The Angry Summer.*

A. G. PRYS-JONES for the poems *St. Govan* from *Poems of Wales*; *Henry Morgan's March on Panama* and translation of *Snowdrops*, a poem by A. E. Jones, both from *Green Places: Poems of Wales.*

LADY HUGHES PARRY and SIR IFAN AB OWEN EDWARDS for passages by Sir O. M. Edwards herein entitled *Tregaron Bog* from *Yn y Wlad*; *Llanuwchllyn Old Chapel* from *O'r Bala i Geneva*; *Owain Glyn Dŵr* from *Y Llynnoedd Llonydd*; *The Soul of a Nation* from *Er Mwyn Cymru.*

SIR H. IDRIS BELL and THE CLARENDON PRESS for translations published in *The Development of Welsh Poetry*: *To the River Clegyr*, from the Welsh poem by Iorwerth C. Peate; *A Love Song* from the Welsh poem *Eifion Wyn* by Eliseus Williams; *I Gaze Across the Distant Hills* from the Welsh hymn by Williams of Pantycelyn; *Lo, Between the Myrtles* from the Welsh hymn by Ann Griffiths.

DAVID BELL for the translation *The Owls* from the Welsh poem of R. Williams Parry.

PROFESSOR J. LLOYD-JONES for translations from his *Rhŷs Memorial Lecture* (P.B.A., vol. XXXIV): *Bardsey of the Saints* from the Welsh poem by Meilyr; *My Choice* from the Welsh poem by Prince Hywel ab Owain Gwynedd; *A Lament* from the Welsh poem by Dafydd Benfras; *Winter-Time* from the Welsh poem by Bleddyn Fardd.

PROFESSOR GWYN JONES for passage *Mabinogi and Edda* from essay of the same name. Also PROFESSOR THOMAS JONES in collaboration with Professor Gwyn Jones for passage herein entitled *Blodeuwedd* from *The Mabinogion.*

A. O. H. JARMAN and PLAID CYMRU for passage herein entitled *On the Act of Union* from *The Historical Basis of Welsh Nationalism.*

THE GREGYNOG PRESS for extract from the poem *The Ballad of the Welsh Buccaneers* by Lieut. William Peilyn translated by Alfred Percival Graves; extracts from *The Vision of the Sleeping Bard* by Ellis Wynne translated by T. Gwynn Jones herein entitled *At the Gate*, *Seeming Piety* and *Arrant Thieves.*

REV. R. S. THOMAS for the poem *A Peasant.*

HUGH EVANS & SONS LTD., for extracts herein entitled *The Little Old Cottages*, *Knitting*, *Beti Jones's Supper*, from *Cwm Eithin* by Hugh Evans translated by E. Morgan Humphreys as *The Gorse Glen.*

THE TRUSTEES OF SIR HENRY JONES for passages herein entitled *A Country Home*, *A Domestic Scene* and *Church-Membership* from *Old Memories*; passages herein entitled *The True and the Good* and *A Friendly Universe* from *A Faith that Enquires.*

PROFESSOR W. J. GRUFFYDD for the poem *Gwladys Rhys.*

JACK JONES and HAMISH HAMILTON LTD., for passage herein entitled *The Kingdoms of the Earth* from *Off to Philadelphia in the Morning* by Jack Jones; passage herein entitled *Dowlais—Two Generations* from *Unfinished Journey* by Jack Jones.

COLONEL RICHARD C. RUCK, METHUEN & CO., and A. P. WATT & SON, for passages herein entitled *Grinding Poverty* and *An Old Quarryman* from *From Hand to Hand*, translation of Welsh novel *O Law i Law* by T. Rowland Hughes.

DAFYDD JENKINS for passage *The Court Cupboard* translated from a Welsh story of D. J. Williams.

SIEGFRIED SASSOON for the poem *At the Grave of Henry Vaughan.*

UNIVERSITY OF WALES PRESS for extract from *Gruffydd Jones of Llanddowror*, so herein entitled, by R. T. Jenkins.

METHUEN & CO. LTD., for passage herein entitled *The Lady of Llwyn Madoc* from *The South Wales Squires* by Herbert M. Vaughan.

Dr. Thomas Jones, C.H., and Oxford University Press for passage from *Lloyd George*, so herein entitled, by Thomas Jones.

Hughes a'i Fab Publishers Ltd., for poems *Chairing of the Bard* and *War Epitaph*, translated by Sir H. Idris Bell from the Welsh poems of R. Williams Parry and published in *Welsh Poems of the 20th Century in English Verse;* extract herein entitled *Avallon* from the poem *Ymadawiad Arthur* by T. Gwynn Jones.

Walter Dowding for the poem *I'r Hen Iaith a'i Chaneuon*; passage herein entitled *Sisters* translated by Walter Dowding from a short story by Kate Roberts from *A Summer Day and Other Stories.*

Dr. Wyn Griffith for passage herein entitled *Old Age* translated from a short story by Kate Roberts, published in *A Summer Day and Other Stories.*

Dylan Thomas and Pearn, Pollinger & Higham Ltd., for the poem from *Quite Early One Morning* by Dylan Thomas, so herein entitled.

Routledge & Kegan Paul Ltd., for poems *To My Motherland* and *At the Eisteddfod* from *Works of Sir Lewis Morris.*

J. D. Lewis & Sons Ltd., for the poem *Cymru* by D. Gwenallt Jones, herein entitled *Wales*; poems by T. H. Parry-Williams, *Dychwelyd* herein entitled *The Return*, and *Cynefin* herein entitled *Affinity*; poem *Adar Rhiannon* by D. Gwenallt Jones herein entitled *Birds of Rhiannon.*

Editions Poetry London Ltd., for extract from poem *In Praise of a Girl* by Huw Morris translated by Gwyn Williams in *The Rent that's due to Love.*

Mrs. W. H. Davies and Jonathan Cape Ltd., for *Days that have been* from *The Collected Poems of W. H. Davies.*

Dylan Thomas, J. H. Dent & Sons Ltd. and New Directions Inc., for the poem *Fern Hill*, from *Deaths and Entrances* by Dylan Thomas.

Waldo Williams for poem *Cofio* herein entitled *Remembrance.*

Mrs. M. P. Rhys for the poem, *Cymru* by E. Prosser Rhys, herein entitled *Wales.*

Miss Collins and Dodd Mead & Co., Inc., for the poem *Antichrist or the Reunion of Christendom* from *The Collected Poems of G. K. Chesterton.*

Aberystwyth Borough Council for the aerial photograph of Aberystwyth.

D. B. Hutton for the photographs: Harlech Castle; The Menai Straits; South Stack Lighthouse, Holyhead; Llyn Idwal; Moel Siabod and River Llugwy; The Central Buttress, Tryfan.

CONTENTS

PLACES

HISTORY—LITERARY AND GENERAL

PASTORAL AND INDUSTRIAL

PEOPLE, GREAT AND SMALL

HUMOUR, ROMANCE, AND SENTIMENT

CUSTOMS, BELIEFS, AND REFLECTIONS ON LIFE

POEMS, SONGS, BALLADS

RELIGIOUS AND PHILOSOPHICAL

ILLUSTRATIONS

INTRODUCTION

This anthology of prose and verse relating to Wales has been planned as a companion volume to the revised edition of *A Book of Scotland*, a pattern which has been closely followed in the arrangement of the matter. The selections have been chosen from three main sources: (*a*) translations of prose and poetry composed in the Welsh language; (*b*) compositions in English (or in a few instances translations from Latin) by Welshmen; (*c*) writings by Englishmen on Welsh themes. Each of these bodies of literature has its own distinctive qualities, while at the same time there is a richness and wide variety within each.

The earliest extant poetry in the Welsh language dates from the sixth century. It arose from the grim struggle between the Brythonic Celts and the Angles of Northumbria. Several of the place-names in these heroic odes and elegies, by Taliesin and Aneirin, betray their Northern origin far beyond the confines of Wales. For a thousand years, however, until the break-up of the native social order in the Tudor Age, these poems were among the greatest unifying forces in Welsh literature, life and ideals. They were the *Hengerdd*, the 'Old Song,' and constituted the models of succeeding generations of apprentice poets who sedulously studied poems written in this tradition, and who sought not only to imitate their turns of phrase and metrical pattern, but also to uphold the ideal of manhood which was presented and extolled in these compositions. For a thousand years the leaders of Welsh life were represented as lineal descendants and spiritual heirs of the sixth century Owain ab Urien; the valour and loyalty of succeeding generations of Welsh youths were aroused by the eulogy of the men who went to Catraeth (Catterick) and who disdained to flee when confronted by overwhelming odds. It was a dual ideal of skilful and ruthless contest in the field against enemies who threatened the native society, combined with a love of the social graces, deference to women, generosity, a cultivated appreciation of music and well-spoken words cunningly arranged in a traditional verse pattern or in colourful and lively prose, and a proud attachment to the native soil and community. The Welsh community was regarded as a closely woven network of families, binding countless generations and the whole of Wales into a meaningful unity, not necessarily into one state, but a unity of kinship, language, law, social pattern, and literary and historical tradition. Delight in mountains, solitude, and wild expanses, is singularly rare in Welsh literature before the eighteenth century; love of nature being usually expressed in a feeling for the intimate, for woodland, the play of light on running water, the inhabited valley, pastureland, and the haunts of men. Even Prince Hywel ab Owain Gwynedd, who sang of his love for the wide expanses of mountain and shore in Merioneth, hastens to include also his country's habitations and settlements among the objects of his affection.

The best descriptions of Welsh scenery have been written in English, and it is not irrelevant to mention in this connection the present-day controversy regarding the proposed hydro-electric schemes in Snowdonia. It is no accident that a good deal of the opposition has come from English lovers of natural beauty. Local opinion is very divided and uncertain, not because of any philistine disregard for the splendour of the scenery, but due to a haunting fear that the survival of a Welsh community among these mountains is rendered precarious by the present inadequacy of economic means necessary to ensure its survival.

The pattern of Welsh life underwent far-reaching

changes from the Tudor period to the eighteenth century. In Wales the Tudors could do no wrong. They had removed the disabilities which had weighed so heavily on the Welsh people since the fall of the native dynasty in 1282, and which had been particularly severe after the suppression of Glyn Dŵr's Rising early in the fifteenth century. The Tudors had extended full citizen rights and the protection of the law to all 'loyal' Welshmen, with full freedom of movement throughout the realm. The hurt to the nation's pride had been assuaged, and, much to the disgust of Pistol and his ilk, favours were heaped on Fluellyn and his compatriots by the reigning scions of Owain Tudor of Penmynydd. These favours and prospects of advancement, however, caused a gradually widening rift in Welsh society. Wealthier families attached themselves more and more to English interests and ambitions, and in time became a caste apart, severed more and more from the mass of the people in language, religious affiliations and culture. The significance of modern Welsh history has been the increasing ability of these masses, with no central focus of national life such as can be supplied by a capital city, or by native institutions of higher learning, and in spite of meagre material resources, to re-integrate themselves into a new pattern of nationhood, and to throw up new leaders in education, religion, literature, and politics.

The situation in our own day is again changing rapidly. A soul-less cosmopolitanism is making ugly inroads into the life of Wales, but is not going to gain an uncontested victory. The young Welsh University has fostered a new Welsh scholarship and a literary renaissance which have meant a rediscovery of our native heritage with its fourteen centuries of literary tradition. A new synthesis is being created from the finer qualities of the democratic Wales of post-Tudor days and the cultivated aristocratic traditions of mediaeval Wales. The pride born of this new knowledge of the rock from which we are hewn should serve us well in the struggle against the disintegrating forces of modern vulgarity. All three phases of Welsh life and thought, the mediaeval, the post-Tudor and the contemporary, are reflected in the passages translated from Welsh which are to be found in this book.

The earliest effort at literary composition in English by a Welshman, of which we have any record, is very much a *tour-de-force.* It is an eulogistic poem to the Virgin by an Oxford student, composed in the fifteenth century with the express purpose of refuting a taunt by an English fellow-student that the Welsh had no learned art of poetry. The challenger was certainly on weak ground, for Wales had but newly seen the amazing achievement of Dafydd ap Gwilym, our greatest individual poetic genius, and it was also the *grand siècle* of technical accomplishment in Welsh verse. Not before the social changes of the Tudor age, however, was the English language to be widely used as a literary medium in Wales. Members of the landed gentry, like Sir John Wynne of Gwydir in the North, and George Owen of Henllys, in the South, proud of their position and lineage, and of the Welsh community of which they felt themselves still to be a vital part, but at the same time attracted by the new ' civility ' of which the Tudor court in London was the centre, began to express themselves in the tongue and in the manner of that court. But Wales was not to make its earliest great contribution to English literature and thought until the next generation, when the deracination of the land-owning and (by this time) largely English-speaking families was more advanced. In the case of Henry Vaughan, we know that he spoke Welsh throughout his long life in the delectable ' Silurian ' countryside, and that his poetry is not uninfluenced by Welsh literary tradition, but Lord Herbert of Cherbury, and his saintly younger brother, George Herbert, even more so, were at a further remove from the culture which their ancestors had long patronised. Claims are, indeed, sometimes made for the inclusion of Traherne, Carew, and even Donne, among 'Welsh' authors, but they are based on ancestry alone, and on qualities claimed to have been derived from ancestors, for it would be hard to prove that they had any personal awareness of belonging themselves to any Welsh community.

There is no continuity of tradition that can be described as an Anglo-Welsh literary stream until we reach the present century. There are individual poets such as Dyer in the eighteenth century, and in the Victorian age Sir Lewis Morris, a descendant of a versatile Anglesey namesake who is well represented in this book. Lord Herbert of Cherbury's contribution to world thought has been more than rivalled by that of Dr. Richard Price and by Robert Owen, to name only those whose significance is beyond dispute.

With the mingling and movement of population which have accompanied the growth of modern industrialism, and also with the spread of popular education in the English language, the last hundred years have seen a great linguistic change. For the first time in fifteen hundred years the Welsh-speaking people are a minority in Wales. Large English-speaking communities have grown, particularly in Monmouth and Glamorgan, although in intonation and idiom the substratum of Welsh is often prominent enough. The present century has seen a new and vigorous literary movement which within the scheme of this volume can be but meagrely represented. The vitality of Anglo-Welsh literature in our generation is matched only by its variety, but the question remains whether it can ever forge a link between succeeding generations in the way that literature in Welsh has always done. It is the product of a generation at only a short remove from spoken Welsh, a generation still rich in peculiar ways of thought and expression, and in its awareness of being a separate community. It is difficult to foresee how these qualities can, in the world of today, long survive the loss of the native language. The selections from contemporary Anglo-Welsh writers in this book have been chosen mainly from the work of some of those who have been moved to write by feelings arising from their attitude (be it what it may) to the native land and community, either in their current aspects, or their historic past, or both. It is not our concern to question the possibility that individual writers of Welsh extraction may have it in them to break the links that bind them to their country of origin, and yet enrich English literature greatly, but theirs is no prominent place in 'A Book of Wales.'

Welsh people and scenes begin to appear in purely English literature also during the Tudor Age. Admiration of the dynasty, together with the new inter-relationship between the peoples of the newly united countries awoke an interest in the country whence the Tudors had sprung. Churchyard and Drayton, and to a lesser extent, even Spenser and Shakespeare, reflect this new interest. 'Owen Glendower' is nobly portrayed, and the Arthurian legends find a new vogue. The rapid influx of Welshmen of all classes into London provoked the antipathy of many people of whom Pistol is a type. This ill-natured sentiment persists in the *Wallography* and in much seventeenth-century pamphlet literature directed against 'Taffydom.' But Shakespeare's good-natured amusement at Fluellyn's defective but colourful and vigorous use of English, his reckless valour, and inordinate national and family pride also set a fashion, which can be traced through Ben Jonson, Sir Thomas Overbury, and the seventeenth-century burlesque, down to Tobias Smollett.

The next great age of English literary interest in Wales begins with the appearance of 'gothic' taste and is continued through the Romantic Revival. No one in the eighteenth century knew more of our ancient literature than Dr. Johnson's "poor Evan Evans," a scholar who corresponded with Bishop Percy and Thomas Gray on matters of Welsh literary history. The closing of the Continent by the long wars against France, together with the cult of the picturesque and the primitive, led to the establishment of the 'Tour into Wales' by English gentlemen, who were often accompanied by artists. Some of these gentlemen and artists were of Welsh origin, but it was not always so. The new fashion has left us, as a precious legacy, not only the landscapes of Paul Sandby, 'Warwick' Smith, and Rowlandson, to name only a few, but also an extensive body of tourist literature, from the days of Pennant down to the time of Malkin and Coxe, and culminating at a still later period in George Borrow's much read *Wild Wales.* Pennant, Malkin and Coxe knew their Wales, past and present, far more intimately, and could present a far more balanced judgment than the violently anti-Papistical and anti-Methodistical Borrow with his absurd prejudices. But the irascible East-Anglian has more readers today than all the other tourists combined. Welshmen read him with mingled admiration and exasperation. In his book they see a superbly clear but grotesquely distorting mirror turned towards their country. His prejudices, however, are sometimes in our favour, and sometimes against us, so it could have been worse! In the wake of the early tourist literature came the interest in Wales shown by the great English Romantic writers, which was followed by that of Tennyson, who visited the Caerleon district in connection with his interest in Arthurian themes, and of Matthew Arnold, whose rediscovery of Celtic literature was an event of European importance. The crowning glory of the English Romantic interest in our country, however, is found in the sublime passages of meditative description inspired by Welsh scenery, particularly at Tintern and

Snowdon, which are among the great achievements of Wordsworth's muse.

The editor of the Scottish volume on which this book is modelled, expressed in his foreword the hope that his selections would "reflect something of the soul of Scotland." We have, so far, hesitated in this introduction to speak of the soul of a nation. A few years ago, at a conference of Welsh students of philosophy, it was strongly held that it is meaningless to speak of a nation's soul as if it were a metaphysical entity, or in the sense in which we may speak of the soul of a man. However, as the discussion proceeded, it became less and less clear what was meant by the soul of a man, so much of the edge was taken off the initial objection to the belief in a nation's soul! Included in this book is a translation of one of the most widely known passages by the best loved of modern Welsh writers, the late Sir Owen M. Edwards. He knew well enough what he meant when he said that Wales has a soul. He was not worried by metaphysical niceties, and neither was he thinking in terms of racial purity. On racialism we can do no better than quote Sir Ifor Williams, doyen of Welsh scholarship today, who once remarked that the people of England and of Wales are formed of the same racial ingredients, although not necessarily in the same proportions, but that the same is true of Christmas cake and plum pudding, only that one has been baked and the other boiled! The varying racial proportions probably have some bearing on national temperament, modes of feeling and artistic gifts, but in the main our distinctive national characteristics are the fruits of age-long common experiences, the results of having inhabited the same corner of the earth, the incalculable effects of the natural scene and the affinities born of it, of having spoken a common tongue, created our own institutions, shared the same responsibilities, felt the same community sense, and borne the effects of the same national development.

We can still recognise ourselves in the people of Giraldus's Wales of the twelfth century—our faults and our good qualities, though much has changed. The Wales of Giraldus and that of Jack Jones are peopled by the same warm-hearted impulsive folk, often contentious, susceptible to the appeal of oratory, relishers of the finely-turned and bold phrase, and passionately attached to the local community and surroundings. They realise themselves in the interplay of personal relations within the neighbourhood and country to which they feel they belong, and have a deep distrust of any impersonal officialdom, privilege, or remote control. A shrewdness and distrust of vague sentiment are combined with a responsiveness to the appeal of music and clear forcible expression in verse, prose or in pulpit or platform speech. Here is no 'Celtic twilight,' but a love of clarity, brilliance, distinct colours and striking antithesis. These are our prevailing modes.

D. M. *and* E. M. Lloyd

PROLOGUE

All, all is sacred, and the heavenly muse
Of poetry has crowned these lofty hills,
And if my partial strains of patriot love
May aught avail, I bid them now reveal
Our kindred old, and fathers we revere,
Whose names no more we know, whose fame is silent
Mist curling around the age-old mountain peaks—
How on these heights on many a flaming noon
They sang or sorrowed as they found life's way
Bitter or sweet. And may we in our turn
Leave on these slopes a wreath of memories,
Our sighs and meditations steeped in wonder,
For ever to be treasured by the breeze
Or dying ever in the rising mist.
What then is Jacob's Well? In every stream
That flows there shines the image of One greater
Than Jacob. My fathers crossed this river too,
And heavenly breezes sped along its banks,
The moonlight, and the star of many a dawn
Miraculous, the sun, and thunderstorm.
All the world is sacred: and every height
Supports an angel of eternal song;
And the Ægean shores are only part,
A portion of the realm of poesy:
Homer ne'er sang of yonder hills we see,—
He saw them not! What would old Snowdon be
Had she but sheltered once his cradle, pray?
An Ida still more glorious in his song:
A god-like daylight breaking on her crest!

ISLWYN (WILLIAM THOMAS, 1832-78)
translated from the Welsh by
D. M. LLOYD

[R. Cecil Hughes

CONWAY CASTLE

[A. W. Hutton

HARLECH CASTLE

[*Reece Winstone*

CHEPSTOW CASTLE

Places

TINTERN ABBEY

Lines composed a few miles above Tintern Abbey, on revisiting the banks of the Wye during a tour, July 13, 1798.

Five years have passed; five summers, with the length
Of five long winters! and again I hear
These waters, rolling from their mountain-springs
With a sweet inland murmur.—Once again
Do I behold these steep and lofty cliffs,
Which on a wild secluded scene impress
Thoughts of more deep seclusion; and connect
The landscape with the quiet of the sky.
The day is come when I again repose
Here, under this dark sycamore, and view
These plots of cottage-ground, these orchard-tufts,
Which, at this season, with their unripe fruits,
Among the woods and copses lose themselves,
Nor, with their green and simple hue, disturb
The wild green landscape. Once again I see
These hedge-rows, hardly hedge-rows, little lines
Of sportive wood run wild; these pastoral farms
Green to the very door; and wreathes of smoke
Sent up, in silence, from among the trees,
With some uncertain notice, as might seem,
Of vagrant dwellers in the houseless woods,
Or of some hermit's cave, where by his fire
The hermit sits alone.

Though absent long,
These forms of beauty have not been to me,
As is a landscape to a blind man's eye:
But oft, in lonely rooms, and mid the din

Of towns and cities, I have owed to them,
In hours of weariness, sensations sweet,
Felt in the blood, and felt along the heart,
And passing even into my purer mind
With tranquil restoration:—feelings too
Of unremembered pleasure; such, perhaps,
As may have had no trivial influence
On that best portion of a good man's life;
His little, nameless, unremembered acts
Of kindness and of love. Nor less, I trust,
To them I may have owed another gift,
Of aspect more sublime; that blessed mood,
In which the burthen of the mystery,
In which the heavy and the weary weight
Of all this unintelligible world
Is lighten'd:—that serene and blessed mood,
In which the affections gently lead us on,
Until, the breath of this corporeal frame,
And even the motion of our human blood
Almost suspended, we are laid asleep
In body, and become a living soul:
While with an eye made quiet by the power
Of harmony, and the deep power of joy,
We see into the life of things. . . .

WILLIAM WORDSWORTH (1770-1850)

PIERCEFIELD

The present proprietor has spared no expense to render the mansion of Piercefield suitable to the grandeur and beauty of the surrounding scenery: all the apartments unite harmony of proportion with costliness of decoration, and Piercefield scarcely yields to any house in this kingdom in taste and splendour. . . .

In the composition of the scenery, the meandering

Wy(e), the steep cliffs, and the fertile peninsula of Lancaut form the striking characteristics.

The Wy, which is everywhere seen from a great elevation, passes between Wynd Cliff and the Banagor rocks, winds round the peninsula of Lancaut, under a chain of stupendous cliffs, is lost in its sinuous course, again appears in a straighter line at the foot of the Lancaut rocks, and flows under the majestic ruins of Chepstow castle, towards the Severn.

The rocks are broken into an infinite variety of fantastic shapes, and scattered at different heights and in different positions; they start abruptly from the river, swell into gentle acclivities, or hang on the summits of the hills; here they form a perpendicular rampart, there jet into enormous projections, and impend over the water.

But their dizzy heights and abrupt precipices are softened by the woods, which form a no less conspicuous feature in the romantic scenery; they are not meagre plantations placed by art, but a tract of forests scattered by the hand of nature. In one place they expand into open groves of large oak, elm, and beech; in another they form a shade of timber trees, copses, and underwood, hiding all external objects, and wholly impervious to the rays of the sun; they start from the crevices of the rocks, feather their edges, crown their summits, clothe their sides, and fill the intermediate hollows with a luxuriant mass of foliage. . . .

The peninsula of Lancaut, on the opposite bank, in the midst of these impending rocks, and hanging woods, is a farm in the highest state of cultivation. The ground swells gradually from the edge of the water towards the isthmus, on which stands the farm-house, backed by rugged rocks; open groves and single trees are scattered over the meadows and cornfields, and the margin of the river is skirted with a mantle of verdure and fringed with a range of fine elms.

On entering the grounds at the extremity of the village

of St. Arvan's, and at the bottom of Wynd Cliff, the walk leads through plantations, commanding on the right a distant view of the Severn and the surrounding country; it penetrates into a thick forest, and conducts to the Lover's Leap, where the Wind Cliff is seen towering above the river in all its height and beauty, and below yawns a deep and wooded abyss. It waves almost imperceptibly in a grand outline, on the brow of the majestic amphitheatre of cliffs impending over the Wy, opposite to the peninsula of Lancaut, then crosses the park, runs through the groves and thickets, and again joins the bank of the Wy, at that reach of the river which stretches from Lancaut to the castle of Chepstow.

From the Lover's Leap the walk is carried through a thick mantle of forests, with occasional openings, which seem not the result of art or design, but the effect of chance or nature, and seats placed where the spectator may repose and view at leisure the scenery above, beneath and around. This

> *bower'y walk*
> *Of covert close, where scarce a speck of day*
> *Falls on the lengthen'd gloom,*

is consonant to the genius of Piercefield; the screen of wood prevents the uniformity of a bird's eye view, and the imperceptible bend of the amphitheatre conveys the spectator from one part of this fairy region to another without discovering the gradations. Hence the Wy is sometimes concealed or half obscured by overhanging foliage, at others, wholly expanding to view, is seen sweeping beneath in a broad and circuitous channel; hence at one place the Severn spreads in the midst of a boundless expanse of country, and on the opposite side to the Wy; at another, both rivers appear on the same side, and the Severn seems supported on the level summit of the cliffs which form the banks of the Wy. Hence the same objects present themselves in different aspects and with varied accompaniments; hence the magic transition from the impervious gloom of the forests to open groves; from the meadows and lawns, to rocks and precipices, and from the mild beauties of English landscape to the wildness of Alpine scenery.

The summit of Wynd Cliff, which towers above the northern extremity of the grounds, commands in one point of view the whole extent of this interesting scenery. As I stood on the brow of this precipice, I looked down on the fertile peninsula of Lancaut, surrounded with rocks and forests, contemplated the hanging woods, rich lawns, and romantic cliffs of Piercefield, the castle and town of Chepstow, and traced the Wy, sweeping in the true outline of beauty, from the Banagor crags to its junction with the Severn, which spreads into an aestuary and is lost in the distant ocean.

A boundless extent of country is seen in every direction from this commanding eminence, comprehending not less than nine counties; in the midst of this expanse, I principally directed my attention to the subject of my Tour, which now drew to a conclusion; I traced with pleasing satisfaction, not unmixed with regret, the luxuriant vallies and romantic hills of this interesting county, which I had traversed in various directions; but I dwelt with peculiar admiration on the majestic rampart which forms its boundary to the west, and extends in one grand and broken outline, from the banks of the Severn to the Black Mountains

Where the broken landscape, by degrees
Ascending, roughens into rigid hills;
O'er which the Cambrian Mountains, like far clouds
That skirt the blue horizon, dusky rise.

(Thomson's *Spring*)

WILLIAM COXE (1747-1828)
An Historical Tour in Monmouthshire (1801)

AN ENCHANTED LAND

I shall always esteem it as the greatest piece of fortune that has fallen to me that I was born in that noble, fallen Caerleon-on-Usk in the heart of Gwent. . . . The older I grow, the more firmly am I convinced that anything I may have accomplished in literature is due to the fact that when my eyes were first opened in early childhood they had before them the vision of an enchanted land. As soon as I saw anything I saw Twm Barlwm, that mystic tumulus, the memorial of peoples that dwelt in that region before the Celts left the Land of Summer. This guarded the southern limit of the great mountain wall in the west; a little northward was Mynydd Maen—the Mountain of the Stone—a giant, rounded billow; and still to the north mountains, and on fair, clear days one could see the pointed summit of the Holy Mountain by Abergavenny. It would shine, I remember, a pure blue in the far sunshine; it was a mountain peak in a fairy tale. And then to eastward the bedroom window of Llanddewi Rectory looked over hill and valley, over high woods quivering with leafage like the beloved Zacynthus of Ulysses, away to the forest of Wentwood, to the church tower on the hill above Caerleon. Through a cleft one might see now and again a bright yellow glint of the Severn Sea, and the cliffs of Somerset beyond. And hardly a house in sight in all the landscape, look where you would. Here the gable of a barn, here a glint of a whitewashed farmhouse, here blue wood smoke rising from an orchard grove, where an old cottage was snugly hidden: but only so much if you knew where to look. And of nights, when the dusk fell and the farmer went his rounds, you might chance to see his lantern glimmering, a very spark on the hillside. This was all that showed in a vague, dark world; and the only sounds were the faint distant barking of the sheepdog and the melancholy cry of the owls from the border of the brake.

ARTHUR MACHEN (1863-1947)
Autobiography

THE EAGLES DEPART

I, Paulinus am old, at fifty I'm old,
And when I peer to the future it is not to this world I
look;
My days here below almost over,
Enough for me to obey and to bide my hour.
And when I look back I behold how vainly I've striven.
Heavy my days have been,
Memories of youth remain my only delight.
Four years old was I in my father's arms in Caerleon
Gazing at the host of Maxen and Helen the Arvonian
Empress
Marching out of my city,
Under the eyes of the city,
Over the ringing stones of Sarn Helen out of the sound
of the city.
Said my father, behold the world we have known is no
more,
The long-established motion of the sun is no more,
Stability we shall know no more,
No more the carving of stones for the long-lasting
dwellings,
The endless ages of Rome and her peace are no more.
And my father wept.
But my mother replied:
When Rome's tranquillity is gone, the Peace of our Lord
shall stand.
The daily oblations of Christian priests are the stones of
our city's construction,
And our civilisation shall stand united and paved by the
unshaken Creed.

Truly she spoke. For then,
Bereft of centurions and legions and the eagle banners,
And left in our weakness to hold the border,
The barbarians venturing nearer and ever nearer across the land,
And the Scots ever bolder and bolder from over the sea,
Yet in that hour it was that learning and piety
Blossomed like late spring in our land;
To our midst in Dyved and Gwent and Glamorgan
Came a constant stream of sages, teachers of letters and law
From the ravaged lands to the east and the burnt-out cities.
Our lime-washed churches and schools bloom like the cherry-tree's blossom,
And Ambrosius, lord of Caerleon and the South, eagerly welcomes
The heirs of Quintilian and Virgil, the fathers of language,
And the dejected pious disciples of Jerome of Bethlehem.

SAUNDERS LEWIS (1893-)
translated from the Welsh by
D. M. LLOYD

ARTHUR'S FEAST AT CAERLEON

And after restoring order to those countries, on the approach of spring, Arthur returned to the island of Britain. And after his return, with great joy he arranged to hold a court in Britain, in which he would wear on his head the crown of his rightful kingdom, and to summon to that feast all the kings and princes which he had rendered subject to him. And it was his intention to encourage all, with good cheer, to re-establish a state of peace among themselves throughout their domains. And after he had made his mind known to his nearest friends, they took counsel together, and decided to hold that feast in Caerleon-on-Usk in Glamorgan. For that was the fairest place in the isle of Britain, and richest in gold and silver and other treasures, and the most worthy place to honour a festivity of so great renown. For on the one side of the city was that noble river bearing the ships to the city laden with the kings from the four quarters of the world, and on the other side were the green fields and the groves and the forests for its adornment, and within the city and its ramparts were the magnificent houses resplendent with gold. And this was the second city to be compared with Rome for the beauty of its houses, and the abundance of its wealth of gold and silver, and its high dignity. There were two notable churches in the city, one in honour of Julius the Martyr, and containing a nunnery, and the other dedicated to Aaron his companion, containing a house of canons, which was the third seat of an archbishop in the island of Britain. And in that day Caerleon was adorned with two hundred schools with teachers of numerous arts.

The provisions gathered there were well sufficient to honour even so great a feast. . . . And after the assembly had gathered, the three archbishops were called to the court to array the king in the royal robe and to place the crown of the kingdom on his head. The celebration of Mass was entrusted to Dyvrig the Archbishop, for it was at his archepiscopal seat that the court was held. After the robing of the king, they set forth with great dignity to the archbishop's church, one archbishop on his right, and another on his left, bearing his robe; and the kings of Scotland, Gwynedd, Dyved, and Cornwall, chosen for their high degree and their nobility, held four golden swords bare in their hands before the king on his way to the church. And around them on all sides, the communities of monks, canons, and scholars placed in the procession according to their stations, sang various music to the organ, and escorted their king to the mother church to the Mass. And on the other side the queen was brought, clothed in royal dress, with a crown of laurel on her head, with bishops and learned doctors around her, to the nunnery church for Mass. She was preceded by the wives of the four kings already mentioned, who were bearing in their hands four pure white doves. . . .

And they would not have become weary had the whole day been spent in the services of the Mass. But after the termination of divine service in both churches, the king and queen were relieved of their royal robes and clad in lighter dress. Then the king went to the main hall accompanied by all the men-folk, and the queen to her hall with the women-folk. And after all were seated according to their rank, Sir Kay, the chief officer of the feast, arose, clad in ermine, and a thousand noble ones with him, clad in like manner, to serve the food from the kitchen. . . . And then it became apparent that the island of Britain had indeed been restored to its ancient dignity and wealth and jollity, and had been raised to a height where there was no other realm to compare with her. . . .

And when the feasting and drinking were ended, and all had arisen from the tables, they retired outside the city, some to martial exercises on foot or on horse, some to break a lance, others to hurl leaden vessels into the air, others to fence, others to throw a heavy stone, others to play ' throwboard.' And as they were outside the ramparts indulging thus in sport, the ladies whom they most dearly loved stood on the walls watching them, and allowing themselves to be seen by them, in order to arouse their men to greater zest in their play. And the victorious ones in their games received their reward immediately from the hands of the king.

translated by D. M. LLOYD from the *Dingestow Chronicle*, a 13th century Welsh work closely based on Geoffrey of Monmouth's *Historia Regum Britanniae* (1136)

[Reece Winstone

TINTERN ABBEY

[Reece Winstone

ROMAN AMPHITHEATRE AT CAERLEON

[*Ronald Thompson*

CAERNARVON CASTLE

A MARKET SCENE

Pont y Pool is a large straggling place, containing 250 houses and 1500 souls. Several neat habitations, and numerous shops, present an appearance of thriving prosperity, notwithstanding the dusky aspect of the town, occasioned by the adjacent forges. The inhabitants derive great support from the ironworks and collieries, and have been recently benefited by the trade of the canal. The place is the principal mart for the natives of the mountainous district, and the weekly market is not the least considerable, and the cheapest in Monmouthshire. It was a pleasing amusement to mix in these crowded meetings, to observe the frank and simple manners of the hardy mountaineers, and endeavour, in asking the price of their provisions, to extort a *Saxon* word from this *British* progeny. The women were mostly wrapped in long cloth cloaks of a dark blue or brown colour; all of them wore mob caps neatly plaited over the forehead and ears, and tied above the chin; several had also round felt hats like those worn by the men, or large chip hats covered with black silk, and fastened under the chin. This head-dress gives an arch and lively air to the younger part of the sex, and is not unbecoming.

WILLIAM COXE (1747-1828)
An Historical Tour in Monmouthshire (1801)

ABERGAVENNY TOMBS

A Lord that once enjoyde that Seate
Lyes there in sumptious sort:
They say as loe his race was great,
So auncient men report.
His force was much: for he by strength

With Bull did struggle so,
He broke cleane off his hornes at length,
And therewith let him go.
This Lord a Bull hath under seete,
And as it may be thought,
A Dragon under head doth lye
In stone full finely wrought.
The worke and Tombe so auncient is,
(And of the oldest guyse)
My first bare view, full well may mis
To shewe how well he lyes.

A Tombe in deede, of charge and showe
Amid the Chappell stands:
Where William Thomas Knight ye knowe
Lyes long with stretched hands.
A Harbert was he cal'd of right,
Who from great kindred cam,
And married to a worthie wight,
Daughter to Dauie Gam,
(A Knight likewise, of right and name)
This Harbert and his Feere
Lies there like one that purchast fame,
As plainly doth appeere.
His Tombe is rich, and rare to viewe,
Well wrought of great deuice:
Though it be old, Tombes made but newe
Are of no greater price.
His Armes three ramping Lyons white
Behind his head in shield:
A crowned Lyon blacke is hers,
Set out in most rich field.
Behind her head is likewise there,
Loe what our elders did
To make those famous euery where,
Whose vertues are not hid.

* * *

Right ore against this windowe, loe
In stone a Ladie lyes:
And in her hands a Hart I troe,
She holds before your eyes:
And on her breast a great fayre shield
In which she beares no more
But three great Flowerdeluces large:
And euen loe, right ore
Her head another Ladie lyes
With Squirrell on her hand,
And at her feete, in stone likewise,
A couching Hound doth stand:
They say her Squirrell lept away,
And toward it she run:
And as from fall she sought to stay
The little pretie Bun,
Right downe from top of wall she fell,
And took her death thereby.
Thus what I heard I doe you tell,
And what is seene with eye.

A friend of myne who lately dyed,
That Doctor Lewis hight,
Within that Church his Tombe I spyed,
Well wrought and fayre to sight.
O Lord (quoth I) we all must dye,
No lawe, nor learnings lore,
No judgement deepe, nor knowledge hye,
No riches lesse or more,
No office, place, nor calling great,
No worldly pompe at all,
Can keepe us from the mortall threat
Of death, when God doth call.
Sith none of these good gifts on earth
Haue powre to make us liue,
And no good fortune from our birth
No hower of breath can giue,

Thinke not on life and pleasure heere,
They passe like beames of Sunne:
For nought from hence we carrie cleere
When man his race hath runne.

THOMAS CHURCHYARD (? 1520-1604)
The Worthines of Wales (1587)

THE SWAN ON SYFADDON LAKE

Fair swan, the lake you ride
Like white-robed abbot in your pride;
Round-foot bird of the drifted snow,
Like heavenly visitant you show.
A stately ministry is yours,
And beauty haunts your young hours.
From God's hand this day you take
Lordship over Syfaddon lake,
And two noble gifts you have
To keep you safe from the whelming wave:
Master craft in fishery—
On the wide lake could better be?—
And skill to fly on high and far
On strong wings over hill and scaur.
Your eyes discern, high overhead,
Earth's face beneath you spread,
And search all ways the watery deep,
Whose countless crop of fish you reap.
Riding the waves in stately sort
For fish to angle is your sport,
And your fishing rod, beyond compare,
'Tis your long neck, shapely and fair.
Warden you are of the round lake,
Fair-hued as the foam-flake.
Pure white through the wild waves shown;
In shirt as bright as crystal stone
And doublet all of lilies made

And flowered waistcoat you're arrayed,
With jacket wove of the wild white rose;
And your gown like honeysuckle shows.
Radiant you all fowls among,
White-cloaked bird of heaven's throng. . . .

attributed to DAFYDD AP GWILYM (*c.* 1325-*c.* 1385)
translated from the Welsh by
SIR H. IDRIS BELL

OH, ABEREDW, ABEREDW

Oh, Aberedw, Aberedw. Would God I might dwell and die by thee. Memory enters in and brings back the old time in a clear vision and waking dream, and again I descend from the high moor's half encircling sweep and listen to the distant murmur of the river as it foams down the ravine from its home in the Green Cwm and its cradle in the hills. Once more I stand by the river side and look up at the cliff castle towers and mark the wild roses swinging from the crag and watch the green woods waving and shimmering with a twinkling dazzle as they rustle in the breeze and shining of the summer afternoon, while here and there a grey crag peeps from among the tufted trees. And once again I hear the merry voices and laughter of the children as they clamber down the cliff path among the bushes or along the rock ledges of the riverside or climb the Castle Mount, or saunter along the narrow green meadow tree-fringed and rock-bordered and pass in and out of Llewellyn's cave, or gather wood and light the fire among the rocks upon the moor, or loiter down the valley to Cavan Twm Bach and cross the shining ferry at sunset, when the evening shadows lie long and still across the broad reaches of the river. Oh, Aberedw, Aberedw.

FRANCIS KILVERT (1840-79)
Diary

THE PLACES OF MY BOYHOOD

In the places of my boyhood
  The pit-wheels turn no more,
Nor any furnace lightens
  The midnight as of yore.

The slopes of slag and cinder
  Are sulking in the rain,
And in derelict valleys
  The hope of youth is slain.

And yet I love to wander
  The early ways I went,
And watch from doors and bridges
  The hills and skies of Gwent.

Though blighted be the valleys
  Where man meets man with pain,
The things my boyhood cherished
  Stand firm, and shall remain.

IDRIS DAVIES (1905-53)

RHYMNEY

For Ceinfryn and Gwyn

When April came to Rhymney
  With shower and sun and shower,
The green hills and the brown hills
  Could sport some simple flower,
And sweet it was to fancy
  That even the blackest mound
Was proud of its single daisy
  Rooted in bitter ground.

And old men would remember
  And young men would be vain,
And the hawthorn by the pithead
  Would blossom in the rain,
And the drabbest streets of evening,
  They had their magic hour,
When April came to Rhymney
  With shower and sun and shower.

IDRIS DAVIES (1905–53)

SYLVAN RHONDDA

The descent down a long hill brings the traveller to a little brook, abounding with fish, which joins the Rhondda Fawr a little way to the eastward; and at a very short distance from the brook, after descending another hill, you cross a bridge over that river, which has disappeared since its junction with the Rhondda Fach: but from this place the sound of it is never lost, though frequently the sight, till you arrive close by its source at the top of the parish, distant about ten miles. Here, however, it ceases to be the leading feature of the prospect. It fertilizes the valley with its pure transparent stream, rolling over loose stones, but is no longer encumbered, yet ennobled, by massy projections, or stately and aspiring cliffs. Hereabouts, and for some miles to come, there is a degree of luxuriance in the valley, infinitely beyond what my entrance on this district led me to expect. The contrast of the meadows, rich and verdant, with mountains the most wild and romantic, surrounding them on every side, is in the highest degree picturesque. The next object of interest, for such it is in a proportion equal to that of a palace in a better inhabited country, is a substantial farmhouse, placed in a most pleasing solitude, as beautifully situated as any thing in the parish. Its name is Llwyn y Pia signifying the magpie's bush. It is occupied by Jane Davies, a widow, but its situation seems little calculated for the feebler exertions of female industry. . . .

On the farm of Llwyn y Pia, standing alone by the roadside, there is the tallest and largest oak that ever I have happened to meet with. There is also on the same estate, if you pass through a gate on the left, a little beyond the house, a very beautiful field, with a magnificent grove at the upper end of it, under the shelter of a towering rock. A second bridge over the Rhondda, on the other side of which the road winds to the left, furnishes a most interesting point of view, embracing the country just traversed on the one part, and on the other the wilder grandeur of what remains to be explored. I had met with but one person of whom I could ask a question since my entrance into the parish; and then only through the medium of my attendant, whose services as an interpreter were not to be disregarded.

BENJAMIN HEATH MALKIN (1769-1842)
The Scenery, antiquities and biography of South Wales

IN GARDENS IN THE RHONDDA

In gardens in the Rhondda
  The daffodils dance and shine
When tired men trudge homeward
  From factory and mine.

The daffodils dance in gardens
  Behind the grim brown row
Built among the slagheaps
  In a hurry long ago.

They dance as though in passion
  To shame and to indict
The brutes who built so basely
  In the long Victorian night.

IDRIS DAVIES (1905-53)

SWANSEA BAY

In vain by various griefs opprest,
I vagrant roam devoid of rest,
With aching heart, still ling'ring stray
Around the shores of Swansea Bay.

The restless waves that lave the shore,
Joining the tide's tumult'ous roar;
In hollow murmurs seem to say—
Peace is not found at Swansea Bay.

The meek-eyed morning's lucid beam,
The pensive moon's pale shadowy gleam,
Still ceaseless urge—why this delay?
Go, hapless wretch, from Swansea Bay.

'Tis not for me the snowy sail
Swells joyous in the balmy gale;
Nor cuts the boat with frolic play
For me the waves of Swansea Bay.

The glow of health that tints each cheek,
The eyes that sweet contentment speak;
To mock my woes their charms display,
And bid me fly from Swansea Bay.

Haste, smiling nymphs, your beauties lave,
And sport beneath the sparkling wave,

While I pursue my lonely way
Along the shores of Swansea Bay.

The frowning mountain's awful sweep,
The rocks that beetle o'er the deep,
The winds that round their summits play,
All bid me fly from Swansea Bay.

Then, Kilvey hill, a long adieu,
I drag my sorrows hence from you:
Misfortune, with imperious sway
Impels me far from Swansea Bay.

JULIA ANN KEMBLE (ANN OF SWANSEA, 1764-1838)

GRONGAR HILL

Now while Phoebus, riding high,
Gives lustre to the land and sky,
Grongar Hill invites my song;
Draw the landscape bright and strong;
Grongar in whose mossy cells,
Sweetly musing Quiet dwells;
Grongar, in whose silent shade,
For the modest Muses made,
So oft I have, the ev'ning still,
At the fountain of a rill
Sat upon a flow'ry bed,
With my hand beneath my head,
While stray'd my eyes o'er Towy's flood,
Over mead and over wood,
From house to house, from hill to hill,
Till Contemplation had her fill. . . .

Ever charming, ever new,
When will the landskip tire the view!

The fountain's fall, the river's flow,
The woody vallies warm and low;
The windy summit, wild and high,
Roughly rushing on the sky!
The pleasant seat, the ruin'd tow'r,
The naked rock, the shady bow'r;
The town and village, dome and farm,
Each give each a double charm,
As pearls upon an Ethiop's arm.
    See on the mountain's southern side,
Where the prospect opens wide,
Where the ev'ning gilds the tide,
How close and small the hedges lie!
What streaks of meadow cross the eye! . . .

    Be full, ye Courts! be great who will;
Search for Peace with all your skill:
Open wide the lofty door,
Seek her on the marble floor:
In vain ye search, she is not there;
In vain ye search the domes of Care!
Grass and flowers Quiet treads,
On the meads and mountain-heads,
Along with pleasure close ally'd,
Ever by each other's side.
And often by the murm'ring rill,
Hears the thrush, while all is still,
Within the groves of Grongar Hill. . . .

JOHN DYER (1701-57)

ST GOVAN

St Govan, he built him a cell
By the side of the Pembroke sea,
And there, as the crannied sea-gulls dwell,
In a tiny, secret citadel
He sighed for eternity.

St Govan, he built him a cell
Between the wild sky and the sea,
Where the sunsets redden the rolling swell
And brooding splendour has thrown her spell
On valley and moorland lea.

St Govan still lies in his cell,
But his soul, long since, is free,
And one may wonder—and who can tell—
If good St Govan likes Heaven as well
As his cell by that sounding sea?

A. G. PRYS-JONES (1888-

MAENOR PYRR

The castle called Maenor Pyrr, that is, the mansion of Pyrrus, who also possessed the island of Caldey, which the Welsh call Ynys Pyrr, or the island of Pyrrus, is distant about three miles from Pembroke. It is excellently well defended by turrets and bulwarks, and is situated on the summit of a hill extending on the western side towards the seaport, having on the northern and southern sides a fine fish-pond under its walls, as conspicuous for its grand appearance, as for the depth of its waters, and a beautiful orchard on the same side, inclosed on one part by a vineyard, and on the other by a wood, remarkable for the projection of its rocks, and the height of its hazel trees. On the right hand of the promontory, between the castle and the church, near the site of a very large lake and mill, a rivulet of never-failing water flows through a valley, rendered sandy by the violence of the winds. Towards the west, the Severn sea, bending its course to Ireland, enters a hollow bay at some distance from the castle; and the southern rocks, if extended a little further toward the north, would render it a most excellent harbour for shipping. From this point of sight, you will see almost all the ships from Great Britain, which the east wind drives upon the Irish coast, daringly brave the inconstant waves and raging sea. This country is well supplied with corn, sea-fish, and imported wines; and what is preferable to every other advantage, from its vicinity to Ireland, it is tempered by a salubrious air. Demetia, therefore, with its seven cantreds, is the most beautiful, as well as the most powerful district of Wales; Pembroke, the finest part of the province of Demetia; and the place I have just described, the most delightful part of Pembroke. It is evident, therefore, that Maenor Pirr is the pleasantest spot in Wales; and the author may be pardoned for having thus extolled his native soil, his genial territory, with a profusion of praise and admiration.

GIRALDUS CAMBRENSIS (1147-*c.* 1220)
Itinerary through Wales
translated from the Latin by
SIR RICHARD COLT HOARE

THE FISHING LASS OF HAKIN

A new sea song in the sea style set to a new sea tune sung at sea by a seafaring man over a can of sea liquor called Phlip.

Ye sailors bold both great and small
That navigate the ocean,
Who love a lass that's fair and tall,
Come, hearken to my motion;
You must have heard of Milford Haven
All harbours it surpasses,
I know no port this side of Heaven
So famed for handsome lasses.

In Milford on your larboard hand
We found a town called Hakin,
The snuggest place in all the land
For lads inclined to raking;
There all the girls were cleanly drest
As witty as they are pretty,
But one exceeded all the rest,
And this was charming Betty.

A fisherman her father was,
Her mother a fishwoman,
And she herself a fishing lass
Perhaps possessed by no-man;
She'd bait her hook with lug or crab,
No fisherman so nimble,
And at her oar she was a dab,
But never at her thimble.

Assist me, all the wat'ry tribe,
I find my wit a-flagging
As I endeavour to describe
This precious pearl of Hakin;
Ye mermaids tune my merry song,
And Neptune bless my darling,

Your smoking altars shall ere long
Be spread with sole and sparling.

Her fishing dress was clean and neat,
It set me all a-quaking,
I loved her, and could almost eat
This maiden ray of Hakin;
If ere you saw a cuttle fish,
Her breasts are more inviting,
Like shaking blubbers in a dish,
And tender as a whiting.

Her cheeks are as a mackrel plump,
No mouth of mullet moister,
Her lips of tench would make you jump,
They open like an oyster,
Her chin as smooth as river trout,
Her hair as rockfish yellow,
God's Sounds! I view her round about
But never saw her fellow.

When hungry people write for bread,
Whom they call poetasters,
They talk of fires in topmast head,
Of Pollax and of Castor's;
Her eyes afford a brighter mark
Than all those flashy meteors,
Like Milford Lights even in the dark
Revealing all her features.

Whene'er a smile sits on her lip
I'm brisk as bottled cider,
I quite renounce and leave my ship
And never can abide her;
Whene'er she speaks, so sweet her tone
I leap like spawning salmon,
And when she sings I'm all her own,
I serve no Jove nor Mammon.

But if she frowns I'm gone to pot,
As dead as pickled herring,
The muscles of my heart must rot
And split from clew to earring;
Then in my hammock sink me deep
Within the sight of Hakin,
Then sure she'll melancholy weep
As turtles at their taking.

Let doctors kill, let merchants cheat,
Let courtiers cogg and flatter,
Let gluttons feed on costly meat,
Let me have Betty's platter;
To mess with her I'd spend my days
On pilchard and on poor-John,
Let richer folks have if they please
Their turbot and their sturgeon.

LEWIS MORRIS (1700-65)

TREGARON BOG

I had often striven to free my mind from its strong dislike for the place. I would fix my eyes on its peat stacks. I would try to picture in my mind's eye the welcome hearths of the surrounding farmhouses warmed in winter by their cheerful and clean peat fires, their cosiness a gift from the generous bog. But my effort was in vain. My mind was dragged back in spite of myself to the quagmire and slime, to foul creeping things, and the Slough of Despond. . . .

I approached the bog this time as usual from Ystwyth's green and pleasant valley. The heat was intense, for it was July. The light hay-crop was dry and crisp almost fresh from the scythe-stroke, and everyone sought shelter from the sun. From the slope of the hill which

[R. Cecil Hughes

NATIONAL LIBRARY OF WALES

[R. Cecil Hughes

UNIVERSITY COLLEGE OF WALES, ABERYSTWYTH

[*Reece Winstone*

IN CATHAYS PARK, CARDIFF

the train had climbed under the lovely shade of the trees, we could see the glare of the sunlight on the meadows below, and on the hills and valleys beyond. Soon we reached the crest, the spot so keenly longed for by the poet Ieuan the Tall (two centuries ago): "O! Wales of the fair aspect, she is all beautiful, that bright pleasant land! Fortunate is he who sees her, that fair land, elevated and healthy. Summer streams babble brightly there over their pebbly tracks, through clear shallows they flow, where the light weaves through their waters like glass!"

Behold Ystrad Meurig School on the hillside. How delightful was the life of Edward Richard, a teacher there (two hundred years ago), and how melodious are his pastoral songs. Every time that I come to this pleasant spot, his sweet verses come to my mind, and I recollect that he once closed his school for a whole year because his conscience told him he should learn more. And now the bog lies before us; we are by its edge.

But strange to relate, it is not dreary and sad as usual; it is white, as if under a sheet of snow. It is not snow, we know well, not in a summer such as this. The whiteness is more delicate than snow, a warm bright white like angels' wings. The bog was not all white, but the white patches scattered over it seemed to lend their warmth and purity to all the remaining portions of ridge and swamp among which they were interspersed. The ditches had been transfigured under the sunny smile of summer, their dark frowns were not so grim, nor their waters so cold. The peat stacks had a homely look of welcome, and brought to mind the blue smoke which is seen rising from the chimneys of Welsh cottages at noon. The bog was transfigured.

The miracle had been performed by the bog-cotton flowers, old friends of my childhood days. They were there in thousands, patches of delicate and swaying whiteness, living and shimmering in the sun. It was they who gave the grim and dark old bog its white glory. Their feathery tufts were full and yet light. I knew the softness of their touch; one of my childhood pleasures had been to draw them across my cheeks. But never had I seen them looking so young, of such brilliant whiteness, and their movements so lively. They bowed to the lightest breeze, like thousands of worshipping angels. Then suddenly they threw back their heads and swayed like hosts of young girls dancing in white dresses. And then they would stay quiet, rest in their glory, and reflect the light of the sun, making it a gentler and a purer light than when it fell on them. I imagined that the hills and the mountains around were stretching over each other to admire the angelic children of the bog, and that the tracks of men had kept away from them so as not to disturb so gentle a peacefulness, nor to mar so pure a beauty. A blending of whiteness, and light, and warmth, had appeared in the very last place in Wales where I would have sought it. . . .

I have no words to depict the wealth of beauty in the Teivy Valley. But though Llandysul's banks are fair, the charm of Newcastle Emlyn delightful, the country around Cenarth at its prettiest, and the Cardigan sea delectable, yet it is to the cotton flowers in the bog which I had long dreaded that my mind flies back. They are the children of the mountains in their pristine purity, where the breeze awakens the mind into a keen joy, and does not lull it to sleep.

SIR OWEN M. EDWARDS (1858-1920)
Yn y Wlad
translated from the Welsh by
D. M. LLOYD

DEVIL'S BRIDGE

The inn, or rather hospice, for the sounding name of hospice is more applicable to it than the common one of inn, was built at a great expense by the late Duke of Newcastle. It is an immense lofty cottage with projecting eaves, and has a fine window to the east which enlightens a stately staircase and a noble gallery. It fronts the north and stands in the midst of one of the most remarkable localities in the world, of which it would require a far more vigorous pen than mine to convey an adequate idea.

Far to the west is a tall, strange-looking hill, the top of which bears no slight resemblance to that of a battlemented castle. This hill, which is believed to have been in ancient times a stronghold of the Britons, bears the name of Bryn y Castell, or the hill of the castle. To the north-west are russet hills, to the east two brown paps, whilst to the south is a high, swelling mountain. To the north and just below the hospice is a profound hollow with all the appearance of the crater of an extinct volcano; at the bottom of this hollow the waters of two rivers unite; those of the Rheidol from the north, and those of the Afon y Mynach, or the Monks' River, from the south-east. The Rheidol falling over a rocky precipice at the northern side of the hollow forms a cataract very pleasant to look upon from the middle upper window of the inn. Those of the Mynach which pass under the celebrated Devil's Bridge are not visible, though they generally make themselves heard. The waters of both, after uniting, flow away through a romantic glen towards the west. The sides of the hollow and indeed of most of the ravines in the neighbourhood, which are numerous, are beautifully clad with wood.

Penetrate now into the hollow above which the hospice stands. You descend by successive flights of steps, some of which are very slippery and insecure. On your right is the Monks' River, roaring down its dingle in five successive falls, to join its brother the Rheidol. Each of the falls has its own peculiar basin, one or two of which are said to be of awful depth. The length which these falls with their basins occupy is about five hundred feet. On the side of the basin of the last but one is the cave, or the site of the cave, said to have been occupied in old times by the Wicked Children, the mysterious Plant de Bat, two brothers and a sister, robbers and murderers. At present it is nearly open on every side, having, it is said, been destroyed to prevent its being the haunt of other evil people: there is a tradition in the country that the fall at one time tumbled over its mouth. This tradition, however, is evidently without foundation, as from the nature of the ground the river could never have run but in its present channel. Of all the falls the fifth or last is the most considerable: you view it from a kind of den, to which the last flights of steps, the ruggedest and most dangerous of all, has brought you; your position here is a wild one. The fall, which is split into two, is thundering beside you; foam, foam, foam is flying all about you; the basin or cauldron is boiling frightfully below you; hirsute rocks are frowning terribly above you, and above them forest trees, dank and wet with spray and mist, are distilling drops in showers from their boughs.

But where is the bridge, the celebrated bridge of the Evil Man? From the bottom of the first flight of steps leading down into the hollow you see a modern-looking bridge, bestriding a deep chasm or cleft to the south-east, near the top of the dingle of the Monks' River, over it lies the road to Pont Erwyd. That, however, is not the Devil's Bridge—but about twenty feet below that bridge and completely overhung by it, don't you see a shadowy, spectral object, something like a bow, which likewise bestrides the chasm? You do! Well! that shadowy, spectral object is the celebrated Devil's Bridge, or, as the timorous peasants of the locality call it, the Pont y Gwr Drwg. It is now merely preserved as an object of curiosity, the bridge above being alone used for transit, and is quite inaccessible except to birds, and the climbing wicked boys of the neighbourhood, who sometimes at the risk of their lives contrive to get upon it from the frightfully steep northern bank, and snatch a fearful joy, as, whilst lying on their bellies, they poke their heads over its sides worn by age, without parapet to prevent them from falling into the horrid gulf below. But from the steps in the hollow the view of the Devil's Bridge, and likewise of the cleft, is very slight and unsatisfactory. To view it properly, and the wonders connected with it, you must pass over the bridge above it, and descend a precipitous dingle on the eastern side till you come to a small platform in a crag. Below you now is a frightful cavity, at the bottom of which the waters of the Monks' River, which came tumbling from a glen to the east, whirl, boil and hiss in a horrid pot or cauldron, called in the language of the country Twll yn y graig, or the hole in the rock, in a manner truly tremendous.

On your right is a slit, probably caused by volcanic force, through which the waters after whirling in the cauldron, eventually escape. The slit is wonderfully narrow, considering its altitude, which is very great, considerably upwards of a hundred feet—nearly above you, crossing the slit, which is partially wrapt in darkness, is the far-famed bridge, the Bridge of the Evil Man, a work which, though crumbling and darkly gray, does much honour to the hand which built it, whether it was the hand of Satan, or of a monkish architect, for the arch is chaste and beautiful, far superior in every respect, except in safety and utility, to the one above it, which from this place you have not the mortification of seeing. Gaze on these objects, namely the horrid seething pot or cauldron, the gloomy volcanic slit, and the spectral, shadowy Devil's Bridge, for about three minutes, allowing a minute to each, then scramble up the bank and repair to your inn, and have no more sight-seeing that day, for you have seen enough. And if pleasant recollections do not haunt you through life of the noble falls and the beautiful wooded dingles to the west of the bridge of the Evil One, and awful and mysterious ones of the monks' boiling cauldron, the long savage, shadowy cleft, and the grey, crumbling, spectral bridge, I say boldly that you must be a very unpoetical person indeed.

GEORGE BORROW (1803-81)
Wild Wales

THE POET'S PETITION

To the wave that prevented him crossing the Dovey estuary to visit Morfudd.

Hoarse wave, with crest of curling foam,
Back to thy native ocean roam;
And leave the fords of Dovey free,
That Morfudd separate from me!
No bard before hath loved to tell
Thy glassy tower—thy lordly swell—
Thou branch of ocean's mighty stem—
Thou sailor's friend—thou briny gem!
The storm—the rush of hostile ranks,
Jamm'd 'twixt the close and cleftness banks—
The war-steed's sinewy chest of might—
Are faint to thee, thou billowy height!
No organ, harp, no vocal tone,
Are like thy vast and fearful moan.
To her no other pledge I'll give,
The snow-white maid for whom I live,

Than call her beauty like the light,
And as thy circling waters bright!
Thou bright round billow, let me pass
Beyond thy ring of azure glass;
For long my love, awaiting me,
Stands by Llanbadarn's birchen tree.
Of sunken rocks, thou mantle hoar,
Chafed on the wild and rugged shore—
Friend of the sea—knight of the spray—
Oh, did'st thou know, for this delay,
What penalty the bard must pay,
Thou would'st not raise thy gloomy face
Between him and the trysting-place!
What though for Indeg's charms sublime,
My limbs thy dreadful heights must climb;—
Though death were in thy eddies stern;—
Death and thy hate I'll rather spurn,
That back from Morfudd's shore return!

DAFYDD AP GWILYM (*c.* 1325-*c.* 1385)
translated from the Welsh by
ARTHUR JAMES JOHNES (MAELOG)

LLANUWCHLLYN OLD CHAPEL

I confess that I am no objective critic. Childhood impressions are indelible; I am forced to feel that more and more. Although I am no singer the music of Welsh airs and hymn-tunes is part of my soul; in spite of myself I find that I appreciate every other music according as it resembles or differs from these. You have not seen the old chapel at Llanuwchllyn, by the still water, the roof no higher than that of the villagers' houses around it. Its walls were bare, except where patches of damp had given a slight variation to the colour; the benches were sometimes comfortable and sometimes hard—according to the sermon; the windows long and narrow and without ornament, save when the frost drew pictures on them. And yet, that is the most beautiful place where I have ever been. It is the place where I began to think, it was there I fell in love for the first time, there I felt the dread of damnation and the joy of forgiveness; my ambition was first aroused there, and my pride laid low by having it enforced on me that I was wholly without merit—every thought and feeling of greater profundity than the course of daily living, human and divine, direct me back to that old grey chapel. It was void of all architectural and pictorial beauty, but through a window opposite our bench I could see the rain driven by gusts of wind across the mountain-slopes, and a roan tree curved by the prevailing winds into a form of such elegance that it would be the despair of any artist to reproduce the delicate beauty of its branches. The old chapel and its people are greatly changed, now, but when thoughts of heaven visit my unsettled mind,—you will probably smile to hear me say so—but paradise to me is exactly like the old chapel at Llanuwchllyn—the people seated in families on their benches, everyone just the age they then were, the preaching, the jubilant singing, and the plaintive sigh of the wind, and that old roan tree.

SIR OWEN M. EDWARDS (1858-1920)
O'r Bala i Geneva
translated from the Welsh by
D. M. LLOYD

TO THE RIVER CLEGYR

I too have loved the glades that you love, O river,
With longing I think of your waters today in the hotness of June;
The beach I recall where you linger, its bees, honeysuckle, and brambles,

[*R. Cecil Hughes*

PLAS NEWYDD, LLANGOLLEN

[*Reece Winstone*

MARKET HALL, LLANIDLOES

[*The British Travel and Holidays Association*

THE GUILDHALL, SWANSEA

And the copse with its pine and stockdoves and the
pigeons' love-sick tune.
And oh, the hot summer eves, when the kindly darkness
enwrapped us,
And the moon rose big on Bwlch Gwyn, and mist in
the valley spread white;
A bat fluttered over our heads, and a sheep in the distance
bleated,
Athirst for your shimmering stream, far seen from
the waterless height.
My footsteps rang on the roadway, and over them
sounded
The song of a cowman, merry, half-drunk, that louder
and louder rose;
Down by the mill two lovers lingered, long lingered at
parting;
A dog barked in his sleep; at whiles restlessly chattered
the crows. . . .
You watched, O river what came—all laughter, all
weeping;
And ceaseless your merry singing sounded 'twixt
meadow and hill.
You in your wisdom repined not though Time in his
flight should endeavour
To part us two; you knew that my soul from afar
would find you still.

IORWERTH C. PEATE (1901-)
translated from the Welsh by
SIR H. IDRIS BELL

THE RED BANDITS OF MAWDDWY

Arrive at the foot of Bwlch y Groes, or the Pass of the Cross, one of the most terrible in North Wales. The height is gained by going up an exceedingly steep and narrow zig-zag path: the pass itself is a dreary heathy flat on which I suppose the cross stood to excite the thanksgiving of travellers for having so well accomplished their arduous journey. The descent on the other side is much greater, and very tedious, into the long and narrow vale of Mowddwy. It is seven or eight miles long; and so contracted as scarcely to admit a meadow at the bottom. Its boundaries are vast hills, generally very verdant, and fine sheep-walks; but one on the left exhibits a horrible front, being so steep as to balance between precipice and slope: it is red and naked, and too steep to admit of vegetation; and a slide from its summit would be as fatal as a fall from a perpendicular rock. In one place on the right the mountains open and furnish a gap to give sight to another picturesque and strange view, the rugged and wild summit of Aran Fowddwy, which soars above with tremendous majesty.

There is beauty in this vale which is not frequent in others of these mountainous countries. The inclosures are all divided by excellent quickset hedges, and run far up the sides of the hills, in places so steep that the common traveller would scarcely find footing. Numbers of little groves are interspersed, and the hills above them shew a fine turf to the top, where the bog and heath commence, which give shelter to multitudes of red grouse and a few black. But their consequences to these parts are infinitely greater in being the beds of fuel to all the inhabitants. The turberies are placed very remote from their dwellings; and the turf or peat is gotten with great difficulty. The roads from the brows of the mountains, in general, are too steep even for a horse; the men therefore carry up on their backs a light sledge, fill it with a very considerable load, and drag it by means of a rope placed over their breast to the brink of the slope, then go before and draw it down, still preceding, and guiding its motions, which at times have been so violent as to overturn and draw along with it the master, to the hazard of his life, and not without considerable bodily hurt. . . .

Return to Dinas y Mowddwy. On the road was informed of the place, not far from hence, where Lewis Owen, vice-chamberlain of North Wales, and baron of the exchequer of North Wales was cruelly murdered in the year 1555, by a set of banditti with which this county was over-run. After the wars of the houses of York and Lancaster, multitudes of felons and outlaws inhabited this country, and established in these parts, for a great length of time, from those unhappy days a race of profligates, who continued to rob, burn, and murder, in large bands, in defiance of the civil power, and would steal and drive whole herds of cattle, in mid-day from one county to another with the utmost impunity. To put a stop to their ravages, a commission was granted to John Wynn ap Meredydd, of Gwedir, and to Lewis Owen, in order to settle the peace of the country, and to punish all offenders against its government. In pursuance of their orders they raised a body of stout men, and on a Christmas-Eve seized above four score outlaws and felons, on whom they held a jail delivery, and punished them according to their deserts. Among them were the two sons of a woman who very earnestly applied to Owen for the pardon of one: he refused; when the mother in a rage, told him (baring her neck) *These yellow breasts have given suck to those who shall wash their hands in your blood.* Revenge was determined by the surviving villains. They watched their opportunity when he was passing through these parts to Montgomeryshire assizes, to waylay him in the thick woods of Mowddwy, at a place now called, from the deed, Llidiart y Barwn; where they had cut down several long trees, to cross the road and impede the passage. They then discharged on him a shower of arrows; one of which sticking in his face, he took it out, and broke. After this they attacked him with bills and javalins, and left him slain, with above thirty wounds. His son-in-law, John Llwyd, of Ceiswyn, defended him to the last, but his cowardly attendants fled on the first onset. His death gave peace to the country, for most rigorous justice ensued; the whole nest of banditti was extirpated, many suffered by the hand of justice, and the rest fled, never to return.

The traditions of the country respecting these banditti are still strong. I was told that they were so feared that travellers did not dare to go the common road to Shrewsbury, but passed over the summits of the mountains to avoid their haunts. The inhabitants placed sythes in the chimneys of their houses to prevent the felons coming down to surprise them in the night; some of which are to be seen to this day. This race was distinguished by the titles Gwylliaid y Dugoed and Gwylliaid Cochion Mowddwy, i.e. the banditti of the Black Wood, and the red-headed Banditti of Mowddwy.

THOMAS PENNANT (1726-98)
Tours in Wales

PENMAEN POOL

Who long for rest, who look for pleasure
Away from counter, court, or school
O where live well your lease of leisure
But here at, here at Penmaen Pool?

You'll dare the Alp? you'll dart the skiff?—
Each sport has here its tackle and tool:
Come, plant the staff by Cadair cliff;
Come, swing the sculls on Penmaen Pool.

What's yonder?—Grizzled Dyphwys dim:
The triple-hummocked Giant's stool,
Hoar messmate, hobs and nobs with him
To halve the bowl of Penmaen Pool.

And all the landscape under survey,
At tranquil turns, by nature's rule,
Rides repeated topsyturvy
In frank, in fairy Penmaen Pool.

And Charles's Wain, the wondrous seven,
And sheep-flock clouds like worlds of wool,
For all they shine so, high in heaven,
Shew brighter shaken in Penmaen Pool.

The Mawddach, how she trips! though throttled
If floodtide teeming thrills her full,
And mazy sands all water-wattled
Waylay her at ebb, past Penmaen Pool.

But what's to see in stormy weather,
When grey showers gather and gusts are cool?—
Why, raindrop-roundels looped together
That lave the face of Penmaen Pool.

Then even in weariest wintry hour
Of New Year's month or surly Yule
Furred snows, charged tuft above tuft, tower
From darksome darksome Penmaen Pool.

And ever, if bound here hardest home,
You've parlour-pastime left and (who'll
Not honour it?) ale like goldy foam
That frocks an oar in Penmaen Pool.

Then come who pine for peace or pleasure
Away from counter, court, or school,
Spend here your measure of time and treasure
And taste the treats of Penmaen Pool.

G. MANLEY HOPKINS (1844-89)

THE SQUIRE OF CWMBYCHAN

From Corsygedol, I pursued my journey towards Harlech; but, on the road, was tempted by my constant fellow-traveller, the reverend John Lloyd, to make a small deviation to visit a near relation of his, who lived a few miles to our right, in his antient territories of Cwm Bychan. We approached it through Glyn Artro, a little valley watered by a river of the same name, and prettily wooded. The view upwards was extremely picturesque, of a conic rock skirted by a sweet grove; and beyond soared the naked mountains which bounded the object of our ride.

After passing through the wood, and ascending Dinas Porchellyn, we had before us a wild horizon of rocks and rocky mountains. Even these tracts, unfriendly as they seem to vegetation, had once been covered with venerable oaks; and there still remained a few, between eight and nine feet in circumference. We went under their shade, above a rapid torrent, with a delightful view before us of a true wooden Alpine bridge, and a small mill; and, a little farther, an antient arch, flung from rock to rock, giving passage over a still and black water, shaded by trees. Ford the river again near Llyn Sarph, or The Serpent's Hole. Wind up a rocky staircase road, and arrive full in sight of Cwm Bychan, embosomed with rocks of magnificent height. After a short ride, high above a lake of the same name, descend, and reach the house of the venerable Evan Llwyd, who, with his ancestors, boast of being lords of these rocks, at least since the year 1100. This, and the fortified pass of Drws Ardudwy, were most probably occupied by the sons of Cadwgan, in their contests with the sons of Uchtryd ap Edwyn, whom they at last expelled the country.

The following, as it is the true descent of Mr. Evan

Llwyd, and my fellow-traveller, who being brothers' children, are eighteenth in descent from the Bleddyn ap Cynfyn, so it is a genuine copy of the form of a British pedigree:

Evan ap Edward, ap Richard, ap Edward, ap Humphrey, ap Edward, ap Dafydd, ap Robert, ap Howel, ap Dafydd, ap Meurig Llwyd o Nannau, ap Meirig Vychan, ap Ynyr Vychan, ap Ynyr, ap Meuric, ap Madog, ap Cadwgan, ap Bleddyn, ap Cynfyn, prince of North Wales and Powys.

I was introduced to the worthy representative of this long line, who gave me the most hospitable reception, and in the style of an antient Briton. He welcomed us with ale and potent beer, to wash down the Coch yr Wden, or hung goat, and the cheese, compounded of the milk of cow and sheep. He likewise shewed us the antient family cup, made of a bull's scrotum, in which large libations had been made in days of yore. The family lay in their whole store of winter provisions, being inaccessible a great part of the season, by reason of snow. Here they have lived for many generations without bettering or lessening their income; without noisy fame, but without any of its embittering attendants.

The mansion is a true specimen of an antient seat of a gentleman of Wales. The furniture rude: the most remarkable are the Cistiau Styffylog, or the oatmeal chests, which held the essential part of the provision.

The territories dependant on the mansion, extend about four miles each way, and consist of a small tract of meadow, a pretty lake swarming with trout, a little wood, and very much rock; the whole forming a most august scenery. The naked mountains envelope his vale and lake, like an immense theatre. The meadows are divided by a little stream, and are bounded on one side by the lake; on the other, by his woods, which skirt the foot of the rocks, and through which the river runs, and beyond them tumbles from the heights, in a series of cataracts. He keeps his whole territory in his own hands; but distributes his hinds among the Hafodtys, or summer-dairy houses, for the conveniency of attending his herds and flocks; he has fixed his heir on another part of his estates. His ambition once led him to attempt draining the lake, in order to extend his landed property: but, alas! he gained only a few acres of rushes and reeds; so wisely bounded his desires, and saved a beautiful piece of water . . .

Stools and roots of firs, of vast size, are frequently found near the lake. Mr. Llwyd observed one, with the marks of fire on it, which he used to repair the Tyddyn y Traian, or jointure-house of his family; an antient customary appendage to most of the Welsh houses of any note.

THOMAS PENNANT (1726-98)
Tours in Wales

MERIONETH

A foaming white wave drenches the grave,
The mound of bright Rhufawn, chief of rulers. . . .
  I love him who gave me my fill of mead
Where the seas encounter age-long contest.
I love her household troops and her thickly-set habitations, . . .
I love her sea-strand and her mountains,
And her strong-place by her trees, and her fair lands,
And her meadows, and her waters, and her valleys,
And her white seagulls and her lovely women.
I love her soldiers and her fine-looking horses,
And her woods and her strong ones and her dwellings.
I love her fields strewn with small clover. . . .
I love her settled parts where to live is valour's privilege,
And her extensive wild places, and her provisions for man. . . .
A foaming white wave drenches the grave.

A foaming white wave sweeps angrily by the home-
steads,
Brilliant as frost where it spreads.
I love the sea-strand of Merioneth,
Where a white arm has been my pillow.
I love the nightingale on the privet bush
By Kymer of the meeting waters in the much admired
valley. . . .
A foaming white wave sweeps angrily by the home-
steads.

PRINCE HYWEL AB OWAIN GWYNEDD (*d.* 1170)
translated from the Welsh by
D. M. LLOYD

THE CUCKOO'S SONG IN MERION

Though it has been my fate to see
Of gallant countries many a one;
Good ale, and those that drank it free,
And wine in streams that seemed to run;
The best of beer, the best of cheer,
Allotted are to Merion.

The swarthy ox will drag his chain,
At man's commandment that is done;
His furrow break through earth with pain,
Up hill and hillock toiling on;
Yet with more skill draw hearts at will
The maids of county Merion.

Merry the life, it must be owned,
Upon the hills of Merion;
Though chill and drear the prospect round,
Delight and joy are not unknown;
O who would e'er expect to hear
'Mid mountain bogs the cuckoo's tone?

O who display a mien full fair,
  A wonder each to look upon?
And who in every household care
  Defy compare below the sun?
And who make mad each sprightly lad?
  The maids of county Merion.

O fair the salmon in the flood,
  That over golden sands doth run;
And fair the thrush in his abode,
  That spreads his wings in gladsome fun;
More beautious look, if truth be spoke,
  The maids of county Merion.

Dear to the little birdies wild
  Their freedom in the forest lone;
Dear to the little sucking child
  The nurses breast it hangs upon;
Though long I wait, I ne'er can state
  How dear to me is Merion.

Sweet in the house the Telyn's[1] strings
  In love and joy where kindred wone;
While each in turn a stanza sings,
  No sordid themes e'er touched upon;
Full sweet in sound the hearth around
  The maiden's song of Merion.

And though my body here it be
  Travelling the countries up and down;
Tasting delights of land and sea,
  True pleasure seems my heart to shun;
Alas! there's need home, home to speed—
  My soul it is in Merion.

LEWIS MORRIS (1700-65)
translated from the Welsh by
GEORGE BORROW

[1] *Telyn* is Welsh for *Harp*.

ARENNIG VAWR

Having finished my ale, I paid for it, and leaving the Calvinistic farmer still smoking, I departed from Rhyd y fen. On I went along the valley, the enormous hill on my right, a moel of about half its height on my left, and a tall hill bounding the prospect in the east, the direction in which I was going. After a little time, meeting two women, I asked them the name of the mountain to the south.

"Arennig Vawr," they replied, or something like it.

Presently meeting four men, I put the same question to the foremost, a stout, burly, intelligent-looking fellow, of about fifty. He gave me the same name as the women. I asked him if anybody lived upon it.

"No," said he, "too cold for man."

"Fox?" said I.

"No! too cold for fox."

"Crow?" said I.

"No, too cold for crow; crow would be starved upon it." He then looked me in the face, expecting probably that I should smile.

I, however, looked at him with all the gravity of a judge, whereupon he also observed the gravity of a judge, and we continued looking at each other with all the gravity of judges till we both simultaneously turned away, he, followed by his companions going his path, and I going mine.

I subsequently remembered that Arennig is mentioned in a Welsh poem, though in anything but a flattering and advantageous manner. The writer calls it Arennig ddiffaith or barren Arennig, and says that it intercepts from him the view of his native land. Arennig is certainly barren enough, for there is neither tree nor shrub upon it, but there is something majestic in its huge bulk. Of all the hills which I saw in Wales none made a greater impression upon me.

GEORGE BORROW (1803-81)
Wild Wales

A ROYAL SCENE AT HARLECH

Bendigeid Vran, the son of Llyr, was the crowned king of this island, and he was exalted from the crown of London. And one afternoon he was at Harlech in Ardudwy, at his Court, and he sat upon the rock of Harlech, looking over the sea. And with him were his brother Manawyddan the son of Llyr, and his brothers by the mother's side, Nissyen and Evnissyen, and many nobles likewise, as was fitting to see around a king. . . . And one of these youths was a good youth and of gentle nature, and would make peace between his kindred, and cause his family to be friends when their wrath was at the highest; and this one was Nissyen; but the other would cause strife between his two brothers when they were most at peace.

And as they sat thus, they beheld thirteen ships coming from the south of Ireland, and making towards them, and they came with a swift motion, the wind being behind them, and they neared them rapidly. "I see ships afar," said the king, "coming swiftly towards the land. Command the men of the Court that they equip themselves, and go and learn their intent." So the men equipped themselves and went down towards them. And when they saw the ships near, certain were they that they had never seen ships better furnished. Beautiful flags of satin were upon them. And behold one of the ships outstripped the others, and they saw a shield lifted up above the side of the ship, and the point of the shield was upwards, in token of peace. And the men drew near that they might hold converse. Then they put out boats and came towards the land. And they saluted the king. Now the king could hear them from the place where he was, upon the rock above their heads. "Heaven prosper you," said he, "and be ye welcome. To whom do these ships belong, and who is the chief amongst you?" "Lord," said they, "Matholwch, King of Ireland, is here, and these ships belong to him." "Wherefore comes he?" asked the king, "and will he come to the land?" "He is a suitor unto thee, lord," said they, "and he will not land unless he have his boon." "And what may that be?" inquired the king. "He desires to ally himself with thee, lord," said they, "and he comes to ask Branwen the daughter of Llyr, that, if it seem well to thee, the Island of the Mighty may be leagued with Ireland, and both become more powerful." "Verily," said he, "let him come to land, and we will take counsel thereupon." And this answer was brought to Matholwch. "I will go willingly," said he. So he landed, and they received him joyfully, and great was the throng in the palace that night, between his hosts and those of the Court; and next day they took counsel, and they resolved to bestow Branwen upon Matholwch. Now she was one of the three chief ladies of this island, and she was the fairest damsel in the world.

The Mabinogion (*Branwen*)
translated from the Welsh by
LADY CHARLOTTE GUEST

SNOWDON TWICE VISITED

I took much pains to see this prospect to advantage: sat up at a farm on the west till about twelve, and walked up the whole way. The night was remarkably fine and starry; towards morn, the stars faded away, and left a short interval of darkness, which was soon dispersed by the dawn of day. The body of the sun appeared most distinct, with the rotundity of the moon, before it rose high enough to render its beam too brilliant for our sight. The sea which bounded the western part was gilt by its rays, first in slender streaks, at length glowing with redness. The prospect was disclosed like the gradual drawing up of a curtain in a theatre. We saw more and more, till the heat became so powerful, as to attract the mists from the various lakes, which in a slight degree obscured the prospect. The shadow of the mountain was flung many miles, and shewed its bicapitated form; the Wyddfa making one, Crib y Distyll the other head. I counted this time between twenty and thirty lakes either in this county or Meirioneddshire. The day proved so excessively hot, that my journey cost me the skin of the lower part of my face, before I reached the resting-place after the fatigue of the morning.

* * * * *

On this day, the sky was obscured very soon after I got up. A vast mist enveloped the whole circuit of the mountain. The prospect down was horrible. It gave an idea of numbers of abysses, concealed by a thick smoke, furiously circulating around us. Very often a gust of wind formed an opening in the clouds, which gave a fine and distinct vista of lake and valley. Sometimes they opened only in one place; at others, in many at once, exhibiting a most strange and perplexing sight of water, fields, rocks, or chasms, in fifty different places. They then closed at once, and left us involved in darkness; in a small time they would separate again, and fly in wild eddies round the middle of the mountains, and expose, in parts, both tops and bases clear to our view. We descended from this various scene with great reluctance; but before we reached our horses, a thunderstorm overtook us. Its rolling among the mountains was inexpressibly awful: the rain uncommonly heavy.

We remounted our horses, and gained the bottom with great hazard. The little rills, which on our ascent trickled along the gullies on the sides of the mountain, were now swelled into torrents; and we and our steeds passed with the utmost risque of being swept away by these sudden waters. At length we arrived safe, yet sufficiently wet and weary, to our former quarters.

THOMAS PENNANT (1726-98)
Tours in Wales

ON SNOWDON

The Wyddfa is about thirty feet in diameter and is surrounded on three sides by a low wall. . . . Below on all sides are frightful precipices, except on the side of the west. Towards the east it looks perpendicularly into the dyffryn or vale, nearly a mile below, from which to the gazer it is at all times an object of admiration, of wonder, and almost of fear.

There we stood on the Wyddfa, in a cold bracing atmosphere, though the day was almost stiflingly hot in the regions from which we had ascended. There we stood enjoying a scene inexpressibly grand, comprehending a considerable part of the mainland of Wales, the whole of Anglesey, a faint glimpse of part of Cumberland; the Irish Channel, and what might be either a misty creation or the shadowy outline of the hills of Ireland. Peaks and pinnacles and huge moels stood up here and there, about us and below us, partly in glorious light, partly in deep shade. Manifold were the objects which we saw from the brow of Snowdon, but of all the objects which we saw, those which filled us with most delight and admiration were numerous lakes and lagoons, which, like sheets of ice or polished silver, lay reflecting the rays of the sun in the deep valleys at his feet.

"Here," said I to Henrietta, "you are on the top crag of Snowdon, which the Welsh consider, and perhaps with justice, to be the most remarkable crag in the world; which is mentioned in many of their old wild romantic tales, and some of the noblest of their poems, amongst others in the *Day of Judgement*, by the illustrious Goronwy Owen, where it is brought forward in the following manner:

> "*Ail i'r ar ael Eryri,*
> *Cyfartal hoewal â hi.*

"'The brow of Snowdon shall be levelled with the ground, and the eddying waters shall murmur round it.' . . ."

GEORGE BORROW (1803-81)
Wild Wales

SNOWDON—A MOONLIT SCENE

In one of these excursions, travelling then
Through Wales on foot, and with a youthful Friend,
I left Bethgelert's huts at couching-time,
And westward took my way to see the sun
Rise from the top of Snowdon. Having reach'd
The Cottage at the Mountain's foot, we there
Rouz'd up the Shepherd, who by ancient right
Of office is the Stranger's usual guide;
And after short refreshment sallied forth.

It was a Summer's night, a close warm night,
Wan, dull and glaring, with a dripping mist
Low-hung and thick that cover'd all the sky,
Half threatening storm and rain; but on we went
Uncheck'd, being full of heart and having faith
In our tried Pilot. Little could we see
Hemm'd round on every side with fog and damp,

And, after ordinary travellers' chat
With our Conductor, silently we sank
Each into commerce with his private thoughts:
Thus did we breast the ascent, and by myself
Was nothing either seen or heard the while
Which took me from my musings, save that once
The Shepherd's Cur did to his own great joy
Unearth a hedgehog in the mountain crags
Round which he made a barking turbulent.
This small adventure, for even such it seemed
In that wild place and at the dead of night,
Being over and forgotten, on we wound
In silence as before. With forehead bent
Earthward, as if in opposition set
Against an enemy, I panted up
With eager pace, and no less eager thoughts.
Thus might we wear perhaps an hour away,
Ascending at loose distance each from each,
And I, as chanced, the foremost of the Band;
When at my feet the ground appear'd to brighten,
And with a step or two seem'd brighter still;
Nor had I time to ask the cause of this,
For instantly a Light upon the turf
Fell like a flash: I looked about, and lo!
The Moon stood naked in the Heavens, at height
Immense above my head, and on the shore
I found myself of a huge sea of mist,
Which, meek and silent, rested at my feet:
A hundred hills their dusky backs upheaved
All over this still Ocean, and beyond,
Far, far beyond, the vapours shot themselves,
In headlands, tongues, and promontory shapes,
Into the Sea, the real Sea, that seem'd
To dwindle, and give up its majesty,
Usurp'd upon as far as sight could reach.
Meanwhile, the Moon look'd down upon this shew
In single glory, and we stood, the mist

Touching our very feet; and from the shore
At distance not the third part of a mile
Was a blue chasm; a fracture in the vapour,
A deep and gloomy breathing-place through which
Mounted the roar of waters, torrents, streams
Innumerable, roaring with one voice.
The universal spectacle throughout
Was shaped for admiration and delight,
Grand in itself alone, but in that breach
Through which the homeless voice of waters rose,
That dark deep thoroughfare had Nature lodg'd
The Soul, the Imagination of the whole.

WILLIAM WORDSWORTH (1770-1850)
The Prelude

NANT GWYNANT

From Capel Curig down the justly celebrated vale of Nant Gwynant to Beddgelert. In this vale are two small lakes, the higher of which is the only Welsh lake which has any pretentions to compare with our own; and it has one great advantage over them, that it remains wholly free from intrusive objects. We saw it early in the morning; and with the greenness of the meadows at its head, the steep rocks on one of its shores, and the bold mountains at *both* extremities, a feature almost peculiar to itself, it appeared to us truly enchanting.

WILLIAM WORDSWORTH (1770-1850)
Letters

NEAR LLANBERIS

A little before sunset we came in sight of Llanberis Lake, Snowdon, and all the craggy hills and mountains surrounding it; the foreground a beautiful contrast to this grandeur and desolation—a green sloping hollow, furnishing a shelter for one of the most beautiful collections of lowly Welsh cottages, with thatched roofs, overgrown with plants, anywhere to be met with: the hamlet is called Cwm-y-Glo.

WILLIAM WORDSWORTH (1770-1850)
Letters

THE OWLS

When night lit up the gleaming
  Of dust along the road,
And at Pen Llyn the empty bridge
  The placid stream bestrode,
I heard the owls from far below
Hooting through the groves in Cwm-y-Glo.

When the wild duck rode at anchor
  And rocked beneath the moon,
And the forest mere in icy spray
  Across their backs was strewn,
To the wind which roared on Mynydd Du
They made their answer piteously.

When the Glaslyn slid into a shadow,
  Like a sword into its sheath,
And red the mansion windows burned
  The rookeries beneath,
They cried when the dogs gave cry no more,
And night came down on Ynys-for.

And when the twilight wraps creation
  After its demented day,
And over worker and the work
  The voiceless hush holds sway,
Their tongue will have, I promise you,
Nor joy nor pain—Too-whit, too-whoo!

R. WILLIAMS PARRY (1884-)
translated from the Welsh by
DAVID BELL

HELEN OF SEGONTIUM

Then spoke the king of the Romans unto the emperor. "Lord," said he, "go forth to hunt by the way thou didst seem to go, whether it were to the east, or to the west." So the emperor went forth to the hunt, and he came to the bank of the river. "Behold," said he, "this is where I was when I saw the dream, and I went towards the source of the river westward."

And thereupon thirteen messengers of the emperor's set forth, and before them they saw a high mountain, which seemed to them to touch the sky. Now this was the guise in which the messengers journeyed; one sleeve was on the cap of each of them in front, as a sign that they were messengers, in order that through what hostile land soever they might pass no harm might be done to them. And when they were come over this mountain, they beheld vast plains, and large rivers flowing there through. "Behold," said they, "the land which our master saw."

And they went along the mouths of the rivers, until they came to a mighty river which they saw flowing to the sea, and the vast city, and the many-coloured high towers in the castle. They saw the largest fleet in the world, in the harbour of the river, and one ship that was larger than any of the others. "Behold again," said they, "the dream that our master saw." And in the great ship they crossed the sea, and came to the island of Britain. And they traversed the island until they came to Snowdon. "Behold," said they, "the rugged land that our master saw." And they went forward until they saw Anglesey before them, and until they saw Arvon likewise. "Behold," said they, "the land our master saw in his sleep." And they saw Aber Seint, and a castle at the mouth of the river. The portal of the castle saw they open, and into the castle they went, and they saw a hall in the castle. Then said they, "Behold, the hall which he saw in his sleep." They went into the hall, and they beheld two youths playing at chess on the golden bench. And they beheld the hoary-headed man beside the pillar, in the ivory chair, carving chessmen. And they beheld the maiden sitting on a chair of ruddy gold.

The messengers bent down upon their knees. "Empress of Rome, all hail!" "Ha, gentles," said the maiden, "ye bear the seeming of honourable men, and the badge of envoys, what mockery is this ye do to me?" "We mock thee not, lady; but the Emperor of Rome hath seen thee in his sleep, and he has neither life nor spirit left because of thee. Thou shalt have of us therefore the choice, lady, whether thou wilt go with us and be made empress of Rome, or that the emperor come hither and take thee for his wife?" "Ha, lords," said the maiden, "I will not deny what ye say, neither will I believe it too well. If the emperor love me, let him come here to seek me."

The Mabinogion (*The Dream of Maxen Wledic*)
translated from the Welsh by
LADY CHARLOTTE GUEST

CAERNARVON

Carnarvon was founded two thousand years ago as the outpost of a great Empire—the greatest Empire that the world had seen. It was the Buluwayo of the Roman Empire, the very extreme of barbarism and savagery, just a fortified camp. The ruins are still there, and little children go to a school close by. They learn a language in that school, a dead language; it is the language of that great Empire. They go out and play amongst the ruins, and they talk a language, a living one; it is the language of the conquered and the savages. Let no man despise Wales, her language or her literature. She has survived many storms; she has survived many Empires. Her time will come. When the last truckload of coal reaches Cardiff, when the last black diamond is dug out of the earth of Glamorgan, there will be men then digging gems of pure brilliants from the inexhaustible mines of the literature and language of Wales.

D. LLOYD GEORGE (1863-1945)
Speech at St. David's Festival Dinner at Cardiff, 1906

BARDSEY OF THE SAINTS

Me, the poet Meilyr, a pilgrim to Peter,
The gate-ward who assesses qualities of perfection,
When the time to rise will come for us
All who are entombed, support Thou me.
Awaiting the call, may I be in the precincts
Of the monastery against which beats the tide,
Which is secluded, and of undying fame,
With its graveyard in the bosom of the sea,
The Isle of wondrous Mary, holy isle of the saints—
Glorious within it resurrection to await.

Christ of the prophesied Cross, who knows me, will
deliver me
From a banished existence in violent hell;
The Creator, who created me, will receive me
Among the saintly parish of the band of Enlli.

MEILYR (early 12th century)
translated from the Welsh by
J. LLOYD-JONES

ON HOLYHEAD

There stood I on the cairn of the Grey Giant, looking around me. The prospect, on every side, was noble: the blue interminable sea to the west and north; the whole stretch of Mona to the east; and far away to the south the mountainous region of Eryri, comprising some of the most romantic hills in the world. In some respects this Pen Santaidd, this holy headland, reminded me of Finisterrae, the Gallegan promontory which I had ascended some seventeen years before, whilst engaged in battling the Pope with the sword of the gospel in his favourite territory. Both are bold, bluff headlands looking to the west, both have huge rocks in their vicinity, rising from the bosom of the brine.

For a time as I stood on the cairn, I almost imagined myself on the Gallegan hill; much the same scenery presented itself as there, and a sun equally fierce struck upon my head as that which assailed it on the Gallegan hill. For a time all my thoughts were of Spain. It was not long, however, before I bethought me that my lot was now in a different region, that I had done with Spain for ever, after doing for her all that lay in the power of a lone man, who had never in this world anything to depend upon, but God and his own slight strength. Yes, I had done with Spain, and was now in Wales; and after a slight sigh, my thoughts became all intensely Welsh. I thought on the old times when Mona was the grand seat of Druidical superstition, when adoration was paid to Dwy Fawr, and Dwy Fach, the sole survivors of the apocryphal Deluge; to Hu the Mighty and his plough; to Ceridwen and her cauldron; to Andras the Horrible; to Wyn ap Nudd, Lord of Unknown, and to Beli, Emperor of the Sun. I thought on the times when the Beal fire blazed on this height, on the neighbouring promontory, on the cope-stone of Eryri, and on every high hill throughout Britain on the first of May. I thought on the day when the bands of Suetonius crossed the Menai Strait in their broad-bottomed boats, fell upon the Druids and their followers, who with wild looks and brandished torches lined the shore, slew hundreds with merciless butchery upon the plains, and pursued the remainder to the remotest fastnesses of the isle. I figured to myself long-bearded men with white vestmants toiling up the rocks, followed by fierce warriors with glittering helms and short, broad, two-edged swords; I thought I heard groans, cries of rage, and the dull, awful sound of bodies precipitated down rocks. Then as I looked towards the sea I thought I saw the fleet of Gryffith Ab Cynan steering from Ireland to Abermenai, Gryffith the son of a fugitive king, born in Ireland in the Commot of Columbcille, Gryffith the frequently baffled, the often victorious; once a manacled prisoner sweating in the sun, in the market-place of Chester, eventually king of North Wales; Griffith, who, "though he loved well the trumpet's clang loved the sound of the harp better"; . . . Then I thought—But I should tire the reader were I to detail all the intensely Welsh thoughts which crowded into my head as I stood on the Cairn of the Grey Giant.

GEORGE BORROW (1803-81)
Wild Wales

LLANDUDNO

The summer before last I spent some weeks at Llandudno on the Welsh coast. The best lodging-houses at Llandudno look eastward, towards Liverpool; and from that Saxon hive swarms are incessantly issuing, crossing the bay, and taking possession of the beach and the lodging-houses. Guarded by the Great and Little Orme's Head, and alive with the Saxon invaders from Liverpool, the eastern bay is an attractive point of interest, and many visitors to Llandudno never contemplate anything else. But, putting aside the charm of the Liverpool steamboats, perhaps the view, on this side, a little dissatisfies one after a while; the horizon wants mystery, the sea wants beauty, the coast wants verdure, and has a too bare austereness and aridity.

At last one turns round and looks westward. Everything is changed. Over the mouth of the Conway and its sands is the eternal softness and mild light of the west; the low line of the mystic Anglesey, and the precipitous Penmaenmawr, and the great group of Carnedd Llewelyn and Carnedd David and their brethren fading away, hill behind hill, in an aerial haze, make the horizon; between the foot of Penmaenmawr and the bending coast of Anglesey, the sea, a silver stream, disappears one knows not whither. On this side, Wales, —Wales, where the past still lives, where every place has its tradition, every name its poetry, and where the people, the genuine people, still knows this past, this tradition, this poetry, and lives with it, and clings to it; while, alas, the prosperous Saxon on the other side, the invader from Liverpool and Birkenhead, has long ago forgotten his. And the promontory where Llandudno stands is the very centre of this tradition; it is Creuddyn, where every stone has its story; there, opposite its decaying rival, Conway Castle, is Deganwy, not decaying but long since utterly decayed, some crumbling foundations on a crag-top and nothing more;—Deganwy, where Maelgwn, a British prince of real history, a bold and licentious chief . . . shut himself up in the church to avoid the Yellow Plague, and peeped out through a hole in the door, and saw the monster and died. Behind among the woods, is Gloddaith, where the bards were entertained; and farther away, up the valley of the Conway towards Llanrwst, is the Lake of Ceirionydd and Taliesin's grave. Or, again, looking seawards and Anglesey-wards, you have Penmon, Seiriol's isle and priory, where Maelgwn lies buried; you have the *Sands of Lamentation* and Llys Helig, a mansion under the waves, a sea-buried palace and realm. *Hac ibat Simois; hic est Sigeia tellus.*

MATTHEW ARNOLD (1822-88)
On the study of Celtic Literature

THE VALE OF CLWYD

The North-wind (calme become) forgets his Ire to wreake,
And the delicious Vale thus mildly doth bespeake;
  Deere *Cluyd*, th'aboundant sweets, that from thy bosome flowe,
When with my active wings into the ayre I throwe,
Those Hills whose hoarie heads seeme in the clouds to dwell,
Of aged become young, enamor'd with the smell
Of th' odoriferous flowers in thy most precious lap:
Within whose velvit leaves, when I my selfe enwrap,
They suffocate with sents; that (from my native kind)
I seeme some slowe perfume, and not the swiftest wind.
With joy, my *Dyffren Cluyd*, I see thee bravely spred,
Survaying every part, from foote up to thy head;

Thy full and youthfull breasts, which in their meadowy
    pride,
Are brancht with rivery veines, Meander-like that glide.
I further note in thee, more excellent than these
(Were there a thing that more the amorous eye might
    please)
Thy plumpe and swelling wombe, whose mellowy gleabe
    doth beare
The yellow ripened sheafe, that bendeth with the eare.

MICHAEL DRAYTON (1563-1631)
Polyolbion

IN THE VALLEY OF THE ELWY

I remember a house where all were good
  To me, God knows, deserving no such thing:
  Comforting smell breathed at very entering,
Fetched fresh, as I suppose, off some sweet wood.
That cordial air made these kind people a hood
  All over, as a bevy of eggs the mothering wing
  Will, or mild nights the new morsels of spring:
Why, it seemed of course; seemed of right it should.

Lovely the woods, waters, meadows, combes, vales,
All the air things wear that build this world of Wales;
  Only the inmate does not correspond:
God, lover of souls, swaying considerate scales,
Complete thy creature dear O where it fails,
  Being mighty a master, being a father and fond.

G. MANLEY HOPKINS (1844-89)

SYCHARTH

The home of Owain Glyn Dŵr

Twice have I pledged my word to thee
To come thy noble face to see;
His promises let every man
Perform as far as e'er he can!
Full easy is the thing that's sweet,
And sweet this journey is and meet;
I've vow'd to Owain's court to go,
And I'm resolv'd to keep my vow;
So thither straight I'll take my way
With blithesome heart, and there I'll stay,
Respect and honour, whilst I breathe,
To find his honour'd roof beneath.
My chief of long lin'd ancestry
Can harbour sons of poesy;
I've heard, for so the muse has told,
He's kind and gentle to the old;
Yes, to his castle I will hie;
There's none to match it 'neath the sky;
It is a baron's stately court,
Where bards for sumptious fare resort;
There dwells the lord of Powis land,
Who granteth every just demand.
Its likeness now I'll limn you out:
'Tis water-girdled wide about;
It shows a wide and stately door
Reached by a bridge the water o'er;
'Tis formed of buildings coupled fair,
Coupled is every couple there;
Within a quadrate structure tall
Muster the merry pleasures all.
Conjointly are the angles bound—
No flaw in all the place is found.

Structures in contact meet the eye
Upon the hillock's top on high;
Into each other fastened they
The form of a hard knot display.
There dwells the chief we all extol
In timber house on lightsome knoll;
Upon four wooden columns proud
Mounteth his mansion to the cloud;
Each column's thick and firmly bas'd,
And upon each a loft is plac'd;
In these four lofts, which coupled stand,
Repose at night the minstrel band;
Four lofts they were in pristine state,
But now partitioned form they eight.
Tiled is the roof, on each house top
Rise smoke-ejecting chimneys up.
All of one form there are nine halls
Each with nine wardrobes in its walls.
With linen white as well supplied
As fairest shops of fam'd Cheapside.
Behold that church with cross uprais'd
And with its windows neatly glaz'd;
All houses are in this comprest—
An orchard's near it of the best,
Also a park where void of fear
Feed antler'd herds of fallow deer.
A warren wide my chief can boast,
Of goodly steeds a countless host,
Meads where for hay the clover grows,
Corn-fields where hedges trim inclose,
A mill a rushing brook upon,
And pigeon-tower fram'd of stone;
A fish-pond deep and dark to see
To cast nets in when need there be,
Which never yet was known to lack
A plenteous store of perch and jack,
Of various plumage birds abound;

Herons and peacocks haunt around.
What luxury doth his hall adorn,
Showing of cost a sovereign scorn;
His ale from Shrewsbury town he brings;
His usquebaugh[1] is drink for kings;
Bragget he keeps, bread white of look,
And, bless the mark! a bustling cook.
His mansion is the minstrel's home,
You'll find them there whene'er you come.
Of all her sex his wife's the best;
The household through her care is blest;
She's scion of a knightly tree,
She's dignified, she's kind and free.
His bairns approach me, pair by pair,
O what a nest of chieftains fair!
Here difficult it is to catch
A sight of either bolt or latch:
The porter's place here none will fill:
Here largess shall be lavish'd still,
And ne'er shall thirst or hunger rude
In Sycharth venture to intrude.
A noble leader, Cambria's knight,
The lake possesses, his by right,
And midst that azure water plac'd,
The castle, by each pleasure grac'd.

IOLO GOCH (*c.* 1320-98)
translated from the Welsh by
GEORGE BORROW

CASTLE CAEREINION

It was situated in a pleasant glen, fertile and well-wooded, opening out into the great valley of the Severn. Offa's Dyke could be traced a mile or two to the eastward, and the line of demarcation between English and

[1]The original refers to ale, spirits and bragget. (*Editor*)

Welsh ran through the parish. The lower division was entirely English, and the upper Welsh; while the village situated about the centre was a sort of Debatable Land. Both languages were known pretty generally, especially by the elder folk, though English was mostly spoken: as to the children, they used English exclusively. And in external features also the country partook of the characteristics of both countries: on the one hand we had a rich, fat valley, thoroughly English in its look of abundance and comfort; on the other, there was a Welsh succession of hills and dales, less rich but very pleasing to look at. On the English side the houses were mostly of brick, red, square, and rather ugly, but the huge ricks, sleek cattle, and blooming orchards took off much of the barrenness. In the Welsh division the houses were built in that most picturesque of styles, with frames of oak, the interstices being filled up with lath and plaster. The poorest thatched cottage had its garden, well filled with fruit trees; the poverty that the richest land is not totally exempt from, was well hidden beneath a mask of picturesqueness, and one might well forget for a time that it had any existence. Coming as I did from a part of the country very uninviting to the eye, the beauty of Castle Caereinion was more striking than it would have been to one familiar with a richer landscape: to me it had all the beauty of Carmel and Sharon combined.

ROBERT ROBERTS (1834-85)
The Life and Opinions of R. R., a wandering scholar

IN PRAISE OF OSWESTRY

Hill-countryman in younger days,
Now with grey hairs I've changed my ways;
My faltering steps prefer the town,
Within its walls I'll settle down.
My jaded stomach milk would scorn,

And calls for physic night and morn.
A wandering poet near life's goal
Prefers his flask and pewter bowl,
Warmth and comfort and friendly cheer,
Fresh meat, white flour, and good beer.
The timbered homes of lowland lea
Restore my health like the green tree,
Hence the home which shall be mine
In Marchland where are mead and wine;
Generous and true, a friendly town,
Gracious, gifted, of high renown;
The castle with its curtain wall
Famed far as Rome above them all:
Oswald's town, where Christ is loved,
To the Conqueror a treasure proved.

The London of our Owain's land,
With orchards rich and wine-shops grand,
A school that's free, and of wide fame,
The town of preachers of good name;
In a temple rich the Host they raise—
Men in grammar and metrics beyond all praise,
A church supreme, and jewelled chalice,
Clear bells, and an organ in God's palace,
A tuneful choir—a well-trained band,
Vestments famed throughout the land;
Where find you clergy as good and bright
As they who serve in that temple white?
In coiffure and dress no women excel
Those who in Oswald's city dwell.
Adorned in Cheapside's merchandise,
Harmonious her citizens, and wise.

A tall Earl rules that city bright,
An Earl who is England's proud delight;
May God in his grace preserve him long
To maintain his rule, a guardian strong

[R. Cecil Hughes

YR WYBRNANT: HOME OF BISHOP MORGAN

Translator of the Bible into Welsh

[R. Cecil Hughes

Y GARREG WEN, NEAR BORTH-Y-GEST

Home of famous harpist

[W. Morris Mendus

ST. DAVID'S CATHEDRAL: THE NAVE

Over commons and yeomen proud and free,
And citizens too of higher degree.
Among these men I, too, would stay
As one of them to live my day.
My muse to leave this town no more
Would strive than the sea to leave the shore.
Long wedded here, a burgess am I,
To whom should I pay my fee, should I try?
May Oswald's citizens hold their hand
Till hair on my head again will stand!
If suddenly I'm called five pounds to pay,
My fellows will aid me without delay.

Among gracious folk whose hearts were true,
Owain Waed Da was a burgess too;
He had only to sing among his friends
To gain his greatly coveted ends.
The privilege I seek is what came his way,
My burgess rights let none gainsay!
A cowyth I offer, a song in court—
Good poetry avoids great hurt.
The muse's solace is a gift more blest
Than a noble of gold in the city chest;
More lasting than gold, of greater fame,
As Welshmen have sung, is our good name.
To my fellow-townsmen sing then will I
And my welcome will hold until I die:
No more will I wander without consent
To offer my song where once I went.

GUTO'R GLYN (*c.* 1412-*c.* 1493)
translated from the Welsh by
D. M. LLOYD

History—Literary and General

CELTIC MAGIC

The Celt's quick feeling for what is noble and distinguished gave his poetry style; his indomitable personality gave it pride and passion; his sensibility and nervous exaltation gave it a better gift still, the gift of rendering with wonderful felicity the magical charm of nature. The forest solitude, the bubbling spring, the wild flowers, are everywhere in romance. They have a mysterious life and grace there; they are Nature's own children, and utter her secret in a way which makes them something quite different from the woods, waters, and plants of Greek and Latin poetry. Now of this delicate magic, Celtic romance is so pre-eminent a mistress, that it seems impossible to believe the power did not come into romance from the Celts. Magic is just the word for it,—the magic of nature; not merely the beauty of nature,—that the Greeks and Latins had; not merely an honest smack of the soil, a faithful realism, —that the Germans had; but the intimate life of Nature, her weird power and her fairy charm. . . . Gwydion wants a wife for his pupil: "Well," says Math, "we will seek, I and thou, by charms and illusions, to form a wife for him out of flowers." So they took the blossoms of the oak, and the blossoms of the broom, and the blossoms of the meadow-sweet, and produced from them a maiden, the fairest and most graceful that man ever saw. And they baptized her, and gave her the name of Flower-Aspect." Celtic romance is full of exquisite touches like that, showing the delicacy of the Celt's feeling in these matters, and how deeply Nature lets him come into her secrets. The quick dropping of blood is called "faster than the fall of the dewdrop from the blade of reed-grass upon the earth, when the dew of June is at the heaviest." And thus is Olwen described: "More yellow was her hair than the flower of the broom, and her skin was whiter than the foam of the wave, and fairer were her hands and her fingers than the blossoms of the wood-anemony amidst the spray of the meadow fountains." For loveliness it would be hard to beat that; and for magical clearness and nearness take the following:

"And in the evening Peredur entered a valley, and at the head of the valley he came to a hermit's cell, and the hermit welcomed him gladly, and there he spent the night. And in the morning he arose, and when he went forth, behold, a shower of snow had fallen the night before, and a hawk had killed a wild-fowl in front of the cell. And the noise of the horse scared the hawk away, and a raven alighted upon the bird. And Peredur stood and compared the blackness of the raven, and the whiteness of the snow, and the redness of the blood, to the hair of the lady whom best he loved, which was blacker than the raven, and to her skin, which was whiter than the snow, and to her two cheeks, which were redder than the blood upon the snow appeared to be."

And this, which is perhaps less striking, is not less beautiful:

"And early in the day Geraint and Enid left the wood, and they came to an open country, with meadows on one hand and mowers mowing the meadows. And there was a river before them, and the horses bent down and drank the water. And they went up out of the river by a steep bank, and there they met a slender stripling with a satchel about his neck; and he had a small blue pitcher in his hand, and a bowl on the mouth of the pitcher."

And here the landscape, up to this point so Greek in its clear beauty, is suddenly magicalised by the romance touch:

"And they saw a tall tree by the side of the river, one-half of which was in flames from the root to the top, and the other half was green and in full leaf."

Magic is the word to insist upon,—a magically vivid and near interpretation of nature; since it is this which constitutes the special charm and power of the effect I am calling attention to, and it is for this that the Celt's sensibility gives him a peculiar aptitude.

MATTHEW ARNOLD (1822-88)
On the Study of Celtic Literature

MABINOGI AND EDDA

There is hardly any question to which an otherwise well-educated man will return a less correct but a more confident answer than: What are the qualities that distinguish early Welsh writing? For if there is a Celtic Twilight, it drenches with its mists and half-tones some other landscape than the Welsh; its haze and melancholy must be sought elsewhere than in the writings we are now considering. However filled with light and shadow, with humour, pathos and magic, we discover them to be, all is clean and sheer and shaped by the fine dry hand of a craftsman. But the popular Ossianic notions of the subject suggest that many still underwrite a conception of old Welsh literature no more accurate than early eighteenth-century conceptions of the blood-swilling viking, skulls, snake-pits and all. The Four Branches are not wind-filled, obfusc, gloomy, extravagant, whimsical, stuffed with sentiment, or garnished with romance. They are at once delicate and strong, rich in emotion but devoid of emotionalism, magical yet matter-of-fact, and their atmosphere is that of rainbow-hued Dyfed and Gwynedd. They are as remote from mysticism as from realism. They show a great love of colours and contrasts, so that at times the texture of narrative appears impregnated with a purity and soft brilliance of greens, blues, reds and yellows. Above all they are strong and translucent.

If now I praise Snorri for the clarity of his style, for the charm which accompanies his precision and resilience, I shall be puzzled to express adequately the difference that every reader will find between the Welsh writer and the Icelandic. The Icelander's page is lit with a dry intellectual light; the Welshman's is refulgent with imagination. What in Snorri is a clear beam, in his fellow, is a warm glow.

GWYN JONES (1907-)
Mabinogi and Edda

AN EARLY EISTEDDFOD

1176. At Christmastide in that year, the Lord Rhys ap Gruffudd held a court with great splendour in Cardigan Castle, and arranged two kinds of contests there, one for bards and poets, and the other for harpists and crowthers and pipers and other musicians. He had two chairs placed for the winners, and honoured them with lavish gifts. Among the harpists, a youth of Rhys's own court was successful, and of the poets, those of Gwynedd were supreme. All seekers of largesse obtained from Rhys all that they asked for, and no one met with refusal. That feast, before it was held, had been proclaimed a year in advance throughout Wales, and England, Ireland, and the other islands.

The Chronicle of the Princes
translated from the Welsh by
D. M. LLOYD

HOW TO PRAISE EACH THING

Furthermore one must know how to praise each thing which one would wish to select as the subject of a poem. There are two kinds of things about which poems should be composed, namely a spiritual thing, and a corporeal thing; a spiritual thing, such as God and the saints; a corporeal thing, such as man, or an animal or a place. God should be praised for divine quality, and strength, and almightiness, and supreme wisdom and complete goodness and entire mercy and truth, and righteous judgements, and purity, and holiness, and creative power, and fatherliness, and spirituality, and honour, and heavenly beauty, and every honourable spiritual quality. . . .

Two kinds of human beings should be praised, man and woman. There are two kinds of man, a man in religion and a man in the world. There are two kinds of man in the world, laymen and clerics. There are two kinds of clerics, prelates and subordinates. Prelates, such as bishops and archbishops are praised for wisdom, and prudence, and the skilful accomplishment of their church government, and their firmness in maintaining the rule of the church, and their mercy to the poor, and their deeds of charity, and their prayers, and their spiritual actions, and their discriminating generosity, and the maintainance of their courts, and their meekness, and other honourable ecclesiastical qualities. . . .

Teachers are praised for wisdom and accomplishment, and mastery over laws and canons, and depth of insight, and skills, and triumphs in disputations, and meekness, and fairness, and good breeding, and generosity, and good manners, and amiability, and other praiseworthy qualities. . . .

A ruler is praised for ability, and power, and military skill, and courage, and pride, and meekness, and wisdom, and accomplishment, and generosity, and mildness, and amiability towards his men and his friends, and beauty of countenance, and a dignified bearing, and magnanimity of mind, and nobleness of actions, and other honourable and kindly qualities. . . .

Three kinds of women are praised; a matron, a maid, and a nun. A matron is praised for wisdom, and orderliness, and chastity, and generosity, and beauty of countenance, complexion and figure, and guilelessness of speech and actions. And it is not fitting to compliment a matron for prowess in love-making or dalliance, for a wooing-song to her is not seemly.

A maid is praised for her appearance, and beauty, and neatness, and innocence, and perfection of manners and behaviour, and generosity, and chastity, and good name, and breeding, and delicacy, and kindness, and it is to her that love-making and dalliance are fitting. . . .

A nun is praised for saintliness and chastity and purity of life, and other devout qualities. . . .

It is not becoming for a *prydydd* (a poet of high grade) to dabble in *clerwriaeth* (the practices of low grade poets, *c.f. clerici vagantes*), for such base things are opposed to the art of the *prydydd.* For it is the habit of the *clerwr* to mock and to belittle, and to arouse feelings of shame and disgrace, whereas it behoves the *prydydd* to praise and compliment, and to procure fame and joy and glorification. And, moreover, *clerwriaeth* is not reducible to rule, for it is a disorderly art, and for that reason may it be avoided by the *prydydd.* On the other hand it is becoming for a *prydydd* to concern himself with *teuluwriaeth* (the middle grade art of the 'household' bards), and to treat it critically, for it is an art that submits itself to rule and to the discipline of the *prydydd.* Wherever the *prydydd* practises his art, it is not right to credit the disparaging productions of the *clerwr*, for the *prydydd's* song of praise should outweigh such mean effusions. Incantations, sorcery, and magical practices, are not worthy of the *prydydd's* indulgence, and he should not meddle with them. Ancient song of high repute, and tales preserved in writing, questions reflecting honour on those who asked them, and replies rendered excellent by art and truth—these are the things that are good for the *prydydd* to know when called upon to converse with wise men, to delight young maidens, and to entertain gentlemen and ladies of breeding. For the *prydydd's* art is a portion of natural wisdom, and is derived from the Holy Spirit, and its inspiration is a fruit of genius mated to artistic assiduity.

The Welsh Poetic Art
From *Llanstephan 3*, an early 15th century manuscript, translated from the Welsh by
D. M. LLOYD

THE BARDIC FUNCTIONS[1]

The Office and functione of the Bruttish or Cambrian Bards was to keepe and preserve *Tri chof ynys Brydain*: That is the Three Records or Memorialls of Bryttaen, which otherwise is called the Bruttish antiquitie which consisteth of three parts and is called *Tri chof*. ffor the preservatione wheareof when the Bards were graduated at there comencements, they were rewarded wyth treble reward one reward for every *Cof*: as the auncient Bard Tudur Aled doth recite of this *Tri chof* and his reward for the same at his comencement and graduacione at the Royall wedding of Ieuan ap Davyd ap Ithel vychan of Northopp in Inglefield in fflintshire which hee vppon the *Cerdd marwnad* of the sayd Ieuan ap Davyd ap Ithel recited thus

Cyntaf neuadd im graddwyd
vy oror llys f'eryr llwyd
am Dri chof im dyrchafodd
yn neithior hwnn a thair rhodd

[1]We wish to acknowledge the kindness of Mr. D. J. Bowen, M.A., of the staff of the National Library of Wales, in transcribing this text from the manuscript. (*Editors.*)

[The first hall where I was graduated was the Borderland court of my grey eagle. For the '*tri chof*' did he raise me up in his marriage feast, and gave me three gifts.]

And soe you may see that hee was exalted and graduated at the sayd wedding for his knowledge in the sayd *Tri chof*, and was rewarded wyth thre severall rewards one for every *Cof*.

The one of the sayd three *Cof* is the History of the notable Acts of the kings and princes of this land of Bruttaen and Cambria;

And the second of the sayd three *cof* is the languaige of the Bruttons for which thee Bards ought to giue accompt for every word and sillable there in whey they are demaunded thereof and to preserue the auncient tonge and not to intermix ytt wyth any forrayne tonge or to bring any forrayne word amongest yt to the preiudice of there owne words wheareby they might eyther be forgotten or extyrped.

And the Thyrd *Cof* was, to keepe the genealogies or Descents of the Nob[il]itie, there Division of lands and there Armes; for there Descents Armes and Divisione of lands were but one of the Three *Cof*.

The auncient Bards had a stipend out of every plowland in the countrey for there mayntenance And the sayd Bards had alsoe a Perambulacione or a Visitacione once every three yeares to the houses of all the Gentlmen in the Countrey (which was called *Cylch clera*) for preservinge of the sayd *Tri chof*. At which Perambulacione they dyd collect all the memorable things that were donne and fell out in every Countrey that concerned there profession to take notice of and wrotte yt downe: soe that theye could not be ignorant of any Memorabl actes, the death of any great persone, his descent, Division or porcione of lands, Armes and Children in any Countrey wythin theyre Perambulacione.

At which Perambulacione the sayd Bards receaved

there Rewards beinge a sett and a certenn Stipend from every gentlman to whose house they were intertayned in there Perambulacione which Stipend or Reward was called *Clera*.

Cerdd foliant is the Poemes of laude and prayse made in the Commendacione of a gentlman or gentlewoman in his lif time, and *Cerdd farwnad*, are Mournfull Poems made in lamentacione of a gentlmans death after his decesse.

Those menn that I call and tearme heare by the title of Gentlman, is called in oure languaige *Gwr bonheddic*, and there is no mann admitted by the Lawe to be called *Gwr bonheddic*, but hee yt paternally descendeth from the Kings and Princes of this lande of Bruttaen for *Bonheddic* is as much as *Nobilis* in Laten.

And the Paternall ascent of every gentlman most asscend to Royall persons from whom every gentlman did hould his Lands and his Armes.

And if a gentlman be soe descendded by father and mother then is hee stiled or lituled by the Lawe *Bonheddic canhwynawl*, which signifieth a perfect Noblman, by father and by mother. And this Title *Bonheddic*, is the first title that a man hath and remayneth in his blood from his byrth to his death and this Title *Bonhedd* can not be really given by any man whatsoever to any man or any that hath yt really deprived of yt.

All other Titls may be taken from man and may extinguish by his death or other casualties but this can not for hee bringeth this Title into the world and is not extinguished by his death for yt remayneth in his blood to his posteritie soe that he cannot be severed from ytt.

Comon persones of late yeares haue taken vppon them the title of *Bonhedd* or *Generositie*, but they are not really *Bonheddic* but are soe called or tearmed for fashione sake by reason of theyre welth, Offices or behavioure which are but Transitory things And *Bonedd* consisteth in noe Transitory thing but in a permanent. Soe that hearby you may vnderstand the gentrie of the Countrey had a speciall Interest in the *Tri chof*, for th[e] Histories were the Acts and deeds of theyre Ancestors and kinsmen; and the preservatione of the Languaige, Armes, descents, and Divisione of lands were theyreo wne proper service, and therefor the Stipend payd by them to the Bards was not constituted wythout good cause there vnto nor there Intertaynments in the perambulatione allowed vnto them but vpon good cause and reasone.

And all the Histories and Acts of the kings and Nobilitie were Collected by them all the Battells were recorded by them, and expresly remembred, vppon the *Cerdd foliant* of such noble persones as had performed the service in feelde and vppon there *cerdd farwnad* soe that there could be noe mistakinge of Truth in setting downe Histories from three yeare to three yeare.

And there was a greate punishment inflicted by the lawe vppon the Bards wyth long Imprisonement losse of place and dignitie wyth great disgace if any of them should sett downe for truth but truth in any Historicall treatie whatsoever. for noe man dyd treate of any Battell but such as was an eye witnes thereof for some of the cheefest of the Bards were the Marshalls of all Battells, and of Counsell for directinge the field and the kings or Generalls Inteligences how the Battell went on, soe that they could not be ignorant of any passaige or thinge donne in field. They dyd not write of Battells by hearesay afarr or by relacione vnles yt were some suddayne fight or skirmish vnexpected, for in all Battells of moment they were present as I shall express yt at large in an other place and my warrant and authorytie to prove the same.

Our Histories were not written by Scoolmasters that trafayled noe further for his knowledge than a Childs iourney from his Brekfast to his lesson, nor by any munck that iourned no further then from masse to meate nor by any prentise that had noe other educatione but from shopp to market nor by any Base persone of byrth condicion or calling But by noble Bards noblie descended Barons and fellowes to lords and princes.

ANONYMOUS
From *Llanstephan MS. 144* in hand of John Jones,
of Gelli Lyfdy (early 17th century)

STYLE AND THE CELTS

This something is *style*, and the Celts certainly have it in a wonderful measure. Style is the most striking quality of their poetry. Celtic poetry seems to make up to itself for being unable to master the world and give an adequate interpretation of it, by throwing all its force into style, by bending language at any rate to its will and expressing the ideas it has with unsurpassable intensity, elevation, and effect. It has all through it a sort of intoxication of style,—a *Pindarism*, to use a word formed from the name of the poet, on whom, above all other poets, the power of style seemed to have exercised an inspiring and intoxicating effect; and not in its great poets only, in Taliesin, or Llywarch Hen, or Ossian, does the Celtic genius show this Pindarism, but in all its productions:—

The grave of March is this, and this the grave of Gwythyr;
Here is the grave of Gwgawn Gleddyfrudd;
But unknown is the grave of Arthur.

That comes from the Welsh *Memorials of the Graves of the Warriors.*

Take the well-known Welsh prophecy about the fate of the Britons:—

Their Lord they will praise,
Their speech they will keep,

Their land they will lose,
Except wild Wales.

To however late an epoch that prophecy belongs, what a feeling for style, at any rate, it manifests! And the same may be said of the famous Welsh triads. We may put aside all the vexed questions as to their greater or less antiquity, and still what important witness they bear to the genius for literary style of the people who produced them!

MATTHEW ARNOLD (1822-88)
On the Study of Celtic Literature

WELSH AND ENGLISH POETRY

Donnington, February 21st, 1753

Dear Sir,

Nothing could have been more agreeable to me, than to employ my Muse on the subject you sent me; but the more agreeable the Subject, the more I regrett the vast inequality of my poor Muse to such an arduous task. If therefore it is not so well executed as I could wish, I readily own it was owing to my incapacity, and not to any defect in our Language. For *That* is (at least I am willing to believe it is) adequate to the highest strains of Panegyrick, and abundantly fitted for copiousness and significancy, to express the sublimest thoughts in as sublime a manner as any other Language is capable of reaching to. But still we must not think it is priviledged above all other Languages of the Universe, and exempted from all difficulties and restraints. No, it has it's own proper Idioms as all other have, and consequently when it is tied down, to keep pace with another, it is strait'ned and fetter'd, like David in Saul's armour, and like him had rather it's own sling and stone (the meanest of weapons) than be armed Cap a pè in such armour, as it has not prov'd, knows nothing of. Thus with regard to Translations, it fares with all Languages, but more especially where there is such a very great (I had almost said, irreconcileable) difference between the proprieties and Idioms of two Languages, as confessedly there is between our's and the English. This difficulty (great as it is) is again doubly augmented, when our translation is requir'd to be in Verse. There (besides the usual difficulty of making what is a beautifull thought in the one appear like common sense in the other) we are tied to find out, and range in order, letters and Syllables. What an exquisite nicety is requir'd in this literal Muster (if I may so call it) you very well know, so that it is sufficient for me only to mention it. Perhaps it were to be wish'd that the Rules of Poetry in our Language were less nice and accurate: we should then undoubtedly have more writers but perhaps fewer good ones. I would never wish to see our Poetry reduc'd to the English Standard, for I can see nothing in *that* that should entitle it to the Name of *Poetry*, but only the number of Syllables (which yet is never scrupulously observ'd) and a choice of *uncommon*, or if you please *Poetic* words, and a wretched Rhyme, some times at the end, and in blank Verse, *i.e.* the best kind of English Poetry no Rhyme at all. Milton's Paradise Lost is a Book I read with pleasure, nay with Admiration, and raptures: call it a great, sublime, nervous, etc. etc., or if you please a Divine Work, you'll find me ready to subscribe to anything that can be said in praise of it, provided you don't call it *Poetry*, or, if you do so, that you would likewise allow our *Bardd Cwsg* [one of the best classics of imaginative Welsh prose] to take his seat amongst the *Poets*. As the English Poetry is too loose, so ours is certainly too much confin'd and limited, not in the Cynghaneddau [a scheme of sound correspondences in Welsh poetry], for without them it were no Poetry; but in the length of Verses and Poems too, our longest lines not exceeding ten syllables (too scanty a space to contain anything *Great* within the compass of *Six* or *Seven* Stanzas, the usual length of our *Gwawdodyn Byrr*) and our longest Poems not above *Sixty* or *Seventy* Lines, the standard Measure of *Dafydd ap Gwilym's cywyddau*; which is far from being a length adequate to a Heroic Poem. However, these are, I apprehend, difficulties that will never be remedied; these Models our wise Forefathers left us, and *these* I presume, they judg'd most agreeable to the genius of our Nation and Language. Some freedom and ease of composition is, and was always observ'd to be productive of happier effects than an over-rigid and starch'd nicety. Thus the Greeks were much less confin'd as to Quantities than the Romans. And, not to detract from Virgil's deserv'd praise, I think Homer may be justly allow'd to be preferable to him, almost in such a measure and proportion, as an original Writer is to a Translator. The Romans had several words even in their own language, that by reason of their Quantities, could not possibly be put into Verse. Thus, Horace was at a loss to name the Town *Equotutium*, and was fain to describe it by a round-about sort of Paraphrase. And Martial was hard put to it, to name the favourite Boy *Earinus*, Domitian's valet. But on the contrary, every harsh word sounded smooth in a Greek's mouth: they might sound "Ἆρες, Ἄρες," with an air, tho' they made the same syllable in the same word to be, first, *long*, and then with the *same* breath, *short*. This, Martial wittily observes of 'em, and at the same time as wittily laments the over-rigidity of his own Country Muses:—

Nobis non licet esse tam disertis
Musas qui colimus severiores.

But, with all their severity, if Martial had been acquainted with the obstinate, coy, and incompliant temper of our British *Awen*, he would certainly have taken the Roman Muses for a bevy of City Courtezans. Besides, our Muse, by long disuse, has almost forgot to converse with Princes, at least in the mode and language of the present times. . . .

Eich rhwymedig wasanaethwr
[Your indebted servant]

Directed to
Mr. Richard Morris
At the Navy Office, London

GRONWY DDU O FON
Dark Gronwy from Mona

GORONWY OWEN (1723-69)

THE ESSENCE OF WELSH POETRY

During the wars of Napoleon there was a country squire of the name of Lloyd living in the old house of Cwmgloyn, inland a little from Trefdraeth (or Newport in the English maps) on the north coast of Pembrokeshire. He was a justice of the peace. His father had been high sheriff of the county in 1771. The family had been much concerned with the sea, and squire Lloyd had ships built for him at Trefdraeth and at Aberystwyth. One of these, the Hawk, was a fifty ton schooner made from his own woods at Trefdraeth, partly for trade, partly for his pleasure voyages. It was later sunk by the French. At its launching a local poet, one Ioan Siencyn, wrote a poem to greet it and its captain, and its squire-owner. After a finely imaged description of the Hawk breasting the sea, the poet visualises squire Lloyd on board, travelling to England and Ireland, but especially visiting his friends in North and South Wales. There the gentry and local poets come to meet him and one verse describes their welcome to him:

Around their tables laden with steaming dishes,
He shall hear histories of those good men, our ancestors,
And cywydd *and* englyn *and odes of Taliesin,*
And he shall drink his fill of golden barley beer.

That poem was written close to the beginning of the nineteenth century. It speaks simply and naturally of odes of Taliesin and *cywydd* and *englyn* as part of the pertinent welcome to squire Lloyd of Cwmgloyn. Taliesin was a poet of the sixth century. *Cywydd* and *englyn* were metrical forms of the Welsh Middle Ages. But for Ioan Siencyn at the very end of the eighteenth century they were all necessary for the proper entertainment of the Welsh squire in any Welsh country house. Poetry was part of the tradition of hospitality.

Now will you imagine with me that a poet of the fifteenth century, some great figure such as Tudur Aled, had been released to revisit Pembrokeshire at the launching of the Hawk, and had listened to the reading of Ioan Siencyn's verses to squire Lloyd? What would our fifteenth century master have thought or said? He would note with warm approval the occasion of the poem. Just such an event, the completion of a new house or a new ship, had in his time also been the appropriate moment for a complimentary poem to the head of a family. And Tudur Aled would have relished Ioan Siencyn's development of the image of the Hawk as it was launched on the water:

Spread now your wings, forget the green woodlands,
Learn to live mid the mouthing of seas.

When Siencyn calls on Neptune and Triton to protect the schooner, Tudur Aled would remember that he, in the early sixteenth century was beginning to learn the use of those Greek gods from his friends in the circle of Cardinal Wolsey; and that when the poet returns to his bird-schooner and describes the Hawk:

Your wings playing high as the clouds,
Your breasts cleaving the salt billows,
Let your beak pierce the waves, your belly furrow them,
Your rudder scatter them in spray-suds . . .

the fifteenth-century poet would have recognised it as just that serious playing with image that was part of the technique of poems inspired by manual craft in his own day. And as the poem grew to the final eulogy of squire Lloyd and his society, to the reference to Taliesin and talk of the deeds of his forefathers storied over the yellow beer on the laden dining table, Tudur Aled might well exclaim: "My art still survives in this last decade of the eighteenth century and the great technique and the old mastery are not all forgotten. This country poet, this Ioan Siencyn, is truly an heir of our ancient discipline; he also sings the immemorial ideals and the pattern of behaviour of the leaders of the Welsh people, and I recognise him as a poet of the long line that began with Taliesin in the North."

There, I think, we capture something essential in the progress of Welsh poesy. We call it the literary tradition of Wales. It means you cannot pluck a flower of song off a headland of Dyved in the late eighteenth century without stirring a great Northern star of the sixth century. And all the intermediaries are involved. The fourteenth century gave the technique of *dyfalu* or image-making, the sixteenth century brought in the Virgilian echoes, the seventeenth gave the measure. The whole body of Welsh poetry from the sixth century onward has contributed directly to Ioan Siencyn's verses. And, mark you, the poem I am discussing is an obscure piece of work by a little known poet whose name is in no history of Welsh literature nor in any anthology. It was last published in a forgotten volume at Aberystwyth in 1842. Why do I use it as a peg for this talk? Because it reveals the nature and continuity of the Welsh poetic tradition and because it reveals its quality and creative virtue: for the virtue of that tradition is that it may enable a quite minor poet to write a major poem. . . .

SAUNDERS LEWIS (1893-)

A PRINCE PREPARES FOR DEATH

And then Gruffudd ruled smoothly and powerfully for many years, in gentleness and peace, a good neighbour to all the kings around him, namely Henry, king of England, Murchath, king of Ireland, and the king of the Danish isles. His fame was resplendent in the near-by and in the far-away kingdoms. Hence, all good things were multiplied in Gwynedd, and the citizens began to build churches in every part, to replant the old woods, and to make orchards and gardens with enclosures and ditches around them. They built of stone, and fed of the fruits of the earth in the manner of the men of Rome. And he, Gruffudd, built large churches where his greatest courts were, and maintained his courts at all times with feastings worthy of his honour. Then it was that Gwynedd sparkled with lime-washed churches like the firmament of stars. He ruled his people with an iron rod, securing peace and agreement with neighbouring kingdoms, and while his sons were yet striplings, he placed them over distant border territories to hold and maintain against foreign nations of alien speech lest these might think of rising again to oppose him. Other minor rulers directed their steps to his court and sought his protection and his counsel whenever they were harassed by foreigners.

But at long last, Gruffudd, having become old, and losing the sight of his eyes, directed his energy to deeds of mercy. After having fashioned for himself a name long to be remembered for his military skill, he prepared to go himself to a secluded and sheltered place where he could lead a holy life and count utterly as nought his whole earthly dominion. And already, as his departure from this world was approaching, he called together his sons and arranged his end as did King Ezechias on another occasion; and then it was that he divided all his possessions, and his justice will remain for ever and ever. He sent twenty shillings to the Church of Christ in Dublin, where he was born and reared, an equal amount to all the chief churches of Ireland, and to the church of St. David's, the monasteries of Chester and of Shrewsbury; and more to the church of Bangor; ten shillings to Holyhead, to Penmon, Clynnog, Bardsey, Meifod, Llanarmon, Dineirth and many of the other noblest churches. This wealth he gave to the bishop, the arch-deacon, priests, dignatories, teachers, and Christian poor. For his protection I invoke the Holy Spirit who knows all things, and can distinguish them.

Life of Gruffudd ap Cynan (12th century)
translated from the Welsh by
D. M. LLOYD

DEATH OF A YOUNG PRINCE

1146. Late that year died Rhun ab Owain, a praiseworthy youth, in whose manners nature revealed the high quality of his stock, fair in appearance and attractive of speech, self-possessed in all company, generous and amiable at home, stern to his enemies and pleasing to his companions. He was tall and fair of complexion, his hair was wavy and fair, he was long-featured, his eyes were large and blue and full of merriment, his neck long and sleek, his chest wide, his body and legs were long, his thighs well-fleshed, his feet long and slender, and his toes long and straight. When the news of his death was brought to Owain, he fell into such great sadness that neither the fair aspect of his kingdom, nor the entertainment of bards, nor the cheer of noble company, nor the sight of the most precious objects, could avail to arouse him from his grief and dejection. God, however, in his wonted goodness, had fore-ordained mercy to the Welsh nation, so that it might not be lost completely, like a ship bereft of its captain and head, for Owain was still spared to her for a ruler. When unendurable grief had troubled the mind of the prince, and had weighed down cruelly on him, then it was that divine Providence restored him, for there was a castle called Mold which had been vainly attacked by many, and had remained untaken. When the most splendid prince and his nobles and his household troops came to besiege it, neither the natural strength of the place, nor its ramparts nor its garrison could protect it. All was burnt and destroyed, many of its defenders were killed and others captured; and when the prince knew that, he bestirred himself from all his sadness and grief, he recaptured his usual vigour of mind, and the joy of living returned to him.

The Chronicle of the Princes
translated from the Welsh by
D. M. LLOYD

POWYS BEREFT OF HER PRINCES (1160)

On the field of Acton hill, a hundred warriors I counted,
With my red blade on my thigh,
In one ebb-tide three hundred men of battle . . .
May they reach heaven in one company.

In Dudleston field our leader was roused,
Not grudging of praise was he,
Every gentle one on a sleek breathless horse,
Every lion-hearted one with sword by his side.

In Maes y Croesau we crossed the path of warriors,
Mounted on bay steeds,
Pillagers making for the herds,
Brave ones ready with their red swords.

In Maes Tref the summons of our leader's mounted host
Is clearly heard,
The onrush of men on sweating horses
Like the roar of whirlwind through shrubbery.

In Mathrafal field sods are broken
By the feet of magnificent horses
Engaged in the support of the true and successful ruler—
A portent of a gift-bearing victory.

God only, and the wise men of the world,
And the learned seers alone know
The number of our splendid gold-torqued host
At the Rhiweirth River.

Many a foaming steed by the churches of Llanfor,
Prancing in January,
And many a powerful man of battle
With Llywelyn, patron of the men of art.

Many the man and many the mount in Maesing today,
That wide and peaceful land,
And many a man strong in the strife of battle
With the generous one of Cadell's stock.

In Llangwm strath my mind dwelt on our leader,
And men's minds dwell on my song;
The host of gentle Madog, a bulwark against onslaught,
The host of Llywelyn did I see.

The portion of Llywelyn, lord of battle,
From Rhug even to Buddugre;
Many a rider on his lively mount,
Many a youth along the green hill.

When we were summoned to Cynwyd of the great battle
Our counsel was offered,
Proud warriors with broken shields,
As far as the pasture-land were we scattered.

God will not allow alive any longer any man
With two cloaks, for what has happened:
The death of Madog, loud is my complaint,
The slaying of Llywelyn is complete extinction.

A greeting to thee, Waelest Edwy,
And the hall on the bank of the Dee,
And the delectable place, like a sea-beach,
Which has awakened my longing more and more.

A greeting to thee, Cwm Brwynog,
And the houses, and the far-famed borders,
And the place where a chieftain no longer holds court,
And the church which once was above Madog's hall.

Since blessed Madog is dead,
Many the high-born who are no longer glad,
The whole world which is known to me is in a state of
woe,
And privileges are vain things now.

For the bull of conflict is dead,
And my leader of the far-reaching hand no longer lives;
If a heart can break with grief
Mine will be in two halves.

If the gentle one of Lleision's stock were alive,
The men of Gwynedd would not be encamped in the
heart of Edeirnion,
The lord of battle bereft of fighting men—
The feed of grey and sated birds of prey.

In Madog's lifetime no man would venture
To seize the fair borderland:
Vain it is to think of appropriating
Anything of this world that comes not from God.

CYNDDELW (*c.* 1135-*c.* 1200)
translated from the Welsh by
D. M. LLOYD

THE BERWYN INVASION

1164. The next year Dafydd ab Owain laid waste the province of Tegeingl, and withdrew all its people and cattle and movable wealth to the Vale of Clwyd. And when the King of England had reason to believe that his castles in that region were being attacked, he stirred up a host in great haste, and reached Rhuddlan, and encamped there three nights; after which he returned to England and assembled a very powerful army of the picked warriors of England, and Normandy, and Flanders, and Gascony, and Anjou, and the whole of the North. He reached Oswestry with the intention of wiping out the Welsh completely, once and for all. He was met by Owain and Cadwaladr, the sons of Gruffudd ap Cynan, with all the host of Gwynedd, Rhys ap Gruffudd with the host of the South, and Owain Cyfeiliog and Iorwerth the Red, son of Maredudd, and the sons of Madog ap Maredudd, and all the host of Powys with them, and the two sons of Madog ab Idnerth with their host, and they assembled together boldly and fearlessly in the Vale of Llangollen, pitching their tents at Corwen. And as the opposing armies were thus remaining in their tents, neither daring to attack the other, the King of England grew enraged and egged his host on to the woods of the Ceiriog Valley. There he caused the trees to be hewn and thrown down to the ground. He was opposed bravely and successfully by a small Welsh force of picked men acting in the absence of their princes, and many of the bravest on both sides were killed. The king pressed onwards with his armies and pitched his tents on Berwyn Mountain where he remained a few days. Then a tremendous storm of wind and foul weather and driving rain broke on them, and they lacked food. He withdrew his camping place back to England, and in his fury he caused to be taken out the eyes of his hostages whom he had long held, namely the two sons of Owain, Rhys and Cadwaladr; and Cynwrig and Maredudd the sons of Rhys, and many others.

The Chronicle of the Princes
translated from the Welsh by
D. M. LLOYD

"ACCORDING TO PLAN"

1210

The King (of England) came to Chester. Llywelyn then withdrew to the heart of Anglesey after causing all the cattle and movable wealth to be withdrawn to the wilds of Snowdonia, and the king came according to plan as far as the castle of Degannwy. Then hunger struck his host to such an extent that one egg was sold for three halfpence, and horseflesh was as acceptable as the choicest gifts. And for that reason the king returned to England about Whitsuntide, feeling greatly abashed, his plan having miscarried completely.

The Chronicle of the Princes
translated from the Welsh by
D. M. LLOYD

'DOMINION STATUS'

7 *Edward* I (1279-80): And the aforesaid Prince Llywelyn says that whereas every province which is constituted under the dominion of the Lord King has its own laws and customs according to the manner and usage of those parts where they are situated, such as the Gascons in Gascony, the Scots in Scotland, the Irish in Ireland, and the English in England, (an arrangement which tends to increase the influence of the Crown rather than to diminish it), he, being a Prince, therefore pleads that he should retain his Welsh law and proceed according to it. He makes this plea especially as, in the making of peace between them, the Lord King had of his own free will granted to him and to all men of Wales their own Welsh law. Thus by common right he ought to have his own law and Welsh customs in the same manner as the other nations already mentioned, all of which are constituted under the rule of the Lord King, have their own laws and customs according to their own tongue. And consequently, by special right and through a special grant from the Lord King he pleads that he may enjoy the privilege thus granted to him.

THE WELSH ASSIZE ROLL, 1277-84
(Claim presented at Oswestry by
Llywelyn ap Gruffudd, Prince of Wales)
translated from the Latin by
E. M. LLOYD

THE FALL OF LLYWELYN, THE LAST WELSH PRINCE

1282

Great Christ, generous Lord, a grace I seek,
Christ Son of God, the guileless One, forget not me,
The righteous, gift-bearing Christ, most powerful Surety,
Whose body bore the keenest pain.

What I relate concerns a man.
He who endures grief may he be the most calm.
He who is endowed with the highest power
May his mind be the lowliest.

Christ came to the world so that Adam
And his people should not be in Hell, an enslaved multitude,
And to people heaven around the Exalted Lord,
Which was lost by that most purblind angel.

Great Wales has lost the manliest of leaders,
Brave his sword-blade, active, splendidly brave and most valiant was he;
A courageous leader no longer lives, how shall I endure his loss?—
Brave and manly, generous, most free bestower of gifts.

It was for us that this man was killed, this man who was supreme,
A man who ruled Wales, boldly I will name him:
Valiant Llywelyn, the bravest of Welshmen,
A man who loved not to slink into the easiest way out.

A strong man in the attack on a host on his border,
The man of the green tents, the maintainer of the camp,
Manly son of Gruffudd, most ungrasping giver of
largesse
In the splendid tradition of Nudd and Mordaf.

A red-speared man, a man grief-stricken like Priam,
A fine man as king over the proudest army,
A man whose fame will spread easily—most generous
his outlay—
As far as the sun travels on his farthest course.

It is a grievous thing that that man is destroyed, a most
courtly leader,
A man bitterly mourned, the truest of kinsmen,
A refined, wise, and upright man, the best from Anglesey
To Caerleon, that fairest of places.

Llywelyn who stood near the limits of the Taff,
A leader of the people, lavish bestower of raiment.
A man above them all, the greatest of soldiers,
As far as Porth Wygyr a calm eagle.

May He who bore the direst and most painful death
For the sake of the five ages of the world, the heaviest and
most grievous agonies,
May He receive my most noble and gentle prince
To his portion of mercy, which is the greatest of great-
nesses.

BLEDDYN FARDD (13th century)
translated from the Welsh by
D. M. LLOYD

YVAN OF WALES

Yvan of Wales lay at siege before Mortayne in Poitou. . . . This siege thus enduryng there issued out of the realme of Englande, and out of the marches of Wales, a squier, a Walshman, called James Lambe. He was but a small gentylman, and that well shewed after, for a very gentylman wyll never set his mynde on so evyll an entent. Some sayde, or he departed out of Englande, he was charged and enfourmed by some knyghtes of Englande, to do the treason that he dyde. For this Yvan of Wales was gretly behated in England. . . . James Lambe, the same season arryved in Bretayne, and dyd so moche, that he came into Poitou, and ever as he went he named hymselfe to be servaunt to Yvan of Wales, for he spake good Frenche: sayeng, howe he was come out of Wales to speke with Yvan. And so he was anone beleved, and was conveyd by them of the countre, to Mortaygne, where the siege was. Then he wente wisely to Yvan, and shewed hym in his owne langage how he was come out of his countre to se hym, and to do hym servyce: Yvan, who thought none yll, lightly beleved him, and gave hym moche thankes for his comynge, and sayd, howe he wolde right gladlye have his servyce. And than he demaunded of him tidynges of the countrey of Wales; and he shewed him trewe tidynges, and untrewe, for he made him beleve howe all the countre of Wales wolde gladlye have hym to be their lorde. These wordes brought this James greatly in love with Yvan, for every man naturally desyreth to go into their owne countres, and to here therof, so that Yvan made him his chamberlayne: and this James every day more and more aquaynted him so with this Yvan of Wales, that he had nat so moche trust in no man, as he had in him. So moch this Yvan loved this James Lambe, that it was his distructyon, and the more pytie, for he was a good and a valyant man of armes . . . and bare himselfe so well that he was greatly praysed and wel beloved of the Frenche kyng, and with all the lordes.

Nowe lette us speke of his ende, the whiche I am lothe to do, savynge to shewe truely what fell in that tyme.

This Yvan of Wales hadde an usage beyng before Mortayne at the siege, that gladly in the mornyng when he was up and redy, he wolde come before the castell, and sytte downe and kembe his heed a good long space, and syt and beholde the castell, and the countrey about, beynge out of doute or feare of any thynge. And lyghtly there went none with him but this James Lambe; and often tymes he made him redy, and none but he, wherby at last came his endyng day. On a mornyng betymes, when the wether was fayre and clere, and the nyght had been so hote that he coulde nat slepe, howebeit, he rose and dyd on him but a syngle jacket and his shyrte, and a mantell or a cloke above, and so went thyder as he was wonte to go, and sate hym downe, and this James Lambe, with hym, every man beynge in their lodgynges aslepe, for it was early in the morning, and ther was made but lytell watche, for they thought themselfe sure of the castell. And when Yvan was sette on an olde stocke of wode, he sayd to James, Go to my lodgyng and fatche my combe, for I wyll refreshe me here a lytell season. Sir, quoth he, it shall be done. And so he wente and came agayne with the combe: and as he was comyng, I trowe the devyll entred into hym, for besyde the combe, he brought with hym a lytell javelyne of Spayne, with a large heed of stele, and with the same strake this Yvan as he sate, clene through out the body, so that he fell downe starke deed. And when he hadde done, he left styll the dart in his body, and so went his way, and drewe under covert of the castell, and soo came to the barryers and was let in, for he made signes to enter, and so he was brought before the Soudic of Lestrade. Sir, quoth he, I have delyvered you of one of the greatest enemyes that ye had. Of whom is that, quod the Soudic. Thus, quoth James, and so shewed him all the hole mater, as ye have herd before, fro poynt to poynt. And when the Soudic herde that, he shaked his heed, and behelde him right felly, and said, A, than thou hast murdred him, knowe for trouthe, all thynges consydred; savyng but that this dede is for our profyte, it shulde cost the thyne heed: but sithe it is done it can nat be undone agayne. Howebeit, it is a great domage of that gentylman to be so slayne: we shall have rather blame therby than prayse.

JEAN FROISSART (1337-1410)
Chronicle, translated out of the French by
SIR JOHN BOURCHIER, LORD BERNERS

A WELSH POLICY

Whereas, most illustrious prince, the under written articles especially concern our state and the reformation and usefulness of the Church of Wales, we humbly pray your royal majesty that you will graciously consider it worthy to advance their object, even in the court of the said lord Benedict : . . .

. . . that the Church of St. David's shall be restored to its original dignity, which from the time of St. David, archbishop and confessor, was a metropolitan church . . .

Again, that the same lord Benedict shall provide for the metropolitan church of St. David's, and the other cathedral churches of our principality, prelates, dignitaries, and beneficed clergy and curates, who know our language.

Again, that the lord Benedict shall revoke and annul all incorporations, unions, annexions, appropriations of parochial churches of our principality made so far, by any authority whatsoever with English monasteries and colleges. That the true patrons of these churches shall have the power to present to the ordinaries of those places suitable persons to the same or appoint others.

Again, that the said lord Benedict shall concede to us and to our heirs, the princes of Wales, that our chapels, etc., shall be free, and shall rejoice in the privileges, exemptions, and immunities in which they rejoiced in the times of our forefathers the princes of Wales.

Again, that we shall have two universities or places of general study, namely, one in North Wales and the other in South Wales, in cities, towns, or places to be hereafter decided and determined by our ambassadors and nuncios for that purpose. . . .

In testimony whereof we make these our letters patent. Given at Pennal on the thirty-first day of March, A.D. 1406, and in the sixth year of our rule.

OWAIN GLYN DŴR (*c.* 1359-*c.* 1416)
Letter to Charles VI, King of France,
translated from the Latin by T. MATTHEWS

OWEN GLENDOWER

OWEN GLENDOWER: at my nativity
the front of heaven was full of fiery shapes,
of burning cressets: and at my birth
the frame and huge foundation of the earth
shaked like a coward.

HOTSPUR: Why, so it would have done at the same season, if your mother's cat had but kitten'd, though yourself had never been born.

OWEN GLENDOWER: I say the earth did shake when I was born.

HOTSPUR: And I say the earth was not of my mind,
If you suppose as fearing you it shook.

[R. Cecil Hughes

CWM, LLANGERNYW
Home of Sir Henry Jones

[R. Cecil Hughes

PANTYCELYN
Home of William Williams, hymnwriter

[*National Museum of Wales*

THE WELSH FOLK MUSEUM: ST. FAGANS CASTLE FROM THE NORTH

OWEN GLENDOWER: The heavens were all on fire, the earth did tremble.
HOTSPUR: O, then the earth shook to see the heavens on fire,
and not in fear of your nativity.
Diseased nature oftentimes breaks forth
in strange eruptions; oft the teeming earth
is with a kind of colic pincht and vext
by the imprisoning of unruly wind
within her womb; which, for enlargement striving,
shakes the old beldam earth, and topples down
steeples and moss-grown towers. At your birth
our grandam earth, having this distemperature,
in passion shook.
OWEN GLENDOWER: Cousin, of many men
I do not bear these crossings. Give me leave
to tell you once again, that at my birth
the front of heaven was full of fiery shapes;
the goats ran from the mountains, and the herds
were strangely clamorous to the frighted fields.
These signs have marked me extraordinary;
and all the courses of my life do show
I am not in the roll of common men.
Where is he living,— clipt in with the sea
That chides the banks of England, Scotland, Wales,—
which calls me pupil, or hath read to me?
And bring him out that is but woman's son
can trace me in the tedious ways of art,
and hold me pace in deep experiments.
HOTSPUR: I think there is no man speaks better Welsh.—
I'll to dinner.
EDMUND MORTIMER: Peace, cousin Percy; you will make him mad.
OWEN GLENDOWER: I can call spirits from the vasty deep.
HOTSPUR: Why, so can I, or so can any man;
but will they come when you do call for them?

OWEN GLENDOWER: Why, I can teach you, cousin, to
command the devil.
HOTSPUR: And I can teach thee, coz, to shame the devil
by telling truth: tell truth, and shame the devil.—
If thou have power to raise him, bring him hither,
and I'll be sworn I have power to shame him hence.
O, while you live, tell truth, and shame the devil!
EDMUND MORTIMER: Come, come, no more of this
unprofitable chat.
OWEN GLENDOWER: Three times hath Henry Boling-
broke made head
against my power; thrice from the banks of Wye
and sandy-bottom'd Severn have I sent him
bootless home and weather-beaten back.
HOTSPUR: Home without boots, and in foul weather too!
How scapes he agues, in the devil's name?
OWEN GLENDOWER: Come, here's the map: shall we
divide our right
according to our threefold order ta'en?

. . . .

. . . .

I'll not have it alter'd.
HOTSPUR: Will not you?
OWEN GLENDOWER: No, nor you shall not.
HOTSPUR: Who shall say me nay?
OWEN GLENDOWER: Why, that will I.
HOTSPUR: Let me not understand you, then;
Speak it in Welsh.
OWEN GLENDOWER: I can speak English, lord, as well
as you;
for I was train'd up in the English court;
where, being but young, I framed to the harp
many an English ditty lovely well,
and gave the tongue a helpful ornament,—
a virtue that was never seen in you.

. . . .

. . . . *Exit.*

EDMUND MORTIMER: Fie, cousin Percy! how you cross my father!
HOTSPUR: I cannot choose: sometimes he angers me
with telling me of the moldwarp and the ant,
of the dreamer Merlin and his prophecies,
and of a dragon and a finless fish,
a clip-wing'd griffin and a moulten raven,
a couching lion and a ramping cat,
and such a deal of skimble-skamble stuff
as puts me from my faith. I tell you what,—
he held me fast last night at least nine hours
in reckoning up the several devils' names
that were his lackeys: I cried "hum," and "well, go to,"
but markt him not a word. O he is as tedious
as a tired horse, a railing wife;
worse than a smoky house:—I had rather live
with cheese and garlic in a windmill, far,
than feed on cates and have him talk to me
in any summer-house in Christendom.
EDMUND MORTIMER: In faith, he is a worthy gentleman;
exceedingly well-read, and profited
in strange concealments; valiant as a lion,
and wondrous affable, and as bountiful
as mines of India. Shall I tell you, cousin?
He holds your temper in a high respect,
and curbs himself even of his natural scope
when you do cross his humour; faith, he does:
I warrant you, that man is not alive
might so have tempted him as you have done,
without the taste of danger and reproof:
but do not use it oft, let me entreat you.

WILLIAM SHAKESPEARE (1564-1616)
From *King Henry the Fourth, Part One*, Act III, Scene 1

OWAIN GLYN DŴR

But the common people of Wales did not lose their respect and their love for the leader in his day of misfortune. For years he wandered among his people and he was never betrayed. Owain Glyn Dŵr's career can be summed-up in two phrases—defender of the common people, and the incarnation of love of country. Love of country prepared him for his life's work; the common people's love for him, and their faith in him, gave him strength to pursue it from day to day. He drew his inspiration from the history of Wales; he saw the splendour, half imagined it is true, of her ancient kings. His letters to the king of Scotland and to the Irish princes are redolent of the dreams of a student of history. He saw the common people of his country writhing under oppression, enduring the tyranny of lordling and official, and with a keener edge on their suffering for having had a glimpse of a better life. He gave them a nobler ideal than merely that of hanging stewards and burning manorial rolls, the pedigree charts of their subjection. He gave a direction to blind resentment—national unity and a university. And no one has ever been loved as the common people of Wales loved Owain Glyn Dŵr. Llywelyn is a figure in history, but Owain Glyn Dŵr is as if he were still alive with the nation, and it is no wonder that like Moses and Arthur, the location of his grave is not known. The poets sang their longing for his return, and the common people awaited his coming. They believed they would encounter him again on their way, that he would lead them to a higher freedom; they would not have it that he was dead.

SIR OWEN M. EDWARDS (1858-1920)
Y Llynnoedd llonydd
translated from the Welsh by
D. M. LLOYD

"MY HOPE IS ON WHAT IS TO COME"

We are in a similar plight, my dear countrymen, to the men of the five epochs of the world, who languished many ages in hell, long ago, in *limbo patrum*, the vale of the enslaved, continually (God knows) waiting the day they would see a brilliant light, and when some liberation would come to them, and the birth of the Prophesied One.

From hour to hour Wales, that once was great, is expecting—and learning. Day after day I may see it. *My hope is on what is to come.*

attributed to SIÔN CENT (floruit 1400-30)
translated from the Welsh by
D. M. LLOYD

A WASP'S NEST

Thus, after many bickerings betweene Howell and David ap Jenkin, David ap Jenkin being too weake, was faigne to flie the countrey, and to goe to Ireland, where he was a yeare or thereabouts. In the end he returned in the summer time, haveing himself and all his followers clad in greene, who, being come into the countrey, he dispersed here and there among his friends, lurking by day, and walkeing in the night for feare of his adversaries; and such of the countrey as happened to have a sight of him and his followers said they were the fairies, and soe ran away. All the whole countrey then was but a forrest, rough and spacious, as it is still, but then waste of inhabitants, and all overgrowne with woods, for Owen Glyndwr's warres beginning in *anno* 1400, continued fifteen yeares, which brought such a desolation that greene grasse grew on the market place in Llanrwst, called Bryn y botten, and the deere fled into the church-yard, as it is reported.

This desolation arose from Owen Glyndwr's policie to bring all things to waste that the English should find no strength nor resting place. The countrey being brought to such a desolation could not be replanted in haste, and the warres of York and Lancaster happening some fifteen yeares after, this countrey being the chiefest fastness of North Wales, was kept by David ap Jenkin, a captaine of the Lancastrian faction, fifteen yeares in Edward the Fourth his time, who sent diverse captaines to besiege him, who wasted the countrey while he kept his rocke of Carreg y Walch; and, lastly, by the Earle Herbert who brought it to utter desolation.

Now you are to understand that in those dayes the countrey of Nantconway was not onely wooded, but alsoe all Carnarvon, Merioneth, and Denbigh shires seemed to be but one forrest haveing few inhabitants, though of all others Nantconway had the fewest, being the worst then, and the seat of the warres, to whom the countrey about paid contribution. From the towne of Conway to Bala, and from Nantconway to Denbigh (when warres did happen to cease in Hiraethog, the countrey adjoining to Nantconway), there was continually fostered a wasp's nest, which troubled the whole countrey, I mean a lordship belonging to St. Johns of Jerusalem, called Spytty Jevan, a large thing, which had privilege of sanctuary. This peculiar jurisdiction, not governed by the King's lawes, became a receptacle of thieves and murtherers, who safely being warranted there by law, made the place thoroughly peopled. Noe spot within twenty miles was safe from their incursions and roberies, and what they got within their limits was their owne. They had to their backstay friends and receptors in all the county of Merioneth and Powisland. These helping the former desolations of Nantconway, and preying upon that country, as their next neighbours, kept most part of that countrey all waste and without inhabitants. In this estate stood the hundred of Nantconway when Meredith removed his dwelling thither, being (as I guesse) about the four and twentieth yeare of his age, and in the beginning of King Henry the Seventh his time. Being questioned by his friends why he meant to leave his ancient house and habitation, and to dwell in Nantconway, swarming with thieves and bondmen . . . he answered that he should find elbowe roome in that vast countrey among the bondmen, and that he had rather fight with outlawes and thieves than with his owne blood and kindred, "for if I live in mine house in Evioneth, I must either kill mine owne kinsmen or be killed by them."

SIR JOHN WYNNE (1553-1626)
The History of the Gwedir Family

A TURBULENT AGE

After Meredith had lived certaine yeares at Dolwyddelan castle, he builded the house at Penanmen, being the principal best ground in Dolwyddelan, and alsoe within certaine yeares after, he removed the church of Dolwyddelan from a place called Bryn y bedd to the place where now it is, being parte of the possessions of the priory of Bethkelert . . . The church, which is very strongly built, the castle, and his house of Penanmen stand three square, like a trivett, either a mile distant from each other. Questioning with my uncle what should move him to demolish the old church, which stood in a thickett, and build it in a plaine, stronger, and greater than it wes before, his answer was, he had reason for the same, because the country was wild, and he might be oppressed by his enemies on the suddaine in that woodie countrey, it therefore stood him in a policie to have diverse places of retreat. Certaine it was that he durst not goe to church on a Sunday from his house of Penanmen but he must leave the same guarded with men, and have the doores sure barred and boulted, and a watchman to stand at the *Garreg big* during divine service, being a rock whence he might see both the church and the house, and raise the crie if the house was assaulted. He durst not, although he were guarded with twenty tall archers make knowne when he went to church or elsewhere, or goe or come the same way through the woodes and narrowe places lest he should be layed for.

SIR JOHN WYNNE (1553-1626)
The History of the Gwedir Family

A CALL TO ARMS

Henry VII minding on his entry to England to clayme the crown against the tyrant Richard the Third, wrote this letter, which is still extant, to John ap Meredith, *in haec verba*:

By the King.

Right trusty and well-beloved, wee greete you well: and whereas it is soe, that, through the helps of almighty God, the assistance of our loveing and true subjects, and the greate confidence that wee have to the nobles and commons of this our principalitie of Wales, we be entred into the same, purposing by the helpe above rehearsed, in all haste possible, to descend into our realme of England, not only for the adoption of the crowne, unto us of right appertaining, but alsoe for the oppression of the odious tyrant Richard late Duke of Gloucester, usurper of our said right; and moreover to reduce as well our said realme of England into its ancient estate, honour, and property, and prosperitie, as this our said principalitie of Wales, and the people of the same to their dearest liberties, delivering them of such miserable servitude as they have piteously long stood in. We desire and pray you, and upon your allegiance strictly charge and command you, that immediately upon the sight hereof with all such power, as ye may make, defencibly arrayed for the warre, ye addresse you towards us, without any tarrying upon the way, untill such time as ye be with us, to our aide, for the effect above rehearsed, wherein ye shall cause us in time to come to be your singular good Lord, and that ye faile not hereof as ye will avoyd our grievous displeasure, and answere it unto your perill. Given under our signet at our . . . (*Date and place omitted in the MS.*)

To our trustie and well-beloved John ap Meredith ap Jevan ap Meredith.

KING HENRY VII (1456-1509)
quoted from SIR JOHN WYNNE (1553-1626)
The History of the Gwedir Family

OLD AND NEW TIMES

DEMETUS (*A Penbrokshire man*): But this may be said of him, if all the nobility and commons of England had been of Owen Glyndoor's mind, and suppressed Henry IV, fought on the defence and restored Richard II, their lawful king, then had not that civil and bloody dissention between the houses of Lancaster and York have plagued England so long: then had the life of many a Duke, Marques, Earl, Baron, and many a valiant knight, and many thousands of good English subjects been saved—but no more of that, God's will must be fulfilled.

BARTHOL (*A Doctor of the Civil Law*): Indeed I have read in the English Cronicles of a notable traitor and rebel of a Welshman called Owen Glyndoor, and I was persuaded he was some notable traitor.

DEMETUS: Judge you if he that seeing his lawful prince suppressed, imprisoned, deprived of his Crown and realm, would stretch forth his force to withstand the usurper, whether he were worthy to be registered for a traitor? But for this the whole nation grew in to marvellous great hatred and endured the rigour of those hard and unreasonable laws of King Henry IV, until God, the consolator of the comfortless, looking down upon the oppression of this poor nation, as he did upon the heavy burdens of the children of Israel under the whip of the merciless taskmasters of Egypt, sent unto us a Moses that delivered us from bondage; for whereas by reason of those rigorous laws which were provided against the Welshmen to keep them poor, to deprive them of good education, and to make them uncivil and brutish, there grew about that time deadly hatred between them and the English nation insomuch that the name of a Welshman was odious to the Englishmen and the name of Englishman woeful to the Welshman. And when they were thus in most disdain, it pleased the Lord of his mercy to send us a prince of our own nation and born in our country to govern both England and Wales: I mean that worthy and grave Prince, Henry VII, who for his wisdom is termed in histories of foreign nations a second Salomon.

This noble prince atchieving the Crown of England and being lineally descended from the ancient British Kings of this land, so drew the hearts of the Welshmen to him, as the loadstone doth the iron, who ever sithence have borne such natural love and affection to the said King Henry VII, his son King Henry VIII, and King Edward VI, Queen Mary, and now doth beare towards our most sovereign

Prince, Queen Elizabeth, now living, whom we pray the Lord of Lords long and long to preserve to govern England and Wales, that there hath not been found in England any country or province more obedient in heart than this country of Wales hath been and is to the progeny of the said King Henry VII that hath here governed after him in this land; for over and besides the dutie and allegiance that we owe unto her Majesty as our sovereign Prince, there is a certain ardent affection in the hearts of Welshmen towards her Majesty which maketh them inwardly to rejoice that God hath blessed our nation (who was so long oppressed by the hatred of divers of the Kings of England) with a prince of our own natural country and name.

GEORGE OWEN, OF HENLLYS (1552-1613)
The Dialogue of the Government of Wales

THE ACT OF UNION

Selections

A.D. 1535) 27 Henry 8, c. 26. An Act for Laws and Justice to be Ministered in WALES in like Form as it is in this Realm.

"Albeit the Dominion Principality and Country of Wales justly and righteously is, and ever hath been incorporated annexed united and subject to and under the Imperial Crown of this Realm, as a very Member and Joint of the same, whereof the King's most Royal Majesty of Meer Droit, and very Right, is very Head king Lord and Ruler; yet notwithstanding, because that in the same Country Principality and Dominion divers Rights Usages Laws and Customs be far discrepant from the Laws and Customs of this Realm, and also because that the People of the same Dominion have and do daily use a Speech nothing like, nor consonant to the natural Mother Tongue used within this Realm, some rude and ignorant People have made Distinction and Diversity between the King's Subjects of this Realm, and his Subjects of the said Dominion and Principality of Wales, whereby great Discord Variance Debate Division Murmur and Sedition hath grown between his said Subjects"; His Highness therefore, of a singular Zeal Love and Favour that he beareth towards his Subjects of his said Dominion of Wales, minding and intending to reduce them to the perfect Order Notice and Knowledge of his Laws of this his Realm, and utterly to extirp all and singular the sinister Usages and Customs differing from the same, and to bring the said Subjects of this his Realm, and of his said Dominion of Wales, to an amicable Concord and Unity, hath by the deliberate Advice Consent and Agreement of the Lords Spiritual and Temporal, and the Commons in this present Parliament assembled, and by the Authority of the same, ordained enacted and established, That his said Country or Dominion of Wales shall be and continue for ever from hence forth incorporated united and annexed to and with this his Realm of England; and that all and singular Person and Persons, born or to be born in the said Principality Country or Dominion of Wales, shall have enjoy and inherit all and singular Freedoms Liberties Rights Privileges and Laws within this his Realm, and other the King's Dominions, as other the King's Subjects naturally born within the same have, enjoy and inherit.

2. And that all and singular Person and Persons inheritable to any Manors Lands Tenements Rents Reversions Services or other Hereditaments, which shall descend after the Feast of All Saints next coming, within the said Principality Country or Dominion of

Wales . . . shall for ever, from and after the said Feast of All Saints, inherit and be inheritable to the same Manors Lands Rents Tenements Reversions and Hereditaments, after the English Tenure, without Division or Partition, and after the Form of the Laws of this Realm of England, and not after any Welsh Tenure, nor after the Form of any Welsh Laws or Customs. . . .

20. Also be it enacted by the Authority aforesaid, That all Justices Commissioners Sheriffs Coroners Escheators Stewards and their Lieutenants, and all other Officers and Ministers of the Law, shall proclaim and keep the Sessions Courts Hundreds Leets, Sheriffs Courts, and all other Courts in the English Tongue; and all Oaths of Officers Juries and Inquests, and all other Affidavits Verdicts and Wagers of Law, to be given and done in the English Tongue; and also that from henceforth no Person or Persons that use the Welsh Speech or Language shall have or enjoy any Manner Office or Fees within this Realm of England, Wales, or other the King's Dominion, upon Pain of forfeiting the same Offices or Fees, unless he or they use and exercise the English Speech or Language.

ON THE ACT OF UNION (1536)

The Act decreed that English was to be the sole official language of all legal and government business in Wales. A Welshman who was ignorant of English was thereby disqualified from holding any public office in his own country. The Welsh system of land inheritance by equal division, known as *gavelkind*, was to be discontinued and replaced by the English system of primogeniture. Out of the Marcher lordships the five new shires of Denbigh, Montgomery, Radnor, Brecknock and Monmouth were created, and other portions of

Marcher territory were added to the English counties of Shropshire, Herefordshire and Gloucestershire. The boundaries of Pembrokeshire and Glamorgan were extended, and Parliamentary representation at Westminster granted to the Welsh counties and county boroughs. The border between England and Wales was not drawn according to any national line of demarcation and districts which were Welsh in tradition and speech, such as Ewyas Lacy and Oswestry, were excluded from Wales. Two commissions were appointed by the Act with instructions to report on the implementation of its provisions. By 1542 their labours were complete and that year's final enactment, defining such matters as shire boundaries in minute detail, set the seal on Henry VIII's Welsh policy. The Welsh problem, it was believed, was now solved, and the country would settle down and accommodate itself to the status of a collection of English counties. Legally the Welshman was an Englishman, and Wales incorporated into England.

The realities of nature and history, however, could not be ignored or brushed aside so easily. The assimilation of Wales to England has never been made final and absolute, and it has at no time been possible to govern the two countries on the assumption that no distinction of any kind existed between them. Even the Acts of Union in some measure acknowledged the distinctiveness of Wales by establishing a Chancery and an Exchequer at Denbigh and at Brecon, modelled on those already existing at Caernarvon, and by the institution of the Courts of Great Sessions to administer English law in Wales. . . .

Unlike the later Acts of Union of 1707 and 1800, which respectively united the national parliaments of Scotland and Ireland with that of England, the Act of 1536 did not abolish a Welsh Parliament. The Norman and Edwardian conquest had denied Wales the possibility of developing parliamentary institutions, and by 1536 her people had long been familiar with English administrators and officials. In large tracts of the country the English laws of inheritance had already supplanted the ancient Welsh custom. In one sense the Act of 1536 was merely the completion of a process which had been manifest locally and intermittently for centuries.

Even so the purpose of the first of the Acts of Union, as of those that followed it, was to bring about uniformity within the realm. Impelled by what appeared to them to be political and military necessity its promoters believed that a state uniform in speech and religion would be better equipped to meet the threat of foreign aggression. Another and quite different factor which influenced them was the prevailing view of cultural values. By this time the manners of London Society had come to be regarded as the standard of civilisation, and the language of culture, in Britain and Ireland at least, was considered to be English. This attitude is well illustrated by the reference in the Act of Union to "the sinister usages and customs" which still persisted in Wales. The lack during these centuries of a Welsh capital city, acting as a focus for the national culture, was an irreparable loss. English writers of the period frequently used the word 'civilitie,' meaning thereby the qualities of urbanity and gentility of which London was, in their view, the obvious centre and source. Among the educated classes it was believed that this metropolitan virtue could be transplanted to Wales and, with tender nurture and a modicum of faith, made to blossom amid the quarrelsome squires and mountain farmers. Sir John Wynne of Gwedir, describing the thriving state of trade and the prosperity of the legal profession at Caernarvon, remarks that

"Civility and learning flourished in that towne, soe as they were called the lawyers of Carnarvon, the merchands of Beaumares and the gentlemen of Conway."

At best this was only an aping of the manners of

English urban life. In England the century following the Act of Union witnessed the flowering of the English Renaissance in the works of Spenser and Sidney, Marlowe and Shakespeare and Jonson, but in Wales, where the last of the great *cywyddwyr* were composing their last eulogies and elegies and the entire mediaeval culture was in decay, the new culture of the Renaissance was denied an opportunity of fully expressing itself in a Welsh garb.

For the Welsh gentry heartily and unanimously welcomed the Tudor new order. To them as a class it brought advancement and increased wealth. London now became for a numerous section of them a centre of activity and a focus of interests, and for the remainder a source of social and cultural standards. . . .

Thus a millenium of Welsh history came to an end. A division now appeared in the national life, an ever-widening breach separating the gentry from the common people. The crystallisation of landlordism into a social system and the anglicisation of the upper classes proceeded simultaneously. Becoming increasingly alienated from its traditions and heritage, the Welsh aristocratic class renounced the duties and obligations which for time out of mind it had discharged and honoured. The change, though gradual, was completed by the end of the eighteenth century. It is this defection of the aristocracy, and its withdrawal from the stage of Welsh national life, that gives unity to the period we are discussing. The common people were left to toil unremittingly, not merely for their own bare sustenance, but for the maintainance of a propertied class which was discarding all sense of responsibility for the well-being of a native Welsh society. From that period till today the main theme of Welsh history has been the effort of the people to recreate a society and to raise up new leaders to take the place of those who had deserted them. A general awakening did not occur until the eighteenth century, and its early manifestations were religious and educational in character. The rebirth of a political national consciousness was delayed till the nineteenth century.

A. O. H. JARMAN (1911-)
In *The Historical Basis of Welsh Nationalism*

THE REFORMATION

Jesus has been made the occasion of wrangling throughout the world, a fearful state of affairs! Some are firm for the new Faith and others staunch for the old. They snarl at each other like dogs—every head is opinionated. Men are known by what they say, and by their noise. Father and son are not inclined to agree in anything; the daughter is against the mother, and they drift to an ugly situation. Brother sullenly and wrongfully filches brother's land; sisters are bitter towards each other, no two of them singing the same tune. None of us is any better, not one being free of the will to do harm.

Let us confess it, and may we strive to live as we should. God, the Trinity, will then hearken to the truly felt yearning of him who knows the commandments and the articles of the Faith.

SIÔN BRWYNOG (floruit 1550)
translated from the Welsh by
D. M. LLOYD

THE BALLAD OF THE WELSH BUCCANEERS

"What befell the Welsh Sea Rovers who adventured to the Indies at the behest of Elizabeth Tudor." The poet is addressing the Pelican. The concluding portion only of this long ballad is given below.

Go tell them boldly, beautious bird,
The Welsh are warriors splendid;
(Of Englishmen we lost a third,
Counting both killed and wounded.)

Captain Bilins, Hector-breast,
On land is our great guider,
In every perilous feat of arms
He was the foremost strider.

Captain Roberts seconds him,
Prince Jason was no prouder;
Like great Duke Theseus with his club
His foes he beats to powder.

Hugh Myddleton has done his share—
So hath each true lieutenant—
Salisbury stout and Heilin rare—
Where'er we flew our pennant.

Robert Bilins, Sergeant Hughes,
Whipped the black foe like flummery!
Will Thomas, William Johnes, and Hugh,
Behold the crew of Cymry!

Tell of our going to Newfoundland,
The cruel Gulf Stream over,
'Tis thence we'll come to Christendom
To meet fond friend and lover.

And if too far to the North we pass,
And thereby miss our sire-land
Then shall we sight Cape Clear aright
And rest awhile in Ireland.

Sure, when within your happy arms
You nursed us, mothers loving,
I' faith how little did you dream
That we should thus be roving!

Our blessings on thee, slender bird,
If Heaven befriend thy mission,
Greet all our kin kind Wales within
And tell them our condition.

LIEUTENANT WILLIAM PEILYN
composed in 1570, translated by
ALFRED PERCEVAL GRAVES

HENRY MORGAN'S MARCH ON PANAMA

Morgan's curls are matted,
His lips are cracked and dry,
His tawny beard is tangled,
And his plumed hat hangs awry:
But his voice still booms like thunder
Through the foetid jungle glade
As he marches, bold as Lucifer,
Leading his gaunt brigade.

Twelve hundred famished buccaneers
Blistered, bitten and bled,
A stricken mob of men accursed
By the monstrous sun o'erhead:
Twelve hundred starveling scarecrows
Without a crumb to eat,
And not a drink for tortured throats

In that grim, festering heat.
Twelve hundred threadbare musketeers
Rotting in tropic mud
Where the reeking, fevered mangroves
Wake havoc in their blood:
Twelve hundred febrile wretches,
A legion of the dead:
But Morgan in his blue brocade
Goes striding on ahead.
Twelve hundred tatterdemalions,
The sorriest, maddest crew
That ever the green savannahs saw
When the Spanish bugles blew:
Twelve hundred rattling skeletons
Who sprang to life, and then
Like a wild wave took Panama,
For they were Morgan's men.

A. G. PRYS-JONES (1888-)

AN OLD AND HAUGHTY NATION

And all this tract that fronts the falling Sun
A noble Peer of mickle trust, and power
Has in his charge, with temper'd awe to guide
An old, and haughty Nation proud in Arms.

JOHN MILTON (1608-74)
A Mask presented at Ludlow Castle (*Comus*)

Pastoral and Industrial

WALES THROUGH EXILES' EYES

GRUFFYDD: It is somewhat more endurable and the heat is less overpowering since we came to this vineyard than it was in the house. For there we were wearied by the intense heat, and the oppressiveness (through lack of a current of air) was enough to smother a man. But here there are the branches and leaves of the vines to shade us from the rays of the sun, and the gentle breeze from the north cools and lightens the air along this walk and around this seat, so that we are not so fretful in the mid-day heat as we have been on previous days.

MORUS: Although this spot is pleasant enough, and delightful enough though it is to see the green leaves shading us from the shimmering sunlight, and however lovely it be to feel this northerly breeze blowing under the tips of the vines to cheer us in this unreasonable heat, which is so hard to bear by any one born and bred in a land as cool as Wales, yet I long for many things which were there to be found, and which enabled us to pass the time pleasantly and to our hearts' content, whilst avoiding the shimmering heat of the long summer day. For in Wales, hot though the day might be, there were ease and comfort for all manner of men. If one were to seek entertainment, a harpist would play sweet airs, and a melodious singer would sing to the tune of the harp either a song of praise to virtue, or a satiric song holding wickedness to scorn, whichever you would prefer. If it were your desire to hear tell of the country's customs in olden days, there were venerable grey-haired men who would recount all the remarkable and commendable deeds throughout the land of Wales over a long period. If you wished to meditate or to read alone, you could choose a suitable place, however intense the heat, either in green summer-houses, or by running waters in a dingle of young sap-laden trees, or in a valley of lush growth, or on a slope in rich meadow-land country full of clover, or in a birch grove, or an ash plantation, or on a breezy conspicuous hill, or some such place where we would not be worried by the exhaustion and the weariness of summer heat.

But around this town there is no such place, for if we enter a grotto or a hollow where the sun never reaches, there is a death-like cold, and if you stay in the open, the heat is enough to melt the crows; if you stay at home the sultriness will afflict you, and as for these vineyards, although they are pleasant enough in appearance, and far more delightful in which to rest than the other places around us, yet a Welshman's heart cannot kindle towards them as it would on the banks of the Dee, or on the floor of the Vale of Clwyd, or in many a place I could name from Maenol Dewi to Holyhead in Anglesey. And even were the place in itself as desirable as the best spot in Wales, still my heart was more glad there in the old days hearing the song of the cuckoo than it has ever been made here by the melodious song of the nightingale; the pleasant song of the thrush or the sparkling note of the blackbird pleased me more there than could be done here by the harmoniously blended heavenly notes of all the singing birds of the world holding concert together.

DR. GRUFFUDD ROBERT, OF MILAN (1531-*c.* 1600)
Prologue to his Welsh Grammar
translated from the Welsh by
D. M. LLOYD

A PEASANT

Iago Prytherch his name, though be it allowed,
Just an ordinary man of the bald Welsh hills,
Who pens a few sheep in a gap of cloud.
Docking mangels, chipping the green skin
From the yellow bones with a half-witted grin
Of satisfaction, or churning the crude earth
To a stiff sea of clods, that glint in the wind—
So are his days spent, his spittled mirth
Rarer than the sun, that cracks the cheeks
Of the gaunt sky perhaps once in a week.
And then at night see him fixed in his chair
Motionless, except when he leans to gob in the fire.
There is something frightening in the vacancy of
his mind.
His clothes, sour with years of sweat
And animal contact, shock the refined,
But affected, sense with their stark naturalness.
Yet this is your prototype, who, season by season,
Against siege of rain and the wind's attrition
Preserves his stock, an impregnable fortress
Not to be stormed even in death's confusion.
Remember him, then, for he, too, is a winner of wars,
Enduring like a tree under the curious stars.

R. S. THOMAS (1913-   )

IN PRAISE OF THE LABOURER

In that day of liberation, when the people of the world through the benefits of life-giving baptism, shall present before God, the gracious Lord, in fair and brave words their works, where there is to be judgement on all, on great Olivet, pleasant hearing will be the unadorned tale of the labourer who trudged the fields. The living God is generous, and if he, good soul, did render his offering and his tithe to God, if it was to God that he rendered them, he is entitled to his reward. It is easy for the labourer from the sunlit meadow to hold fast his trust in God, for he does not refuse lodging, nor alms, to anyone whom he should help. He does not pass judgement except on a ploughbeam. He on his ploughed land does not bear anger; he goes not to war nor pursues it; he does no violence to a man for his wealth; he does not press us hard; he makes no unjust claims in his own interest—nothing is fitting, to his way of thinking, but to endure injustice. But no life, no ordered world, are possible without him. I know he prefers a hundred times in his long-suffering quiet way to grip in his innocence the crouching plough and the ox-goad than to be a pillaging Arthur breaking down strong towers. Yet, without his labours, we would not have the elements of Christ's Sacrifice to sustain Christendom. Neither Pope nor Emperor would have life, well we know it, without him, nor splendidly ruling monarch, generous of his wine, nor any mortal man. Well are we told in the fine old *Elucidarium*: "Blessed is he who holds his hands to the plough . . ." May the hand of the gracious God, who excels all others, and the hand of Mary, be over every labourer.

IOLO GOCH (*c.* 1320-98)
translated from the Welsh by
D. M. LLOYD

THE LITTLE OLD COTTAGES

Poor and cramped as they were, the people who lived in them loved the little old cottages. You remember Ieuan Gwynedd's poem, where he describes the cottage smoke rising from the glen, the white-walled houses on the green hill-side, the beehives at the gable end or by the sheltered garden wall and the roses and the lilies growing in the garden. An idealised picture, perhaps, but many people felt like that about the old houses in which they had been brought up.

The *caban unnos*, a squatter's cottage of turf, was a hut built in one night, hence the name. If a man put up a cottage, if the name may be used in this connection, between sunset and sunrise and if he lit a fire on the hearth and sent smoke through a chimney, it was a recognised custom that he might remain in possession of the house although it was built on common land. Sometimes this happened when a bachelor took it into his head to get married and to set up house. His friends would gather at twilight and work all night to construct the turf hut; it was one of the conditions that the house should be complete with the chimney smoking before sunrise the next morning, and if there was time and labour enough a turf wall would be raised to enclose a garden. Hundreds of such houses were built, and hundreds were filched from the rightful owners by the schemes and trickery of the landowners.

There were several of these turf houses in the neighbourhood of my old home, and when I was a boy I was familiar with the interior of four of them. They were inhabited at the time, and in one of them, I remember, a family of six children was brought up. In that particular house there was some kind of central partition which divided it into two rooms, and the father had made a low loft over the sleeping room as sleeping quarters for some of the children. All the children grew up to be well-respected and religious men and women and most of them lived to a good old age. It is only about two years since the eldest son and the second daughter died, both well over eighty. I never saw a happier-looking woman than Ellen Richards, their mother: her laughter was always ready amid the children and the smoke from the peat fire. The poor cottage was her castle and love transmuted everything into gold.

HUGH EVANS (1854-1934)
The Gorse Glen
translated from the Welsh by E. MORGAN HUMPHREYS

KNITTING

Tears come into my eyes every time I read Tom Hood's *The Song of the Shirt*, and I thank God that our mothers, in all their poverty, did not have to live in the great English towns. They had, at least, the blue sky over their heads, and the green grass for a carpet under their feet, and the clean air of the countryside to breathe, and poor as they were they had something better than a bed of straw to lie on. Their beds of chaff were clean and soft. I am thankful, too, that their work was knitting and not sewing; they had not to sit stooping over their work in dark rooms; they could knit while in the fields with the scent of the wild flowers in their nostrils. My grandmother and my mother could knit very rapidly while reading the Bible on the little round table by their side, and sometimes, as they read and knitted, they would sing of the promises of God.

HUGH EVANS (1854-1934)
The Gorse Glen
translated from the Welsh by E. MORGAN HUMPHREYS

HILL-FARMS OF GWENT

In visiting the farm houses, as well in the hilly districts as in other parts of Monmouthshire, I was struck with the enormous quantity of bacon with which they are stored, frequently observing several ranges of flitches suspended from the ceiling of the kitchen. Bacon is almost the only meat served at the tables of the farmers, and with vegetables and the productions of the dairy, forms their diet. Thin oat cakes are a common substitute for bread, and the repasts are enlivened by the *cwrw*, their national liquor, . . . which is immortalized in the songs of the bards. . . .

The principal articles of diet among the labourers, are oat cakes, potatoes, milk, and cheese, with an inferior species of *cwrw*. Almost every cottage is provided with a small garden, and the greater part are even enabled to keep a cow, which ranges the commons for subsistence. The comforts of the cottager are increased by the abundance of fuel, either of coal or of wood, which prevails in every part of the country; and the price of labour being the same as in most of the counties in England, with these additional comforts, the condition of the peasants in Monmouthshire is very advantageous.

It is impossible to travel in Monmouthshire without being struck with the appearance of neatness and cheerfulness, which results from the custom of whitewashing the houses. On account of the abundance of lime, this operation is annually performed, both within and without, and greatly contributes to the health of the inhabitants. The white colour of these dwellings, scattered along the summits and sides of the hills, and surrounded with foliage of different hues, considerably heightens the picturesque effect of the diversified landscapes.

WILLIAM COXE (1747-1828)
An Historical Tour in Monmouthshire (1801)

A COUNTRY HOME

This house was my real 'home,' the only 'home' I had till I found one of my own. But I was not born in it. I was born in a low, long, thatched, small-windowed, very old-fashioned house at the foot of a little hill close by. My parents moved from it when I was six months old, and every vestige of it has disappeared long ago. I wish I could describe its spacious hearth, with room for fire-place and oven, and chimney-bench (*mainc y simnai*), seated on which neighbours were entertained, and songs were sung and tales of ghosts were told. If you looked up through the great open chimney you would see a wide expanse of sky overhead. If you looked into the room—the kitchen—you would find it rich with flitches of bacon, and very ill-lit by the petty window in front and still smaller one at the back. At the other end was the ground-floor bed-room, and on the other side of the bed-room wall was the barn. Attached to the barn again was a small cow-house, with its gable against a slight slope, on the top of which, looking down at the cow-house, was my father's work-shop, a 'lean-to,' attached to my real 'home.'

I have a distinct memory of this old thatched house, and some of its tenants. Even yet I can hear the thump, thump, thump of the flail, and the fourth gentler thump, as it was swung three times to the left and once to the right, all day long, to thresh the corn grown on the little farm. The threshing, now done in a few hours by a visiting 'fire-engine,' then occupied the farm labourer all the wet days of the winter and occupied him very peacefully. I also remember the excitement of seeing a new calf in the byre, and its being fed; so that it was there that, one way or another, I got my first experience of a wider world.

Returning now to my proper home, I cannot but marvel at the skill that secured its comfort for all of us. A happier household, I believe, there never was; and though my father, I should say, never made a pound a week, we never lacked anything, so far as I could see, whether in the way of wholesome food or of comfortable and respectable clothing. Of course it is not possible to make the 'plenty' of a good working man's home intelligible to the well-to-do. Things which look like impossibilities are achieved every day; and the so-called Laws of Domestic Economy are abstract generalities compared with the concrete sense and skill of the clever mother. Let me illustrate. Seven persons had all their meals every day in that little ten-foot kitchen, where the food was cooked and the family lived. There was no room for us all to sit at our table; neither the table nor the room was big enough. What then? The answer is simple; we took our meals in relays. First came my two elder brothers, both of them apprentice gardeners at the squire's . . . My brothers generally arrived home at mid-day ravenously hungry: for they had had a most hasty breakfast, owing to unfailingly 'sleeping in,' and they had dug and delved all the morning in the open air. Their food was, perhaps by some trifle, a little better, or better served, than what followed. After them came my father bringing his princely good-nature and unselfishness and splendid appetite; and with him came one (or sometimes two) of his workmen. What meal I had I generally took standing, being always in a hurry to go out to play. When my younger sister fed I cannot remember; but everything that concerned her was 'special.' My mother sat at peace to her dinner later on, after she had attended to all our needs, and she ate it at leisure. On Sundays, when we had fresh meat, we all dined at the same time, one, or perhaps two of us, sitting on the doorstep if the weather was fine, with the plate on our knees. But neither on Sunday nor on week-day was the meal scanty, or the fun and chatter lean, or was there any faintest hint of scarcity or poverty.

Let me give another example. There was no room for the cradle in the day-time on that crowded ten-foot floor, when my second, little, short-lived sister was born. What was to be done? Well! the cradle was put upstairs, a string was let down from it through a hole in the low ceiling, and whenever the baby cried my mother bade one of us pull the string. I can hear the rick-rock of the cradle above my head even yet, when I sit down to listen to old memories. . . .

Our food was somewhat monotonous, and possibly we might have done better with less buttermilk and more sweet-milk. But, while the latter was plentiful and cheap and good, the former was to be had in big canfulls for the mere fetching. It was the customary return made by our neighbours for some kindly deed or another of my father's or mother's. On the whole the victualling was as wholesome as it was plentiful. It consisted of bread-and-milk or of 'shot,' that is, ground oat-cake and milk, or of bread and soup—the soup made out of dripping bought at the squire's hall, being, I understand, the cook's perquisite. And the bread was of my mother's own making—the best in all the land! Even yet I think that no bread can rival the big loaves turned out of the domestic ovens of Wales and Brittany.

SIR HENRY JONES (1852-1922)
Old Memories

A MERRY EVENING AT THE HAFOD

Where then shall we go? Which will be the more pleasing, the recesses of Snowdonia, or the secret places of the Berwyn? Which is the more delightful, the floor of the Conway Valley or the majesty of Cader Idris? Where is the deepest peace to be found: between the green Montgomeryshire hills, or in the wilds of Ystrad Yw, or in the Vale of Towy? Let us go to Cwm Cowrach. What kind of place is that? Where is it? Never mind, but let us go to Cowrach, and spend a whole night in the Hafod. Where will we have food and drink? All is well if only we go to Cowrach. The valley is some two miles long, with a river, of course, running through it teeming with trout. Houses on both sides of the valley, some with their gable ends towards the slope, and others facing away from it. A kind of *lane*, not a road and not a path, meanders along, and leads us to a level tract, which once was a bog, but is now a flat and smooth common. At the top end of the valley stands an immense crag which appears as if it were perpetually straining itself with the urge to topple over. It has an old, rough, and glowering face. But the Hafod is built right underneath its frown: an old long house in the shape of a cross, which has never seen lime except at a distance. But let us go in. There is a hearty welcome here for all who call. . . . What kind of place is the Hafod? It has a very large kitchen with a chimney-place as large as a fair-sized parlour, with a hole big enough to contain a bed if it were necessary. When we knocked the door, we were greeted by the barking of some half-dozen hairy *corgis* and two or three terriers. But someone came to the door, and in the handshaking that followed there was a stirring of hearts too; it was not a perfunctory conventional greeting, but a heart could be felt in the fingers and in the grip of the hand. After drinking whey, and eating a thin slice of oatmeal bread, we are ready to discuss the world and its affairs. There is a roaring fire where the flames race up the chimney. We two are seated in a pair of armchairs, one of black oak and the other of white sycamore wood. Opposite us, around the fire, was my Uncle Rolant, engaged in conversation as he attended to his jew's harp. Aunt Gwen's happy face was turned towards the three-piece cupboard where she was looking for some wax to rub on her violin bow, whilst the eldest son is tuning his harp alongside the big table. Although the note of the clarinet is always unpleasant to my ear, and like the sound of an old goose cackling after a gander, here in the Hafod—in a mountain recess, I was in the mood to endure any musical instrument.

After setting the candles in their proper places, and attending to the fire, and seeing that everything was in order, the man of the house favoured us with a solo performance on the jew's harp. Although his head had for many a year blossomed white like the almond tree, and time had scored his cheeks with its sharp nails, nevertheless he entertained us with his playing. "Tut, Roli," said Aunt Gwen, "give over now," and to the harpist she said, "Let us have now *The Men of Dyfi's Entertainment*," on which we were given a skilfully executed duet, which was followed by combined efforts on the jew's harp, the harp, the *crwth*, and the clarinet, together with Deio Wmffra's contribution on the fife and the tambourine! The house re-echoed to the noise, and everyone played his part as he should. When this performance was at its height, there was a knock at the door, and who was there but Deio Puw, a very amusing character. For some forty years he had been coming to the Hafod every three weeks or so; he was always very happy and droll, and could relate all the ghost stories of the country around. He could also play the fiddle well. After a tune on the fife—a lively, wild, and springy tune Aunt Gwen shouted the second time: "Roli, come on the floor," and the old man obeyed the call at once. To show his eagerness he flung away his two clogs, and made his way towards her to lead the dance! Soon there were seven of them, at least, all shaking their ankles in lively merriment. Old and young were enjoying themselves with the same zest and eagerness. After having exercised their feet to their hearts' content, everyone sat down to as fine a cup of tea as ever was poured through a teapot's spout. The Hafod tea was really excellent. Everyone was in good humour, and there were no unkind words or dry looks. Then came the singing to the harp. Everyone was well versed in the art, and there was no danger at all of its intricacies being bungled. On being asked if they often spent an

[Llew. E. Morgan

CWMPARC, RHONDDA VALLEY

[R. Cecil Hughes

RURAL SERENITY, CARMARTHENSHIRE

[*Reece Winstone*

THE MONNOW GATE, MONMOUTH

evening in this delightful way, the good people of the house replied that it only happened some three times a week! It is thus, to the sound of poetry, singing, and the harp, that the members of this family spend their lives. And yet, I can assure you that when the time comes for a family devotional service, no one is more serious and deeply moved whilst on his knees before the Throne of Grace than my Uncle Rolant;—nor anyone with a cleaner heart, a purer life, and a more unsoiled tongue than my Aunt Gwen. No beggar leaves their door hungry, none of the children from the mean cottages around ever goes away without a can of thick creamy milk and a thick slice of well-buttered bread; at Christmastide the carcase of a well-fed sheep is shared there among many, and throughout the year the words of Ieuan the Tall Poet are true of the Hafod:—

Agor dy drysor, dod ran yn gallwych
Tra gelli i'r truan;
Gwell ryw awr golli'r arian
Na chau'r god a nychu'r gwan.

[Open your treasure, give a portion to the unfortunate, wisely and splendidly while you are able; better to lose your money sometimes than to tie up your bag, and to let the weak suffer.]

Just so, and as if it were in observation of the teaching of that *englyn* these good people love to practise kindliness rather than merely to talk about it. And above all, never was a false tale known to travel from the Hafod. Rather than live on slander, jealousy and scandal, they escape to the world of song. In all the country around, no one is so little talked about as the members of this family, and although they are not well-to-do, there is no gentleman's house in the county, provided that the occupant is a Welshman, in which some one of them has not been a welcome guest at some time or other; and besides, there is no one in all the country around who would not do all in his power to help them in case of need. But what am I driving at? This, that the old Welsh way of life, as exemplified in the Hafod family, is better—more free from harmfulness, more honest—and therefore more godly than is the sourness and subterfuge, the pride and the wastefulness of the country today.

GLASYNYS (O. W. JONES, 1828-70)
Cymru Fu
translated from the Welsh by D. M. LLOYD

A FARMHOUSE SUNDAY SCHOOL

It is a bright Sunday afternoon—the weather is fine for our part of the country, that is, it is dry and the sun is cheerful though there is not much heat in its rays. The mid-day dinner is over and the house is set in order for the Sunday School. The people living in the upper part of Cwmcannas lived far from any place of worship. The church was three miles lower down the valley, and the nearest chapel was about two miles off, over the hills in a *cwm* which ran parallel to ours. To remedy in some measure, this want of spiritual accommodation, a Sunday School had been held at Hafod for some years. Our house was the largest of the farm-houses about, and had therefore been fixed upon as the most convenient to hold the school, though there were other houses more centrally situated. Shortly after dinner the neighbouring farmers and their families began to drop in, each with his Welsh Bible under his arm. They liked to come early that they might enjoy a little gossip before school commenced. Here they discussed the preachers at the chapel, the news of the week, and sometimes a little politics. When the kitchen got pretty full, my father would ask some "religious" man to commence by singing a hymn and offering a prayer. They would then disperse through the house to their several classes, for the large kitchen would not hold them all. We had one class of women in the parlour, presided over by my grandfather; another occupied one of the bedrooms. Young and old were there, from my great-grandmother in my grandfather's class down to the young children of five or six who sat on the hob by my mother's side. My father, who was reputed to be a better educated man than any of the others, had a "teacher's class" at the large kitchen table. In this class I was permitted to sit as a genius who was fitter for the company of grown-up men than that of the boys of my age who were puzzling over their horn books away by the dresser. I was privileged further to read out to the class such portions of the commentary as were wanted to elucidate difficult passages, and great was my state of glory as I sat on the window seat with the large folio spread on the table before me. Most of the adults can read pretty fairly, for the reading of Welsh is an easy matter and does not take long to learn. But to some of our older scholars, reading was a great mystery. There is old Robert Hughes, of Moelogan, for instance, a man of seventy and upwards, who sits on a form at my right hand with two of his middle-aged sons by his side. They have been attending school regularly from its first commencement and they have not passed the "a, b, ab" yet.

ROBERT ROBERTS (1834-85)
The Life and Opinions of R. R., a wandering scholar . . .

GWLADYS RHYS

Prayers, Dorcas, Fellowship, and Children's Groups!
And day and night my father's mournful tone
Tiresome as wind, the wind that day and night
Blew shrill through pine twigs round the manse. And
mother,

Seeking the speech of heaven, knew no speech
But talk of meetings, Fellowship, and Dorcas.
What could I ever do, I, Gwladys Rhys,
The Reverend Thomas Rhys's eldest child—
The Minister of Horeb on the Moor?
What but to yearn, and ever listlessly
Cast weary eyes across the down's bare slope,
And rise at mornings to await the nights,
And toss through endless nights longing for morn?
And winter, Oh my God, drawing the blinds
O'er windows at four in the afternoon,
And hear the wind bewailing through the pines,
And listen to my father's talk and mother's!

And then one day, Someone drew nigh the house,
And Something strange I felt within my heart;
The wind bewailed no longer through the pines,
Nor listlessly were weary eyes now cast
Across the down's bare slope. I felt the cool
Touch of a playful breeze from brighter lands,
I drew the blinds across the window-pane,
Nor made reply to father's weariness,
I heard my mother render long account
Of North Wales Women's Temperance League, and then
Through snow I sallied forth without a word,
Although the wind was sighing through the pines
And it was Fellowship and Dorcas Night.

And therefore, wayfarer, 'tis here I lie
By Horeb Chapel's walls—I, Gwladys Rhys,
Aged thirty years; father and mother pass
To services, and Fellowship, and Groups,
Dorcas, Prayer Meetings, and Committees of
The North Wales Women's Temperance League; yes, here
In dark Oblivion's Vale, because the gust

Of that light playful breeze from brighter lands
Was nothing but the sigh of wind through pines.

W. J. GRUFFYDD (1881-1954)
translated from the Welsh by D. M. LLOYD

COUNTRY CHURCHYARDS

It would be impossible to relate the story of the rural life of Wales in the present century (*i.e.* the nineteenth) without giving a prominent place to the chapel and the church. He that would attempt to tell the story otherwise would only succeed in showing how blind he was to its significance, or that he knew nothing of the 'land of song.' Let it be noted that I am referring to the present century. For to whatever commote of Wales one may go, wherever there is a human community, however small and scattered, on looking around, one of the first and most prominent objects that will meet the eye will be a chapel belonging to some religious denomination or other. The edifice will often be plain enough —four walls, a roof, a few windows and a door. If the human settlement is older than the present century, it is likely that there will also be a grey-looking church, and a churchyard with its sad yew tree casting a gloomy shade around. To this resting place generation after generation will have been brought in their turn, as can be seen from the tombstones, most of which will be tilted to one side as if by a stroke of paralysis. On some of these stones will be found an 'englyn,' skilfully or indifferently composed, but I could not other than feel a sort of respect for the crudest of these brief metrical compositions; for the men who had felt the impulse to express their loss in these rude lines, and they who had carved them, now rest here alike, and maybe with no 'englyn' or even a stone above their heads.

I don't quite know why, but somehow I feel on visiting

these places that it is the graveyard that makes the church holy rather than the opposite. And strong though my prejudice against the Establishment may be, and however worldly may have been some of those who, bareheaded and in white surplice, read in unseemly haste that magnificent burial service over hundreds of their fellow men who now quietly rest, completely forgotten, under the green sod, my heart softens, and if it were in my power I would forgive them all their shortcomings and would canonise them everyone. Whatever we may say, there is a spirit in these quiet old churchyards which creates a common fraternity, and a common and catholic humility before our Creator.

DANIEL OWEN (1836-95)
Gwen Tomos
translated from the Welsh by D. M. LLOYD

THE COUNTRY DOCTOR

Anyone who has lived in these mountain regions knows what sickness means there. There are miles of track, broken and rutted by the winter rains, before you even reach the high road. The people there never send for medical aid for petty ailments. The doctor is not even summoned for important family events. He is only called in when life is in jeopardy. Here in this district you have fifty square miles without a doctor. Ask anybody who has lived on a wayside farm in these districts or in the villages in the valleys, and they will tell you that one of the most vivid memories of their youth was to be wakened up in the dead of night by hearing the clatter of a horse ridden furiously past in the dark, and everyone knew there was a dire struggle for life going on in the hills.

DAVID LLOYD GEORGE (1863-1945)
House of Commons speech, 1912, on Disestablishment and Disendowment of the Church in Wales

THE WHITE FLEET-FOOTED STEED

See the white fleet-footed steed,
Lively, joyous, of pure breed;
Slender flanks, hair fine as down,
And silky mane like a maiden's gown;
Restless ears, nervous and taut,
Staglike, erect, and thinly wrought;
White-hot guns are his nostrils wide,
Scattering the dew on every side;
Narrow cheeks, bright-hued and strong,
Shapely nose, well-turned and long:
A tuneful measure with well-trained feet
He strikes on the paving stones of the street.

ANONYMOUS (15th century)
translated from the Welsh by
D. M. LLOYD

THE KING-TREE

The peasants of this county (Merioneth), still, frequently chant with the harp, some verses composed in celebration of a noted oak tree, which formerly grew on Mr. Oakeley's estate at Ganllwyd in the parish of Llanddwywai. The trunk of fifteen feet in length, and twenty-five feet and a half in circumference, measured 609 cubic feet. From the fork it divided into several branches; three of which extended to a further length of forty-five feet, and were large enough for mill-shafts. These three branches, including the length of the butt, may be said to be each twenty yards in length; which explains the dimension inserted in one of the verses,—"*Tri-ugeinllath tw'r Ganllwyd*" (Three-twenty yards of the Ganllwyd growth). This king-tree was held in such veneration by the people that the verses reprobate the undruidical and execrable deed of depriving the forest of its monarch. Acorns from it were sent for, and planted in different parts of the country, and as many of its offspring as are now standing, verify the axiom in the operations of Nature, that *like begets like*, among the various tribes of the vegetable, as well as of the animal world. There are about half a dozen of its descendants now standing on Tan y Bwlch demesne; one measuring nine feet and a half in circumference at the height of five feet. They are all uniformly of the shape, though not of the size, of their majestic sire: short butts, and widely extending horizontal branches; being a most excellent shape for the shading of cattle in the midst of lawns.

GWALLTER MECHAIN (WALTER DAVIES, 1761-1849)
Agriculture of North Wales, 1810

PEMBROKESHIRE COAL

Most of the gentlemen of the shire are well served with wood for their fuel, but for the most part those that dwell near the coal or that may have it carried by water with ease, use most coal fires in their kitchens and some in their halls, because it is a ready fire and very good and sweet to roast and boil meat; and void of smoke where ill chimneys are, and doth not require a man's labour to cleave wood and feed the fire continually. Next unto the wood or rather to be preferred before it for smell is the coal fire for the generality of it, as that which serveth most people and especially the chief towns. This coal may be numbered as one of the chief commodities of this countrey and is so necessary as without it the countrey would be in great distress. It is called stone coal for the hardness thereof, and is burned in chimneys and grates of iron, and being once kindled giveth a greater heate than light, and delighteth to burn in dark places. It serveth also for smiths to work, though not so well as the other kind of coal called the running coal; for that when it first kindleth it melteth and runneth as wax, and groweth into one clod, whereas this stone coal burneth apart and never clingeth together.

This kind of coal is not noisome for the smoke, nor nothing so loathsome for the smell as the ring coal is, whose smoke annoyeth all things near it, as fine linen and men's hands that warme themselves by it, but this stone coal yieldeth in a manner no smoke after it is kindled, and is so pure that fine cambric or lawn is usually dried by it without any stain or blemish, and is a most proved good drier of mault therein passing wood, fern, or straw. This coal for the rare quality thereof was carried out of this country to the city of London to the late Lord Treasurer Burleigh by a gentleman of experience to shew how far the same excelled that of Newcastle, wherewith the city of London is served, and I think, if the passing were not so tedious, there would be great use made of it. . . .

The digging of this coal is of ancient time used in Penbrokeshire but not in such exact and skilful sort as now it is, for in former time they used no engines for lifting up of the coals out of the pit, but made their entrance slope, so as the people carried the coals upon their backs along stairs which they called landways, whereas now they sink their pits down right four square about six or seven foot square, and with a windlass turned by four men they draw up the coals a barrell full at once by a rope; this they call a downright door. The lord of the land hath either rent, or the third barrell after all charges of the work deducted. . . .

They now most commonly sink down right twelve, fourteen or twenty fathom before they come to the coal, whereas in old time four fathom was counted a great labour. When they find it, they work sundry holes, one for every digger, some two, some three or four, as the number of diggers are: each man working by candle light and sitting while he worketh. Then they have bearers, which are boys that bear the coals in fit baskets on their backs, going always stooping by reason of the lowness of the pit, each bearer carrieth this basket six fathom where, upon a bench of stone he layeth it, where meeteth him another boy with an empty basket, which he giveth him and taketh that which is full of coals, and carrieth it as far, where another meeteth him, and so till they come under the door where it is lifted up. In one pit there will be sixteen persons, whereof there will be three pickaxes digging, seaven bearers, one filler, four winders, two riddlers, who riddle the coals when it is aland—first to draw the small coal from the big by one kind of riddle, then the second riddling with a smaller riddle with which they draw small coals for the smiths from the culm, which is indeed but very dust, which serveth for lime burning. These people will land about eighty or hundred barrells of coal in a day. Their tools about this work is pickaxes with a round poll, wedges and fledges to batter the rocks that cross their work.

All times of the year is indifferent for working, but the hot weather is worst by reason of sudden damps that happen, which often times causeth the workmen to swound, and will not suffer the candles to burn, but the flame waxing blue of colour will of themselves out. They work from six o'clock to six o'clock, and rest an hour at noon, and eat their allowance, as they term it, which is ob. (halfpenny) in bread to every man, and iiijd. in drink among a dozen: this is of custom on the charge of the pit, although they worke on their own charge. All their worke is by candle light throughout the year. . . .

The dangers in digging these coals is the falling of the earth and killing of the poor people, or stopping of the way forth, and so die by famine, or else the sudden irruption of standing waters in old works. The workmen of this black labour observe all abolished holy days and cannot be weaned from that folly.

GEORGE OWEN OF HENLLYS (1552-1613)
The Description of Penbrokshire

A BAD SYSTEM

I was, however, also engaged in forming a new partnership for carrying forward the establishment at New Lanark. I was completely tired of partners who were merely trained to buy cheap and sell dear. This occupation deteriorates, and often destroys, the finest and best faculties of our nature. From an experience of a long life, in which I passed through all the gradations of trade, manufactures, and commerce, I am thoroughly convinced that there can be no superior character formed under this thoroughly selfish system. Truth, honesty, virtue, will be mere names, as they are now, and as they have ever been. Under this system there can be no true civilization; for by it all are trained civilly to oppose and often to destroy one another by their created opposition of interests. It is a low, vulgar, ignorant, and inferior mode of conducting the affairs of society; and no permanent, general, and substantial improvement can arise until it shall be superseded by a superior mode of forming character and creating wealth.

ROBERT OWEN (1771-1858)
The Life of Robert Owen by himself

'THE KINGDOMS OF THE EARTH'

A lot more could be said about Rosser Beynon and his work as a musician in the town of Tydfil the Martyr and throughout the Principality of Wales. The life of the soul of the place was partly if not mainly the creation of men like Rosser Beynon, Ieuan Ddu and Moses Davies, to name but three musicians of many. Then there were a dozen preachers of the Gospel who also laboured to make the life of the soul more abundant in the dark and the dirt and under the smoke heavy and constant over the town of Tydfil the Martyr. Those who were referred to as 'impractical men' kept the soul of the place alive and were content to let whoever wanted riches and honours go on gathering those things. Come cholera, explosions in the mines, burnings and maiming in the ironworks, come want and disease and still the body of the place maintained its productive and procreative capacity, the momentum of the body of the place was no longer subject to arrest by the sum-total of bodily ills. But the soul of the place as yet had little momentum beyond what the preachers and poets, musicians and others referred to as 'impractical men' gave it. This is, we know, a mystery of sorts, something about which it is not seemly to be too positive. It is a thing of feeling, of the spirit, and such comparisons as I have made may be worthless. Yet when we remember how things were in those days, those days of immense wealth and productivity on the one hand and mass poverty and stinking conditions on the other, we must try to discover who it was that brought the mass of the people out of that dirt and darkness into whatever light there is in these days.

I could refer to those days in Merthyr as 'the good old days' and leave it at that, for in some ways they were good, as these days are good in some ways. But that does not alter the fact that a great and terrible crime was committed on the body of mankind in those days. The image of God was undoubtedly debased by . . . by who? Well, say by man himself in the first place and by the great industrialists of the times in the second degree. Perhaps I have already said too much about all the millions of pounds sterling made out of the place and about the people of the place having no water supply other than wells and springs that dried up in summer, and stank most of the time. I have also said enough and perhaps too much about the decayed animal matter in the water of the dozen wells on which upwards of forty thousand people were mainly dependent for water for all purposes. I do not want to rub this in. But I respectfully suggest that no man of any greatness whatsoever would or should leave, after having made millions of pounds sterling, these people before he had spent some of his millions in providing them with at least a supply of water for all purposes. But they left us without water, without a hospital in which to be patched up after we had been broken and torn and burnt in their service. Not a hall in which to meet or hold any sort of local event. Nothing worthy the name of sanitation—and I could go on. Those who were often referred to as 'our great benefactors' just took what paid out of the pay-dirt and left the dirt to us. Still, we had the Cyfarthfa Brass Band.

Our real benefactors were those who laboured mightily to keep the soul of the place alive, and Rosser Beynon was one of the foremost of those. This night he is smiling as he looks at Joseph Parry, who has worked down the mine twelve hours for which he will receive fivepence, after his twelve hours' work in his pit-clothes wanting to sing. Let the boy alone, Van, said Rosser Beynon to Myfanwy. Only one with music in his soul would want to sing more than eat after twelve hours down the pit. Go to your place in the choir, my boy.

Lend him my spare copy, Robert James. But he will dirty it, Rosser Beynon, unless he goes out to one of the houses to wash his hands first, said Robert James. Let him dirty it, said Rosser Beynon. Come on now, all of you. There was the usual coughing and scraping of throats and Rosser said: I hope you all sing as good as you cough. Now, do your best, please. We'll take it right through from beginning to end and see how it goes. Then we can treat the weak spots afterwards. Right, Robert. Robert James played the introduction on the piano and Rosser beating time with his baton until he brought the choir into it. They sang the piece entitled 'Teyrnasoedd y Ddaear,' which I would translate into English as 'The Kingdoms of the Earth.' And Joseph Parry, in his pit-clothes and his stomach feeling empty, after having worked hard for twelve hours to earn fivepence, sang of 'The Kingdoms of the Earth.'

JACK JONES (1884-)
Off to Philadelphia in the Morning

GRINDING POVERTY

It was from my grandparents' house in Anglesey that the dresser came here. Fashioned more than a century ago for my great-grandfather by some country joiner Amlwch way, it reigned over the humble kitchen in the little homestead where my grandfather was brought up. After he had grown into a youth and married, he brought his wife, a girl from Pensarn nearby, home to live in the little cottage, and there his two children, my father and Uncle Huw, were born, to be brought up in great poverty, despite my grandparents' ceaseless toil. To my grandmother fell the task of tending the two cows, two pigs and three dozen chickens on the homestead, while her husband was employed in the Parys Mountain Copper Mines, where he had started work at the age of eight for a wage of fourpence for a twelve-hour day. He was only twelve when he went "down below" to mine copper, and there he toiled like a galley-slave for the rest of his life. On many "a settling-up Saturday" he used to return home without a halfpenny to bless himself with, after a whole month of accursedly hard toil; for the owners followed a system of "stoppages" against the cost of candles, powder, sharpening augers and hoisting the ore from the mine. There were times, indeed, when my grandfather returned home, at the month's end, actually in debt to his owners, since this shameful levy totalled more than the wage he had earned in a month of sweated, sweltering labour underground. My grandmother tried to induce him to give up the work, but they could not make a living out of the homestead with its three small, mean fields, and food had to be provided for themselves and their two children.

So, day by day and week by week, my unfortunate grandfather had to go down the Coronation Shaft, to kill himself in the effort to provide for his little family. And every morning at six, in the Prayer Meeting that was held in the smithy on the surface, he gave thanks to God that he was able to keep his children from starvation.

T. ROWLAND HUGHES (1903-49)
From Hand to Hand
translated from the Welsh by RICHARD C. RUCK

A GOOD AND STEADY TRADE

The 'Corner Shop' where I was apprenticed was one of the oldest establishments in the town, and Abel Hughes, my master, was considered a meticulous, fair-minded and far-seeing man. His shop contained general drapery, but his chief trade was in cloth and flannel, which were always of the best quality. In those quiet days there was seldom any bustle in the shop, except on fair days, and it is my belief that it was no cause for regret in Abel Hughes's mind that fairs did not occur oftener than four times a year. Yet, the Corner Shop was the scene of a good and steady trade. . . . It was patronised by old customers whose families had ' dealt ' there longer than could be recollected. They were mostly country people, and the majority were Methodists, for those words of Scripture, ' Let us do good unto all men, especially unto them who are of the household of faith,' were well observed in those days. As I remarked, Abel Hughes stocked the best quality material, and expected reasonable profit. He never over-praised his wares, and would not reduce his price by a halfpenny. If the customer did not like the goods, he begged him, by all means, not to buy them. I never once heard him ' swear ' that this or that material was worth more than he asked for it. Petty lying in business was not so general in those days that any man should find it necessary to ' swear.' I don't believe that Abel Hughes ever spent a halfpenny on advertising; the only service which he ever sought from the printer was the making of bill-heads. His shop-window was small, and the panes about a foot square, for plate-glass had not then come into fashion What little window-dressing there was could easily be done in an hour, and needed repeating only about once a fortnight.

The shop was rather dark even on a bright day, and the smell of moleskin, cotton cord, and velveteen, was so thick that I felt it could be cut with my scissors. When a customer entered, the first thing Abel would do would be to hand him a chair and start a conversation. And that is how the customer would be engaged for half an hour,—sometimes an hour, or even longer. But usually he would buy a valuable parcel, and the transaction would end with an invitation into the ' house ' to have a ' cup of tea ' or a ' bit of dinner.' Very little trade was carried out after sunset, and although the shop was fitted with gas, only one jet was lit—something to show that the shop was not closed. There was very little book-keeping. One book was sufficient, a long narrow one, which served as day-book and ledger, and when a customer paid his account, there was need only to draw a cross on the book in his presence, which served as a receipt.

There was nothing in the business methods of the shop which one could not imagine Noah having performed in the same way had he kept shop before the Flood. And yet Abel Hughes was doing well and making money. What would have happened to him today? Yes, today—when people are scheming so much to add to their customers anyhow;—no matter how; when winning a customer, and making money are, to many, matters of greater consequence than eternity, and eternity of no greater significance than a yard of grey calico.

DANIEL OWEN (1836-95)
Rhys Lewis
translated from the Welsh by D. M. LLOYD

THE COURT CUPBOARD

There's no definite evidence whether Harri Bach—little Harry—was born in his shirtsleeves or not; but it's known for certain that he lived the greater part of his life in that dress, and that he died in it. For Harri was a countryman to the roots of his hair—a piece of the rock from the uplands of the Cothi, that had slipped into the cogs of the modern machine. He came from the parish of Caio, Red Caio of the Romans long ago, a kindly, restless, beautiful countryside, with Mynydd Mallaen as a grey rim behind it. If any one were to ask for a description of Harry in one word, "little-pig" would get as near the truth as anything. Not a pig, remember, but a little pig, the cleanest, friendliest, jolliest little creature of them all. He was fair, round and short-legged, with the slightest touch of the Berkshire nose; and the bristles of his short, strong neck shone like silver wires. Nobody noticed when his hair and his fierce moustache began to go grey and then white, for its natural tint was grey-white. And this effect was added to by his trade of stonemason, with the stone-dust filling the folds of his shirt that was made from the wool of the Pencilmaren sheep.

That particular evening, Harri Bach was alone in the front room of 13, Bethesda Row, Glanllwchwr, while the rays of an Easter sunset pierced through the blue-grey mist that rose from the ugly coal-tips before him. It was a long, narrow room, with two steps leading up to the kitchen behind. Most of it was filled by a big table with a crimson cloth on it, and a row of cheap leather chairs close against the walls. On the walls there were the usual pictures that you see in the homes of the first generation of people who have come from the country—poor pictures of beloved parents, enlarged at the Jew's shop, together with all sorts of china ornaments and little nicknacks gathering dust on the mantelpiece. There was also a sampler with the date '72. The flames of the fire danced happily over the room, throwing strange patterns over the old court cupboard the *cwpwrdd tridarn*—that stood, shining with beeswax, in the right-hand corner, near to the kitchen door. This was Harry's cupboard, the only piece of furniture that he owned in the house. His aunt, his mother's sister, had left it to him in her will; probably one of his ancestors had made it. In it Harry kept his few private treasures, his account-books, his file of bills from that brief period when he had been a flourishing house-builder. He thought more of this cupboard than of all the rest of his little property put together, though he had only recently come to realise it. Whenever he felt perplexed in this confined little room, he somehow found that he had turned to the old court cupboard. Without his knowing it, this cupboard acted as a sort of anchor in the depths, keeping his personality from being shifted by the ebb and flow around him. He had looked at it so often in this meditative mood that his eyes always seemed to penetrate far beyond it. Through this old court cupboard, the very fibre of the hills like himself, he gazed as through a glass into his own heart, and sometimes into the strange distances beyond. He did not see the glass because of what he perceived beyond it. . . .

D. J. WILLIAMS (1885-)
translated from the Welsh by
DAFYDD JENKINS

DOWLAIS—TWO GENERATIONS

"Blowing again," he muttered, as the glare of the furnaces reddened the window. In Dowlais Works now. Steel—Bessemer. Yes, that was what had finished him and many a-more old iron puddlers. Not wanted now. The year previous the world-famous Cyfarthfa Works where he had worked for the Crawshay who was the greatest of the Iron Kings, had gone on from iron to steel, and he—ay, and many thousands like him—had been scrapped with the old iron-making plant. After having toiled to make eight millions sterling for the great Iron King they had been scrapped and left to die as paupers.

His thoughts were bitter as he sat noting the new furnaces of Dowlais and Cyfarthfa illuminating the district and the sky above. He had worked for them all, all the English ironmasters who had made their millions in Merthyr and Dowlais. Sir Josiah John Guest, yes, he had worked for him before ever he was ' Sir ' or M.P. Just plain Josiah John; ay, and for his lady, Charlotte, who had kept the Dowlais colliers out for two months. Unconditional surrender was what she had demanded. As bad as old Crawshay himself, she was. Now they were gone, gone to live in their parks at Caversham and Wimbourne, leaving their old puddlers with constitutions ruined by too much hard work, drinking, and insanitary home life, to fill workhouses and fatten graveyards.

There's Dowlais blowing again. Iron rails had died hard at that greatest of the world's ironworks—yes, had died harder than the scrapped iron puddlers were dying. Not until that very day had they started rolling steel rails at Dowlais. . . .

"Ay," sighed the old man, "an' it's domino on us old puddlers now that Dowlais has gone from iron to steel. Dai, if old Sam Homfray an' William Crawshay an' Josiah John Guest had lived, them works wouldn't be rolling the steel rails that's put all us puddlers on the road to the workhouse."

Dai said: "Wouldn't they? That's all you know. The bosses always makes what pays 'em best. If it paid 'em to they'd make rails out o' black-pudding—that's if rails could be made out of black-pudding. What the hell do they care? None of 'em b'longs here." . . . He poured strong tea into the saucer to cool. "They came —an' now they're on the wing. They didn't come here for our good . . . No fear. Now that they've turned the place shang-de-vang they're on the wing. We Welsh people couldn't turn it out fast enough for 'em, so they brought the English down, an' shipped the Irish across —ay, an' all nationalities till they've made Merthyr like what it was where they tried to build the Tower of Babel. Humph, an' you talk about what the old bosses would do if they was alive——"

"Dai, you listened too much to that man Halliday,

who only came down here from England—yes, he came from England too, remember, to start unions and make strikes."

"John, if you wasn't my father-in-law I'd tell you something. Halliday? Humph, pity there wasn't more like him, then we'd have wages we could live on—ay, an' houses we could live in, not places like this where we're eaten alive by bugs that we can't get rid of. . . . You old puddlers—with one breath you're talking about being driven to the workhouse, and with the next you're sticking up for them who've driven you there. Ay, voting for 'em. Halliday would have been standing up for us in Parliament instead of one of these two we've got if the likes of you had had enough sense to see which was the best man."

"I shall always vote for Henry Richard, Dai, who is a Welshman—I can't make you young chaps out. There's you, Ned Luke, an' that Harry of mine always talking against the bosses, and about 'em coming here from England to do their eye-good. Yet when this Halliday came here from England to make unions——"

"Yes, unions, not money, remember."

"All right, we'll leave it at that. . . . What are them women laughing about up there?"

"A boy, a boy," the old woman his wife was crying as she fell over herself coming down the almost perpendicular, ladder-like stairway. "No, no, I didn't hurt myself a bit," she assured the two men as they helped her to her feet. "Oh, Dai, Saran's got a lovely boy up there— Go an' see. A lovely boy he is . . ."

JACK JONES (1884-)
Unfinished Journey

MRS. EVANS FACH

Mrs. Evans fach, you want butter again.
How will you pay for it now, little woman
With your husband out on strike, and full
Of the fiery language? Ay, I know him,
His head is full of fire and brimstone
And a lot of palaver about communism,
And me, little Dan the Grocer
Depending so much on private enterprise.

What, depending on the miners and their
Money too? O yes, in a way, Mrs. Evans,
Yes, in a way I do, mind you.
Come tomorrow, little woman, and I'll tell you then
What I have decided overnight.
Go home now and tell that rash red husband of yours
That your grocer cannot afford to go on strike
Or what would happen to the butter from Carmarthen?
Good day for now, Mrs. Evans fach.

IDRIS DAVIES (1905-53)

People Great and Small

DEATH OF SAINT DAVID

And after he had bestowed his blessing on all, he (Saint David) spoke these words: "Noble brothers and sisters, be glad, and guard your faith and religion, and do the little things which you have heard from me, and which I have shown you. And I shall go the way which our fathers go. And fare you well," said David, "and may your conduct be steadfast on the earth. For we shall never meet here again." And then was heard a cry arising from all, a wail and lamentation and weeping, and people exclaiming "Woe to us that the earth does not swallow us, that fire does not burn us, would that God would raise the sea over the land, and cause the mountains to fall on us," and almost all that were present were near unto death. From the Sunday to the Wednesday after David's death they took no meat or drink, but prayed piteously. And Tuesday night, close on cock-crow, lo, a host of angels filled the city, and all places in the city were filled with song and joy. And in the morning hour, behold, Jesus Christ came, accompanied by the nine orders of heavenly beings, as when He is surrounded by them in majesty. And the brilliant sun shone over the whole host. And that Tuesday the first day of March, Jesus Christ bore away David's soul in great triumph and gladness and honour. After his hunger, his thirst, and cold, and his labours, his abstinence and his acts of charity, and his weariness, and his tribulation, and his afflictions, and his anxiety for the world, the angels received his soul, and they bore it to a place where the light does not fail, and there is rest without labour, and joy without sadness, an abundance of all good things, and victory, and brilliance, and beauty; where Christ's champions are commended, and the undeserving rich are ignored, where there is health without sickness, youth without old age, peace without dissension, glory without vain ostentation, songs that do not pall, and rewards without end. . . .

The Book of the Anchorite of Llanddewibrefi (*1346*)
translated from the Welsh by
D. M. LLOYD

PRAISEWORTHY WAS HE

Issac, a fine youth from the South,
Like unto the flow of the sea were his manners,
Of modesty and gentleness,
And elegant mead-drinking;
Where he buries his weapon
Retaliation can be forgotten.
He saw not the cruel as uncruel nor the sure as uncertain.
His swordstroke rang through the heads of mothers.
A bulwark in battle, praiseworthy was he, son of
Gwydneu.

? ANEIRIN (6th century)
Y Gododdin
translated from the Welsh by D. M. LLOYD

THE LADY OF WALES

1237

The next year died the Lady of Wales, wife of Llywelyn ap Iorwerth, and daughter of (John), the King of England. Her name was Joan. (She died) in Llywelyn's court in Aber, in February, and her body was buried in a consecrated garden near the seashore. And after that,

Bishop Hywel consecrated the religious house of the barefooted friars in honour of the Blessed Virgin Mary, the prince having built it at his own cost for the soul of his Lady.

The Chronicle of the Princes
translated from the Welsh by
D. M. LLOYD

YVAN ASSERTS HIS CLAIM

This Yvan of Wales was son (*recte* grand-nephew) to a prince of Wales, whom kyng Edwarde had put to dethe, I can nat say for what cause, and so gave the principalyte to his sone, and made hym prince of Wales. So this Yvan came into Fraunce, and complayned to kyng Charles of Fraunce, of the injuryes that the kyng of Englande had done to hym, as in slayeng of his father, and takyng away of his herytage. So the Frenche kyng retayned him, and advaunsed him greatly, and made him governour of certayn men of warr. . . .

The Spanyerdes who had taken the erle of Penbroke, . . . they taryed a certayne space on the see, bycause the wynde was contrary to them; howbeit, at last they arryved at the porte saynt Andrewe in Galyce, and so entred into the towne about noone, and so brought all their prisoners into the Castell. . . . The same day Yvan of Wales was arryved with his shyppe in the same porte, and so toke lande, and entred into the same house. . . . And so it was shewed Yvan, as he was in his chambre, howe the Englysshemen were in the same house as prisoners: and this Yvan had great desyre to se them, to knowe what they were. And so he went forthe into the hall, and as he went thyder he encountered with the erle of Penbroke, whome he knewe ryght well, yet he had nat often sene him before: then he sayd to him, as in reproch, A erle of Penbroke, are ye come into this countre to do homage to me for suche landes as ye holde in the principalyte of Wales, wherof I am rightfull heyre, the whiche your kyng hath taken fro me by evyl counsayle and advyse? The erle of Penbroke was abasshed, whan he sawe that he was a prisoner, and in a strange lande, and knowyng nat the man that so spake to hym in his language; and so answered shortely, and sayd, What are you that gyve me this langage? I am, quoth he, Yvan, sonne to prince Aymon of Wales, whome your kyng of Englande put to dethe wrongfully, and hath disheryted me: but whan I may, by the helpe of my right dere lorde, the Frenche kyng, I shall shape therfore a remedy. And I wyll ye knowe, that if I may fynde you in any place convenyent, that I may fyght with you, I shall do it, and shewe you the right that ye have done to me . . . for by your fathers, with other counsaylours, my lorde, my father was betrayed, wherof I ought to be displeased, and to amende it whan I maye. . . . Ye are a prisoner: I can have none honour to apele you, for ye have nat the rule of yourselfe, for ye are under the rule of them that have taken you; but whan ye be quyte, than I shall speke with you more of the mater, for it shall nat rest thus.

JEAN FROISSART (1337-1410)
Chronicle, translated out of the French by
SIR JOHN BOURCHIER, LORD BERNERS

A CONTRAST[1]

The above-mentioned abbot John Powell bore great sorrow at the unhappy estate of these Welsh people whom he had failed in all his preaching and exhortations to call back from their evil ways, along which they had walked to their grievous hurt. But in spite of this he

[1]These incidents are recounted as having occurred during the wars of Owain Glyn Dŵr (Glendower).

did not cease to preach and to rail at them until his throat became hoarse, and his eyes failed him as a result of his long night watches spent in too much study. Yet scarcely was he able to rouse the slothful remnants of the Britons to resist the Saxons. Then when on one occasion as they were used to do, the Saxons invaded Wales, the Britons were gathered together by the exhortations of the above-mentioned abbot, until they were seven times more in number than the English, and he had indeed filled these Britons with confidence to fight for their native country, to defend their lands and possessions, to save their children and wives, and to suffer unto death for their traditional freedom. And indeed the abbot himself heard their confessions and pronounced absolution before the battle, and did not cease from declaiming and preaching earnestly until it was time to gird on his sword in readiness for the conflict. Yet the abbot was in no wise alarmed, but was so zealous for the liberty of his country and his people that, although he had every right to withdraw from the fray it did not please him to do so. He chose rather to remain with the rest of his Welshmen, killing the Saxons fiercely at Brynbuga (Usk town) above the river at Usk, showing equal proficiency in learning and in arms. In this manner the canon suffered death in this world with seven hundred Britons, and thus won eternal life, as is hoped.

But such was not the behaviour of that friar of whom we hear the following story. As he was preaching to the soldiers and hearing their confessions it came to a conflict. For this reason the friar brought his sermon to an end with a loud voice, saying, "O ye men, be of good cheer, and act manfully, for you are in the right, and if any of you should happen to fall in this battle for the defence of your land, I venture to assert, and by the Faith in which you stand I promise that those very men, this very night, before their innocent blood shed by this enemy is cold, shall feast with Christ." But immediately it came to blows the words of the friar ended, for the good reason that that friar, hastening to save himself from danger, with girded loins took flight, and vanished into thin air. Yet not before the people had shouted to him, "O holy friar, stay and rejoin the battle, for according to your promise, you will then be worthy to feast with Christ." But he, still pursuing his flight, is said to have replied, "Good luck to you; the truth is that today is my fast day, and for that reason it is not for me to feast with Christ tonight!"

W. BOWER'S supplement to FORDUN'S *Scotichronicon*
translated from the Latin by
E. M. LLOYD

CATHERINE OF BERAIN

I must not omit the portrait of a lady, exceedingly celebrated in this part of Wales; the famous Catherine Tudor, better known by the name of Catherine of Berain, from her seat in this neighbourhood. She was daughter and heiress of Tudor ap Robert Fychan, of Berain: she took for her first husband John Salusbury, heir of Llewenni, and on his death gave her hand to Sir Richard Clough. The tradition goes, that at the funeral of her beloved spouse she was led to church by Sir Richard, and from church by Morris Wynn, of Gwedir, who whispered to her his wish of being her second: she refused him with great civility, informing him that she had accepted the proposals of Sir Richard on her way to church, but assured him (and was as good as her word) that in case she performed the same sad duty (which she was then about) to the knight, he might depend on being her third. As soon as she had composed this gentleman, to shew that she had no superstition about the number three, she concluded with Edward Thelwall, of Plas y

Ward, esq; departed this life August 27, and was interred at Llanyfydd on the 1st of September, 1591.

Her portrait is an excellent three-quarters, on wood. By the date, 1568, it seems to have been painted by Lucas de Heere; the only artist I know of in that period equal to the performance. I was told that in the locket she wore to the gold chain was the hair of her second and favourite husband.

THOMAS PENNANT (1726-98)
Tours in Wales

A WELSH ENGINEER

I now speak of the sixth son, Hugh; a person whose useful life would give lustre to the greatest family. This gentleman (afterwards Sir Hugh) displayed very early his great talents and began, as we are told by himself, by searching for coal within a mile of his native place. His attempts did not meet with success: his genius was destined to act on a greater stage. The Capital afforded him ample space for his vast attempts: few readers need be told, that he planned, and brought to perfection, the great design of supplying the city with water. This plan was meditated in the reign of Elizabeth; but no one was found bold enough to attempt it. In 1608, the dauntless Welshman stept forth, and smote the rock: and on Michaelmas 1613, the waters flowed into the thirsting metropolis. He brought it, in defiance of hills and vallies, reckoning every winding, near thirty-nine miles; conveyed it by aqueducts in some places; in others pierced the high grounds, and gave it a subterranean course. He was a true prototype of the later genius of similar works; but he sacrificed private fortune to the public good. Two thousand pounds a month, which he gained from the Cardiganshire mines were swallowed up in this river. He received the empty honour of seeing himself attended by the king, his court, and all the corporation of London, among whom was his brother (designed mayor for the ensuing year.) The waters gushed out in their presence, the great architect received their applause, and knighthood; and, in 1622, the title of baronet. His own fair fortune being expended on an undertaking, which now brings in to the proprietors an amazing revenue, he was reduced to become a hireling surveyor, and was eminently useful in every place where draining or mining was requisite.

THOMAS PENNANT (1726-98)
Tours in Wales

AT THE GRAVE OF HENRY VAUGHAN

Above the voiceful windings of a river
An old green slab of simply graven stone
Shuns notice, overshadowed by a yew.
Here Vaughan lies dead, whose name flows on for ever
Through pastures of the spirit washed with dew
And starlit with eternities unknown.
Here sleeps the Silurist; the loved physician;
The face that left no portraiture behind;
The skull that housed white angels and had vision
Of daybreak through the gateways of the mind.
Here faith and mercy, wisdom and humility
(Whose influence shall prevail for evermore)
Shine. And this lowly grave tells Heaven's tranquillity
And here stand I, a suppliant at the door.

SIEGFRIED SASSOON (1886-)

A POET'S MOTHER

I flatter myself, that I am Master of a fluency of words, and purity of diction; and, if so, be the Poetical vein ever so slender, all the *Cynghaneddau*[1] must be equal, if equally understood. Cornelia, the Mother of the Gracchi, is commended in History for having taught her Sons in their infancy the purity of the Latin Tongue. And I may say in Justice to the memory of my Mother, I never knew a Mother, nor even a Master, more careful to correct an uncouth, inelegant phrase or vicious pronounciation than her; and that, I must own, has been of infinite service to me.

GORONWY OWEN (1723-69)
Letters

A PORTRAIT OF A POET

I wonder how the poor devil of an *offeiriad* (priest) goes on now. I don't hear anything of his being to be turned out. I suppose they dont drink as much as they did, poverty hinders them, and the alehouse will not give them credit. *Nawdd Duw rhag y fath ddyn!* (God protect us from such a man!) a surprizing composition! What poet ever flew higher? What beggar, tinker, or sowgelder ever groped more in the dirt? A tomturd man is a gentleman to him. The juice of tobbacco in two streams runs out of his mouth. He drinks gin or beer till he cannot see his way home and has not half the sense of an ass, rowls in the mire like a pig, runs through the streets with a pot in his hand to look out for beer; looks wild like a mountain cat, and yet when

[1] Welsh traditional patterns of sound correspondence and internal rhyme. The verse of G. Manley Hopkins is greatly influenced by these.

he is sober his good angel returns and he writes verses sweeter than honey and stronger than wine. How is this to be solved? His body is borrowed or descended from the dregs of mankind and his spirit from among the celestial choir: what a stinking dirty habitation it must have.

LEWIS MORRIS (1700-65)
Morris Letters

WILLIAM EDWARDS, BRIDGE BUILDER

But the change on reaching the brow of a very steep hill is instantaneous and delightful. The vale of Taff displays itself at once, in the very spot where its artificial and natural beauties are most eminently combined. The confluence of the Taff and Rhondda Fawr, each rolling impetuously over its bed of rocks; the brawling of smaller and nearer rills, whose waters are unseen, but the sound of their fall distinct; the amphitheatre of hills, of which two, the boldest and most grand, seem to defend the passes of the Taff, and to be connected by that stupendous bridge, viewed from this spot in all the triumphs of its art; the luxuriance of the hanging woods diversified by projecting masses of rock, that relieve the eye from the satiety of richness; the hills which close in upon the river above and below this widest part of the vale; all these circumstances, rushing at once upon the sight, after a long interval of dreariness, combine to make up as pleasurable a scene as the traveller can wish for to recompense his labours. . . . The appearance of the bridge from the Llantrisant road has generally been likened to that of a rainbow; from the lightness, width, and elevation of the arch I may safely say that the effect of such a structure, in such a position between two rocky but well-wooded crags, with a considerable reach of the river and valley seen through

[A. W. Hutton

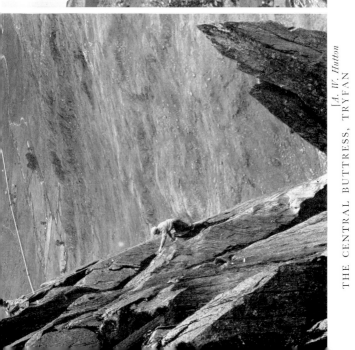

THE CENTRAL BUTTRESS, TRYFAN

[R. Cecil Hughes

TRYFAN

[*E. Emrys Jones*

ABERFFRAW, ONCE A ROYAL SEAT

the lofty arch, affords an instance scarcely to be paralleled of art happily introduced among the wildest scenes of nature.

William Edwards (the builder of this bridge) was the son of a farmer. The family lived in the parish of Eglwys-ilan in the county of Glamorgan. . . . William Edwards was born in the year 1719. His father died when he was only two years old. . . . When he had reached his fifteenth year, he frequently repaired the walls, or stone fences, of the farm. He was observed to perform his work in a style uncommonly neat and firm, and with an expedition surpassing that of most others. . . . Some time after he had exercised his ingenuity in this way, some masons came to the neighbourhood for the purpose of erecting a shed for shoeing horses at a smith's and farrier's shop. William Edwards admired the neatness with which they constructed the pillars, and other parts of the shed and felt an anxious wish for the ability to do the same. . . . He aspired to a higher rank in his profession, and from a dry-wall builder, hoped to become a builder of houses. Soon afterwards he undertook to build a little workshop for a neighbour, and gained great applause for the propriety with which he performed his contract. But a very short period had elapsed before he was employed to erect a mill in his own parish, and it was in the prosecution of this building that he first became acquainted with the principles of an arch. . . .

In 1746, he undertook to build a new bridge over the river Taff, at the spot the singularities of which have introduced him to our attention. This he executed in a style superior to anything of the kind in Wales for neatness of workmanship and elegance of design. It consisted of three arches, elegantly light in their construction. The hewn stones were excellently well dressed and closely jointed. It was admired by all who saw it. But this river runs through a very deep vale that is more than usually woody and crowded about with mountains. . . . The descents into these vales from the mountains being in general very steep, the water in long and heavy rains collects into these rivers with great rapidity and force . . . Such a flood unfortunately occurred after the completion of this undertaking, which tore up the largest trees by the roots, and carried them down the river to the bridge, where the arches were not sufficiently wide to admit of their passage. Here therefore they were detained. Brushwood, weeds, hay, straw, and whatever lay in the way of the flood came down and collected about the branches of the trees, which stuck fast to the arches and choaked the free current of water. In consequence of this obstruction to the flood, a thick and strong dam, as it were, was thus formed. The aggregate of so many collected streams, being unable to get any further, rose here to a prodigious height, and with the force of its pressure carried the bridge entirely away before it. . . .

Of course he was obliged to erect another, and he proceeded on his duty with all possible speed. The bridge had only stood about two years and a half. The second bridge was of one arch, for the purpose of admitting freely under it whatever incumbrances the floods might bring down. The span or chord of this arch was one hundred and forty feet; its altitude thirty-five feet; the segment of a circle whose diameter was one hundred and seventy feet. The arch was finished, but the parapets not yet erected, when such was the pressure of the unavoidably ponderous work over the haunches, that it sprung up in the middle, and the key-stones were forced out. This was a severe blow to a man who had hitherto met with nothing but misfortune in an enterprize which was to establish or ruin him in his profession. William Edwards, however, possessed a courage which did not easily forsake him, so that he was not greatly disconcerted. He engaged in it the third time; and by means of three cylindrical holes through the work over the haunches, so reduced the weight over them, that there was no longer any danger from it. These holes or cylinders rise above each other, ascending in the order of the arch, three at each end, or over each of the haunches. The diameter of the lowest is nine feet; of the second, six feet; and of the uppermost, three feet. They give the bridge an air of uncommon elegance. The second bridge fell in 1751. The third, which has stood ever since, was completed in 1755.

Hitherto the Rialto was esteemed the largest arch in Europe, if not in the world. Its span or chord was ninety-eight feet. But New Bridge is forty-two feet wider; and was till lately, if it is not still so . . . the largest arch in the world of which we have any authentic account. The fame of this bridge introduced William Edwards to public notice, and he was employed to build many other bridges in South Wales. . . .

At length he discovered, not by reading, conversation, or any other mode of extrinsic instruction, but by dint of his own genius matured in the school of experience, that where the abutments are secure from the danger of giving way, arches of much less segments, and of far less altitude than general opinion had hitherto required are perfectly secure, and render the bridges much easier for carriages to pass over, and in every respect adapt them better to the purposes of a ready and free communication.

Caerphilly Castle is in his native parish. He has often been heard to say that he would frequently visit that celebrated ruin, and study the principles of its excellent masonry, with all its various peculiarities, appearing in those venerable remains. He considered himself to have derived more important knowledge from this than from any other circumstance. Indeed, his principles were formed on those of the Caerphilly Castle masonry. He was, what may with sufficient propriety be termed, a mason of the ancient castle, or

Gothic school. His manner of hewing and dressing his stones was exactly that of the old castle-masons. He put them together in a style of closeness, neatness, and firmness, that is never seen but in those ancient, and, as far as we know, everlasting edifices.

William Edwards united with his trade the occupation of a farmer during the whole of his life. Nor was Sunday, though a Sabbath, a day of rest to him, for then he had clerical functions to exercise. In his religious sentiments he was a dissenter, of the denomination styled Independents. About 1750 he was regularly ordained according to the usage of the sect of which he was a member, and about the same time was chosen minister of the congregation meeting at a chapel in his native parish, where he officiated for forty years, and till he died. He was a Calvinist, but of a very liberal description . . . He frequently repeated and enforced a maxim, well worthy the adoption of the most enlightened and eminent divines: that the love of God and of our neighbour is the ultimate end of all religions, which having attained, their possessors had arrived at their object; and that it is against the spirit of Christianity to suppose, that among all parties, be they what they may, there are not many who have indisputably obtained this distinguishing characteristic.

BENJAMIN HEATH MALKIN (1769-1842)
The Scenery . . . of South Wales

A 'CAMBRO-BRITON'

"As for a shentleman in distress," said he, shaking me by the hand, "I lofe him as I lofe my own powels: for, Cot help me! I have had vexations enough upon my own pack." And as I afterwards learned, in so saying, he spoke no more than what was true; for he had been once settled in a very good situation in Glamorganshire, and was ruined by being security for an acquaintance. All differences being composed, he untied his bundle, which consisted of three bunches of onions, and a great lump of Cheshire cheese wrapt up in a handkerchief; and taking some biscuit from the cupboard, fell to with a keen appetite, inviting us to a share of the repast. When he had fed heartily on his homely fare, he filled a large cup, made of a cocoa-nut shell, with brandy and drinking it off, told us, prandy was the pest menstruum for onion and sheese. His hunger being appeased, he began to be in better humour; and being inquisitive about my birth, no sooner understood that I was descended of a good family, than he discovered a particular good will to me on that account, deducing his own pedigree in a direct line from the famous Caractacus, king of the Britons, who was first the prisoner, and afterwards the friend, of Claudius Cæsar. Perceiving how much I was reduced in point of linen, he made me a present of two good ruffled shirts, which, with two more of check which I received from Mr. Thomson, enabled me to appear with decency. Meanwhile the sailor, whom Mr. Morgan had sent to the doctor, brought a prescription for his messmate; which when the Welchman had read, he got up to prepare it, and asked if the man was tead or alive. "Dead!" replied Jack: "if he was dead, he would have no occasion for doctor's stuff. No, thank God, death hasn't as yet boarded him, but they have been yard-arm and yard-arm these three glasses."—"Are his eyes open?" continued the mate. "His starboard eye," said the sailor, "is open, but fast jamm'd in his head; and the haulyards of his under-jaw have given way."—"Passion of my heart!" cried Morgan, "the man is as pad as one would desire to be! Did you feel his pulses?" To this the other replied with—"Anan!" Upon which the Cambro-Briton, with great earnestness and humanity, ordered the tar to run to his messmate, and keep him alive till he should come with the medicine—"And then," said he, "you shall peradventure pehold what you shall see." The poor fellow with great simplicity ran to the place where the sick man lay, but in less than a minute returned with a woful countenance, and told us his comrade had struck. Morgan hearing this, exclaimed—"Mercy upon my salvation! why did not you stop him till I came?"—"Stop him," said the other, "I hailed him several times, but he was too far on his way, and the enemy had got possession of his close quarters, so that he did not mind me."—"Well, well," said he, "we all owe Heaven a teath. Go your ways, you ragamuffin, and take an example and a warning, lock you, and repent of your misteets." So saying, he pushed the seaman out of the birth.

TOBIAS SMOLLETT (1721-71)
Roderick Random

A FORMIDABLE GUEST

I dined at Mr. Myddleton's, of Gwaynynog. The house was a gentleman's house, below the second rate, perhaps below the third, built of stone roughly cut. The rooms were low, and the passage above stairs gloomy but the furniture was good. The table was well supplied except that the fruit was bad. It was truly the dinner of a country gentleman. Two tables were filled with company not inelegant.

After dinner, the talk was of preserving the Welsh language. I offered them a scheme. Poor Evan Evans was mentioned, as incorrigibly addicted to strong drink. Washington was commended. Myddleton is the only man, who, in Wales, has talked to me of literature. I wish he were truly zealous. I recommended the republication of David ap Rhees's Welsh Grammar.

SAMUEL JOHNSON (1709-84)
A Diary of a Journey through North Wales in . . . 1774

MARGARET UCH EVAN

Near this end of the lake lives a celebrated personage, whom I was disappointed in not finding at home. This is Margaret uch Evan, of Penllyn, the last specimen of the strength and spirit of the antient British fair. She is at this time [1786] about ninety years of age. This extraordinary female was the greatest hunter, shooter, and fisher, of her time. She kept a dozen at least of dogs, terriers, greyhounds, and spaniels, all excellent in their kinds. She killed more foxes in one year than all the confederate hunts do in ten: rowed stoutly and was queen of the lake: fiddled excellently, and knew all our old music: did not neglect the mechanic arts, for she was a very good joiner: and, at the age of seventy, was the best wrestler in the country, and few young men dared to try a fall with her. Some years ago, she had a maid of congenial qualities; but death, that mighty hunter, at last earthed this faithful companion of her's. Margaret was also a blacksmith, shoe-maker, boat-builder, and maker of harps. She shoed her own horses, made her own shoes, and built her own boats, while she was under contract to convey the copper ore down the lakes. I must not forget that all the neighbouring bards payed their addresses to Margaret, and celebrated her exploits in pure British verse. At length she gave her hand to the most effeminate of her admirers, as if predetermined to maintain the superiority which nature had bestowed on her.

THOMAS PENNANT (1726-98)
Tours in Wales

GRIFFITH JONES OF LLANDDOWROR

It seemed to him that the Church of which he thought so much was putting up a very poor fight. Of course, there were clergymen who were idle, or even dissolute (such men are found in every country and under the name of every religion), and Griffith Jones's earnestness inclined him to place rather too many of his brethren in this class. But much oftener poverty and lack of education were the bane of the clergy. . . . Altogether, the poor clergyman's actual wage was very small; sometimes the parson received only £9 out of a tithe of £90, and had to take three or four churches together, ten or twelve miles apart, in order to scrape a living. It is difficult to put zeal into your work in circumstances like these. Griffith Jones himself had only £38 a year and his house, and he may be counted rather lucky; and had he not married a wife with some money, he could hardly have travelled as he did, and kept a curate to do his work while he was away from home. . . .

The plan of Griffith Jones's Circulating Schools is so well known that there is no need to dwell at great length upon it. A school would be set up in a given district for three months, as a rule, and that in the winter—a relatively slack time for farmers. The invitation and favour of the parish clergyman were sought; the use of the parish church was asked, the pupils were urged to attend all church services, and the parson was requested to report upon the school and the schoolmaster. The schoolmasters were trained by Griffith Jones himself at Llanddowror. . . . They were paid out of the money which Griffith Jones collected so diligently in Wales and England. (*Welch Piety* is a series of 'annual reports' to these subscribers); from the same fund, Bibles and other books were bought for the schools, and assistance was given to the poorest pupils. Reading, and reading

[The Studio Jon

FISHGUARD

[R. Cecil Hughes

NORTH BEACH, TENBY

[*Aero Pictorial Ltd.*

ABERYSTWYTH FROM THE AIR

[The Studio Jon

FISHGUARD

[R. Cecil Hughes

NORTH BEACH, TENBY

[*Aero Pictorial Ltd.*

ABERYSTWYTH FROM THE AIR

only, was taught, and Welsh was the language of a very great majority of the schools; the Bible and the Catechism were the textbooks. Griffith Jones wrote a set of expositions of the Catechism, each provided on its fly-leaf with an A B C and several rows of syllables and short words, to serve as a "reading primer." A night-school also was to be kept, for the sake of those who could not attend during the day. Sometimes, too, the school was kept in the same place for more than three months, and sometimes it returned to it after some years. . . . When Griffith Jones died, in 1761, *Welch Piety* summed his work up, in so far as figures could sum it up, as follows: 3495 "Schools," that is, school terms in the various neighbourhoods, between 1737 and 1761; and 158,237 pupils, not counting the pupils of the night-schools.

Yet these are but figures. Rightly to assess the work of Griffith Jones, something must be deducted from them: on the other hand, very much more must be added. On the negative side: of course, although the whole time was spent on reading, and although Griffith Jones tells us of some who learned to read well in six weeks, yet three months are only three months, and many a pupil can hardly have learnt more than to recognise the easiest words in his Bible. Then again, the subject-matter of the instruction was, from the point of view of general education, very limited. But, to turn to the other side, Griffith Jones's importance is far greater than the cold figures above would suggest. He saved the life of the Welsh language, in that he raised a great army of readers, familiar, at any rate to some extent, with the standard literary language which is found in the Welsh Bible; without that, Welsh would have crumbled into a heap of disconnected dialects. Without this habit of *reading* Welsh (not that reading was confined to Griffith Jones's people, but *numbers* matter here), in vain would the 'classical' poets and the men of the Eisteddfod have laboured to revive the Welsh tradition. Without it, it may be that even the Methodist Revival would have remained a mere excitation of feelings, a perishable thing soon to be forgotten. . . . Without it, again, . . . men of whom Griffith Jones would have approved hardly at all would have striven in vain to arouse political interest and zeal for education among the Welsh people. . . .

After his day, Thomas Charles had begun to imitate Griffith Jones in North Wales (1785), and had gone on further . . . to establish the Sunday Schools, which for a century were to be the only means of 'Adult Education' in Wales, and for well-nigh a century the chief opportunity for a Welsh child to learn to read his mother tongue. . . . An Englishman who knew Wales testifies that the chief difference between Wales and England was this: that the children were better educated in England than in Wales, but that the middle-aged and the elderly were far better in Wales. If the credit for this must be given to any one man (remembering all the time that there were many schools in Wales besides his), then that man is Griffith Jones.

Griffith Jones was a Churchman, a High Churchman (as the eighteenth century understood High Churchmanship, of course), and it was for his Church—consciously so—that he laboured so hard. He was thinking neither of preserving the Welsh language nor of spreading education in general, but of doing his duty as a faithful priest. He would have desired no better epitaph than to have it said of him that he fought a good fight, that he finished his course, that he kept the faith.

It is exceedingly difficult to form an idea of Griffith Jones personally. We have only two contemporary accounts of him, one by an adoring friend and the other by a furious enemy. The former makes an angel of him, laying on the whitewash so thick that we cannot see the grain of the stone underneath. John Evans on the other hand blackens him—but his book is much the more interesting. Piecing everything together, we gather that Griffith Jones was an asthmatic, melancholy, rather peevish and moody man. During a long journey to Scotland, he saw only "the world's vanity." We can imagine him stalking bleakly through the fashionable streets of Bath, or it may be losing his patience sometimes at the fussing of the "devout and honourable women" who dogged the footsteps of eighteenth century evangelists. We are told that he loved physick, and was fond of doctoring his neighbours. It is John Evans who tells us about the hobby of wood-turning, and it is in his book too that we see (to our great comfort) that this godly man could lose his temper as completely as any of us ordinary people, and that at such times he would say very wild things. We like the great men of History better, and understand them better, for knowing something of their failings.

R. T. JENKINS (1881-)
Gruffydd Jones, Llanddowror

OWAIN MYFYR

Owen Jones ('Owain Myfyr,' 1741-1814) has been depicted for us in a waspish article by Dr. John Jones . . . a Llandybïe man, school-master and afterwards barrister, who in 1824 published a *History of Wales.* According to him, Owain Myfyr "spent his days from 8 to 8 scraping skins in his warehouse," and was during those hours curt and unapproachable. "From 8 till 10 or 12" he spent at the "Bull" in Walbrook Street, (London), where he was a dictator: a loud "hem!" heralded his advent; all made way for him, and he was given three chairs, one to sit upon, the other two to serve as arm-rests. There he consumed "Welchrabbits, pipes, and porter," among "a heterogenous company of . . . harpers, fiddlers, and fifers," talking of "the Welsh language and customs, and the poet whose works he had last paid for transcribing"; at the end of the evening he "discounted a few bills . . . for friendly and deserving Welshmen." . . .

The engraving of Owain Myfyr (in Leathart's book)—the original portrait was painted in 1802 for the Gwyneddigion Society by John Vaughan of Conway—shows us a large, heavy, rather lifeless face, with obstinate chin and lips, and a high forehead.

It is indeed easy to laugh at Owain Myfyr and his pretensions. It may well be that (though he most certainly loved it) he really understood far less than he imagined of the literature on which he spent so much of his money. Without doubt he was a dictatorial man, and without doubt sycophants pandered to him. He *would* have his way, even in matters on which his opinion was worthless . . . Again he had a most violent temper, even if we allow for humorous exaggeration in his friend David Samwel's description of a famous debate at the "Bull":

Myvyr at length indignant rose
Full five feet from the ground . . .
And kicked the table to the ground
With one tremendous crash . . .
He upset candles, arguments,
Pint-pots, and all together.

"Money talked" with him, we can hardly doubt.

But our mockery of his self-esteem pales when we consider his enormous services. There have been very many rich men—very many rich Welshmen too—who have spent their gains on far less laudable objects than did Owain Myfyr. That little remark of John Jones's about "discounting bills" must not be overlooked—nor the generosity which, for instance, sent Gwallter Mechain up to Oxford, and aided Iolo Morganwg and William Owen Pughe. If (to put it at its lowest) it pleased his vanity to parade as "editor" of MSS. which were mostly copied for him, and edited for him, by other men, let it be remembered that he was willing to pay large sums for the copying and the printing. The *Dafydd ap Gwilym* cost him £180 to *print*—in 1789 money. It was he who paid for the transcript of Lewis Morris's *Celtic Remains* which Gwallter Mechain never edited; he paid £80 for the die for the Gwyneddigion Eisteddfodic medals—and paid for the medals themselves; he spent more than £1,000 on the printing of the *Myvyrian Archaiology*, smile as we may at its title . . . Copies of Welsh MSS. made at his expense fill a hundred volumes in the British Museum Library; and students of Welsh literature, from his day to our own, have for the most part had to live on the admittedly imperfect editions of Dafydd ap Gwilym and of the poets of the Age of the Princes which Owain Myvyr's money—and his determination—enabled him to publish. A tenacious man—he clung to his Radical views in politics when some of the more prominent of his fellow-Gwyneddigion wavered under the force of circumstances.

R. T. JENKINS (1881-)
A History of the Hon. Society of Cymmrodorion

ADVICE TO A SON

You hear the Welsh spoken much about you, and if you can pick it up without interfering with more important labours, it will be worth while. I suppose you can easily get a grammar and dictionary. It is, you know, the language spoken by the Britons before the invasion of the Anglo-Saxons, who brought in the principal ingredients of our present language, called from thence English. It was afterwards, however, much mingled with Norman French, the language of William the Conqueror and his followers; so if you can pick up a little of the Cambro-British speech, it will qualify you hereafter to be a good philologist, should your genius turn towards languages. Pray, have you yet learned who Howel Dha was?—Glendower you are well acquainted with by reading Shakespeare. The wild mysterious barbaric grandeur with which he has invested that chieftain has often struck me as very fine. I wish we had some more of him.

SIR WALTER SCOTT (1771-1832)
Letter to his son, Charles, care of the Rev. John Williams, Lampeter, 19th Dec., 1820

EVANS, A CAMBRO-BRITON

The cashier at that time was one Evans, a Cambro-Briton. He had something of the choleric complexion of his countrymen stamped on his visage, but was a worthy sensible man at bottom. He wore his hair, to the last, powdered and frizzed out, in the fashion which I remember to have seen in caricatures of what were termed, in my young days, *Maccaronies*. He was the last of that race of beaux. Melancholy as a gib-cat over his counter all the forenoon, I think I see him, making up his cash (as they call it) with tremulous fingers, as if he feared every one about him was a defaulter; in his hypochondry ready to imagine himself one; haunted, at least, with the idea of the possibility of his becoming one; his tristful visage clearing up a little over his roast neck of veal at Anderton's at two (where his picture still hangs, taken a little before his death by desire of the master of the coffee-house, which he had frequented for the last five-and-twenty years), but not attaining the meridian of its animation till evening brought on the hour of tea and visiting. The simultaneous sound of his well-known rap at the door with the stroke of the clock announcing six, was a topic of never-failing mirth in the families which this dear old bachelor gladdened with his presence. This was his *forte*, his glorified hour! How would he chirp, and expand, over a muffin! How would he dilate into secret history! His countryman, Pennant himself in particular, could not be more eloquent than he in relation to old and new London—the site of old theatres, churches, streets gone to decay—where Rosomond's pool stood—the Mulberry Gardens—and the Conduit in Cheap—with many a pleasant anecdote, derived from paternal tradition, of those grotesque figures which Hogarth has immortalised in his picture of *Noon*,—the worthy descendants of those heroic confessors, who, flying to this country, from the wrath of Louis the Fourteenth and his dragoons, kept alive the flame of pure religion in the sheltering obscurities of Hog Lane, and the vicinity of the Seven Dials!

CHARLES LAMB (1775-1834)
Elia (*The South-Sea House*)

ON LEAVING LONDON FOR WALES

Hail to thee, Cambria! for the unfettered wind,
Which from thy wilds even now methinks I feel,
Chasing the clouds that roll in wrath behind,
And tightening the soul's laxest nerves to steel;
True mountain Liberty alone may heal
The pain which Custom's obduracies bring,
And he who dares in fancy even to steal
One draught from Snowdon's ever sacred spring
Blots out the unholiest rede of worldly witnessing.

And shall that soul, to selfish peace resigned,
So soon forget the woe its fellows share?

Can Snowdon's Lethe from the free-born mind
So soon the page of injured penury tear?
Does this fine mass of human passion dare
To sleep, unhonouring the patriot's fall,
Or life's sweet load in quietude to bear
While millions famish even in Luxury's hall,
And Tyranny, high raised, stern lowers on all?

No, Cambria! never may thy matchless vales
A heart so false to hope and virtue shield;
Nor ever may thy spirit-breathing gales
Waft freshness to the slaves who dare to yield.
For me! . . . the weapon that I burn to wield
I seek amid thy rocks to ruin hurled,
That Reason's flag may over Freedom's field,
Symbol of bloodless victory, wave unfurled,
A meteor-sign of love effulgent o'er the world.

. . . . .

Do thou, wild Cambria, calm each struggling thought;
Cast thy sweet veil of rocks and woods between,
That by the soul to indignation wrought
Mountains and dells be mingled with the scene;
Let me forever be what I have been,
But not forever at my needy door
Let Misery linger speechless, pale and lean;
I am the friend of the unfriended poor,
Let me not madly stain their righteous cause in gore.

PERCY BYSSHE SHELLEY (1792-1822)

A METHODIST 'EXHORTER'

In those days preaching was not usual, and it was looked upon somewhat askance as a new-fangled notion, and a disorderly thing. Among the few 'exhorters,' as they were called, there was an old man known as Iefan Tyclai (Evan of the Clay-house) who would often go on a preaching circuit through Glamorgan. He was lively in appearance, and dressed in a grey coat of homespun cloth, a checked jacket, corduroy knee breeches, coarse black stockings, and wooden shoes with brass buckles. In this dress Iefan would take the everlasting Gospel over hill and through dale, mounted on a brown colt with mane and tail untrimmed. In those days the meetings were held in dwelling houses or in barns. In these places Iefan would walk around as he preached, addressing his words to this person and that, individually, on his way. Sometimes he would walk around the house nine or ten times, proclaiming first the Law and then the Gospel. In one hand he held a short club of ash with an enormous knob weighing a pound or two, and the other fist would be held in the faces of the congregation as if he were determined to belabour the sermon into their brains and hearts.

I can recall being told by the old people how the Tyclai Apostle once came to preach in Llangrallo, a village near the home of the saintly Reverend David Jones, of Llangan. It was a week-night, and many of the villagers had gathered together in a dwelling house for the meeting. They all sat around the walls awaiting the arrival of the visiting preacher. Soon, he came. He read and prayed with great animation, standing in the middle of the assembly. Then he began to move around, from each one to the next, preaching the Gospel to high and low with no distinction of persons. "Come out from among them," said he, "and be ye separate. You know, friends, when you see a hen in and out a good deal among the potatoes, as likely as not, she will make her nest there, and if you spend much more of your time with the things of this vain world, this is where you will abide, and your nest will catch fire. My good people, come out from among them. And you, religious people who are present, ask yourselves what are the things for which you live, which fill your mind and spirit, for the mark of those things will show on you in whatever you do. They tell me that if a lamb sucks the milk of a goat, its wool will become hairy like a goat, and if you suck too much of this world, you are likely to be possessed by the spirit of this world; you will always be striving after the things of this world and forgetting the true worship of God. You will then become corrupt, and in the end you will be out-and-out goats, with nothing of a sheep's nature left in you."

Thus the man from Tyclai would walk hurriedly about the house for half an hour, uttering many maxims and points of theology of this kind, and applying them with no mean skill to each one individually. Eventually the pressure would seem to ease, the wheels would gradually slow down, there was every indication that the Tyclai machine was coming to a standstill. When he found himself by the chair where sat the venerable evangelist from Llangan, Mr. Jones with an angelic smile and a warm heart spoke to the old preacher, saying, "Iefan *bach*, you have been in school a long time now; what have you learnt in all this time?" "Mr. Jones *bach*," said he, "I have been at the same lesson all through the years, and tonight I can tell you honestly that I have learnt it." "But what is it, Iefan *bach*?" "Well, I'll tell you: I've learnt that I don't know anything." "You have?" "I surely have." "Well, well, Iefan *bach*, you have reached the top class in our Lord's school. In spite of all my efforts I've utterly failed to come up to that class." After this conversation, the meeting was terminated with a prayer and a hymn, and everyone went his own way in wonder at the preacher's deep insight and the readiness of his tongue.

EDWARD MATTHEWS, OF EWENNY (1813-92)
Siencyn Penhydd
translated from the Welsh by D. M. LLOYD

FLUMMERY AND CHARACTER

My next recollection is being in school, and a Mr. Thickness, or some such name, was the schoolmaster. I must have been sent young to school,—probably at between four and five years of age,—for I cannot remember first going there. But I recollect being very anxious to be first in school and first home, and the boys had always a race from the school to the town, and, being a fast runner, I was usually at home the first, and almost always the first at school in the morning. On one occasion my haste nearly cost me my life. I used to have for breakfast a basin of flummery,—a food prepared in Wales from flour, and eaten with milk, and which is usually given to children as the Scotch use oatmeal porridge. It is pleasant and nutritious, and is generally liked by young persons. I requested that this breakfast might be always ready when I returned from school, so that I might eat it speedily, in order to be the first back again to school. One morning, when about five old, I ran home as usual from school, found my basin of flummery ready, and as I supposed sufficiently cooled for eating, for no heat appeared to arise from it. It had skinned over as when quite cold; but on my hastily taking a spoonful of it, I found it was quite scalding hot, the body of it retaining all its heat. The consequence was an instant fainting, from the stomach being scalded. In that state I remained so long, that my parents thought life was extinct. However, after a considerable period I revived; but from that day my stomach became incapable of digesting food, except the most simple and in small quantities at a time. This made me attend to the effects of different qualities of food on my changed constitution, and gave me the habit of close observation, and of continual reflection; and I have always thought that this accident had a great influence in forming my character. . . .

During my childhood, and for many years afterwards, it never occurred to me that there was anything in my habits, thoughts, and actions different from those of others of my age; but when looking back and comparing my life with many others, I have been induced to attribute any favourable difference to the effects produced at the early period when my life was endangered by the spoonful of scalding flummery.

ROBERT OWEN (1771-1858)
The Life of Robert Owen by himself

A METHODIST WIFE

Mrs. Williams was a remarkable woman. The daughter of a minister, and the wife of another, she had been brought up close to the altar as she called it, and was, of course, a Methodist to the backbone. But her father, though a Methodist minister, was a Tory of the old school, and accordingly she had been taught to respect the Church as the mother of Methodism and an honoured institution which was now under a cloud in Wales, but which would one day revive to do great things. Hence she showed traits of character which I thought inconsistent. No one could laud Methodism and Methodists more highly than she did, or seemed more thoroughly imbued with Methodist ways, still she did not consider a marriage a proper, or, I believe, a lawful marriage unless it was celebrated according to the rites of the Church, and I have often heard her say that when her time came to die, she could not be satisfied without burial in the old consecrated ground, according to the old rite. This may have seemed to me an inconsistency, but it was natural. It was the effect of old habits and surroundings which are so difficult entirely to efface. She was an earnest missionary, and took a lively interest in the work of converting the heathen. Nothing pleased her better than the account of the conversion of another Indian in Pondicherry, or the history of the Polynesian successes of John Williams. In her zeal for the natives of Borriboola Gha she rivalled Mrs. Jellyby herself, but unlike that worthy lady, she did not neglect her own house for the sake of those interesting people. She rose with daylight, toiled at her work till late at night, and only relaxed from her labours when a visitor (and we had a good many) called her away to the duties of hospitality. And she had a cheery welcome that charmed all who came near her; her beaming face, kind words, and efforts to make every one about her comfortable, endeared her to us all. Among the many faces that memory recalls there is none dearer to me than that of my good friend Mrs. Williams.

ROBERT ROBERTS (1834-85)
The Life and Opinions of R. R., a wandering scholar . . .

MARGARET WILLIAMS

Margaret's mildness and gentleness were exceptional; it could be seen in her bearing, in her voice and in her whole behaviour. She was full of sympathy for all, and a tender godliness made her whole life sweet. I never heard a jarring word cross her lips, true religion was portrayed in her genial face, and a kindly charm was felt in her company. She went through life always quiet and unruffled, like one who felt that she had behind her a store of strength to face all storms.

MYFYR WYN (WILLIAM WILLIAMS, 1849-1900)
Memories of Sirhowy
translated from the Welsh by D. M. LLOYD

A HERMIT AND HIS HAUNTS

The Solitary accompanied us to Pencommon to get the horse and then showed us the way down the lanes towards the Church. The people who met him touched their hats to his reverence with great respect. They recognised him as a very holy man and if the Solitary had lived a thousand years ago he would have been revered as a hermit and perhaps canonized as a Saint. At a gate leading into a lane we parted. There was a resigned look in his quiet melancholy blue eyes. The last I saw of him was that he was leaning on the gate looking after us. Then I saw him no more. He had gone back I suppose to his grey hut in the green cwm.

The evening became lovely with a heavenly loveliness. The sinking sun was shot along the green pastures with a vivid golden light and striking through the hedges here and there tipped a leaf or a foxglove head with a beam of brilliant green or purple. Down the steep stony lane by the ruined Church of Llanbedr, a team of horses came home to Llandeviron from plough with rattling chains.

I crossed the Bach Wye by the short cut at Trewilad leaving Williams to ride round the longer way by Rhyd Lydan and to cross the brook at the Broad Ford lower down. I stood upon the stepping stones at Trewilad to watch the little herd of cows undriven coming lazily through the brook home to Trewilad to be milked. The water, darkly bright, came flowing down and filling the cool shadowy lane, and the red and white cows loitered slowly down to the brook, standing still often in the shallow water as they forded the stream, and the air was full of sunshine and the honey scent of the charlock, and the hedges were luxuriant with the luscious sweetness of woodbine and the beauty of the stars of the deep red rose.

FRANCIS KILVERT (1840-79)
Diary

THE LADY OF LLWYN MADOC

It was my privilege to know intimately for some fourteen years Miss Clara Thomas of Llwyn Madoc and Pencerrig. She offered perhaps the highest example in every sense of the Welsh squires. . . . When I first knew her in late middle-age Miss Clara Thomas was stately and handsome, but I have been told (and I can well believe it) that in her youth she was quite lovely with a wealth of pale golden hair that I only knew as grey. Kindness and sympathy beamed from her face, and she had, I think, the sweetest smile I have ever seen on a human countenance. A spinster to the last, it was commonly reported that the Lady of Llwyn Madoc was afraid of being married for the sake of her money. I doubt it; but in any case, I never met any man worthy of her. But she was clearly satisfied with her own outward life of hospitality, culture and public work, and her interior life of practical virtue. . . .

What a charming peaceful spot was Llwyn Madoc. Nestling in a fold of the narrow valley of the Cammarch, midway between Garth and Abergwesin, amid the wildest scenery, the long low rambling house, set off by a succession of brilliant flower-beds in lawns of velvet smoothness, made a veritable human oasis amidst the solemn woods and moors and swelling hills. Nasturtiums trained on long cords swathed the low-gabled front from base to roof. During the summer months an endless succession of visitors filled the house, so that two carriages and pairs were regularly employed to drive the guests to and fro between Llwyn Madoc and Garth station, some five miles distant. There were no mansions (except Garth House . . .) within calling range in those pre-motor days, so that Llwyn Madoc might be termed a self-contained community. All told, there must have been habitually some two dozen souls sleeping beneath that roof. The life lived was easy, useful, unselfish and spontaneous. The school and church at Eglwys Oen Duw (The Church of the Lamb of God), built and endowed by Miss Thomas, took up much time and attention from the lady of the house and her life-long friend and companion, Miss Gertrude Lewis-Lloyd of Nantgwyllt (not so many miles distant, as the crow flies, across the intervening bogs and mountain-side). On Sunday afternoons the two ladies always taught their classes of boys and girls at Llwyn Madoc House, and never a day passed without some act of kindness or help to poorer neighbours. The district was still quite primitive, even in the first decade of the present century; and I remember Miss Thomas once taking me to a distant farm-house in order to see the house-wife dyeing her cloth with a preparation made from the yellow-flowering genista known as 'dyer's green'. I must confess that the tint produced, which was a dingy yellow, was not very attractive. But the operation was interesting to witness as a survival of a once-common but now almost extinct practice.

For the visitors, many of them young people to whom Miss Thomas had acted as a fairy-godmother in the way of education and financial support, there was tennis and croquet and billiards, as well as fishing and shooting. But better still were the lovely walks with our kind hostess or Miss Lewis-Lloyd over the slopes of Carnwen and Cefn Gardys, whence you looked down on

[*Eagle Photos*

NEAR TAL-Y-LLYN

[*Valentine*

CORACLE FISHING BY CENARTH BRIDGE

[*The British Travel and Holidays Association*

THE DEVIL'S BRIDGE

the buzzards hovering below in the valley. There were delightful picnics too, often so far afield as the Wolf's Leap on the Tregaron road, whither some of us drove and others rode on picturesque mountain-ponies, bred on the home-farm. It was an idyllic visit, with its pleasant house-party and its simple amusements. The one drawback to the place was the climate, for Llwyn Madoc must surely be one of the wettest spots in all Wales, and often for days on end it would pour with rain, and the mist would come rolling down from the bleak hills:—"the grey mare is whisking her tail down the valley," as the country-folk around would describe it.

It was on the heathery hills around Llwyn Madoc, many, many years ago now, that Mr. Henry Thomas (Miss Thomas's father) was out walking one day with a fashionable friend from town, a true Victorian 'swell.' During their walk they happened to meet the famous preacher, Kilsby Jones, who was riding a shaggy pony on his way to some distant chapel. Mr. Thomas and the preacher stopped to converse, whilst the stranger, struck with the uncouth aspect of the reverend gentleman on his humble mount, pulled out his monocle, set it to his eye, and stared quizzically and rudely at this (to him) novel specimen of humanity. But Kilsby was equal to the occasion. With ready wit he slipped one foot out of the stirrup, and lifting the iron to his face and using it as an extempore eye-glass he returned the visitor's stare with interest to the latter's complete discomfiture.

The daily life at both Llwyn Madoc and Pencerrig was conducted on old-fashioned Christian principles. Morning and evening prayers were said by the hostess or by Miss Lewis-Lloyd, and these were often accompanied by music or singing. The servants always attended in full force. I can hear now in my mind's ear old Pearce, the butler, enter the drawing-room during a noisy round game of cards and announce in a tone of mild reproof at our frivolity: "Prayers is waiting, mem!" Whereupon we all hastily threw down our cards, assumed a solemn expression and streamed into the dining-room where the array of domestics awaited our arrival. I suppose it all sounds absurd and sanctimonious to the present generation, but I can assure the reader it was neither.

The life in winter at Pencerrig ran on somewhat different lines, for this place was surrounded by neighbouring houses, for whose benefit Miss Thomas was wont to entertain freely, and early in the New Year always gave a dance to which children in fancy dress were also invited. How truly did our hostess appear the *grande dame* on such occasions, with that sweet face framed in its aureole of soft grey hair and with fine old diamonds and lace round her neck. Yet everything of value that ever she wore was inherited; for herself she never bought costly furs or jewels or dresses out of her vast income, whereof she always regarded herself but the steward for life and ever acted on that principle. Every good thing that this passing life can bestow was hers:—wealth, beauty and high birth, yet she was always the simplest and easiest of mortals, and her wealth she shared with those who were less liberally endowed. Of the high religious tone of her household I have already spoken; but I may add that the conversation was always bright, wholesome and intellectual. One came away from a visit to Llwyn Madoc or Pencerrig refreshed and improved both in mind and body.

HERBERT M. VAUGHAN (1870-1948)
The South Wales Squires

AN OLD QUARRYMAN

Strange, how silence makes one notice things! When the eleven o'clock hooter sounded a hush fell on the whole of the pit; on trucks, crowbars, wedges, and hammers; and in the three-minutes' interval before the blasting-hooter everyone hurried to the shelter-cabin. Everyone, that is, except my father, who lingered by my side until I sent him packing.

I watched him moving slowly away, pausing for a moment to gaze at the flock of crows hovering above the pit; they, too, knew that it was firing-time. I heard the crunch of his boots on fragments of slate, and then it ceased for a moment as he halted to watch Richard Roberts—"Dick Mysterious," as we called him—bending over his fuse on the other side of the pit. Yes, I said to myself, my father has aged of late. In the stillness, I looked at the white hair below the old bowler hat he always wore in the quarry, at the thin neck, the bowed shoulders, the feet that moved so slowly. He ought not to be in the quarry at all today, I thought; his place was at home by the fire. He looked so lonely, so dejected, on his way to the shelter-hut, this skilled, conscientious quarryman who knew that his working days were over. The quarry, his home, and his chapel—those were the three interests of his life, and one of them was slipping quickly from his enfeebled grasp.

T. ROWLAND HUGHES (1903-49)
From Hand to Hand
translated from the Welsh by
RICHARD C. RUCK

A BACKWOODSMAN

Yesterday I visited the old village where I was brought up. I wandered through the woods familiar to my boyhood. There I saw a child gathering sticks for firewood, and I thought of the hours which I spent in the same pleasant and profitable occupation, for I also have been something of a 'backwoodsman.' And there was one experience taught me then which is of use to me today. I learnt as a child that it was little use going into the woods after a period of calm and fine weather, for I generally returned empty-handed; but after a great storm I always came back with an armful. We are in for rough weather. We may be even in for a winter of storms which will rock the forest, break many a withered branch, and leave many a rotten tree torn up by the roots. But when the weather clears you may depend upon it that there will be something brought within the reach of the people that will give warmth and glow to their grey lives, something that will help to dispel the hunger, the despair, the oppression and the wrong which now chill so many of their hearths.

D. LLOYD GEORGE (1863-1945)
Speech at Caernarvon, 1909 in defence of his famous first Budget and his social legislation

LLOYD GEORGE

His tenor voice was admirable; musical, beautifully modulated, and of remarkable carrying power. Lloyd George had not the rich overflowing organ tones of Gladstone, rolling out sentences, clauses, parentheses 'like the Atlantic waves on the Biscayan coast'; its compass was narrower, its quality lighter, it was flexible, caressing, a melodious witchery, mockery, savagery.

On the topmost notes his voice became rough and shrill. He played on all the strings of the human heart and matched with each the mobile landscape of his face and bodily posture—the alluring smile, the scowling visage, the thrilling whisper, the eloquent pince-nez dangling from its black silk ribbon, the menacing finger, the arms outstretched to the uttermost. If his voice had not the sonorous rotundity of Gladstone's or the unrelieved pugnacity of Joseph Chamberlain's, he abounded in a sense of fun; his humorous sallies convulsed his audience and there were moments when he reduced them to tears. S. K. Ratcliffe comments: "It was all done with absolute mastery. Not a paragraph bungled; not a stroke, or a joke, goes awry." Emotional, dramatic, rhetorical, and never too long, he was always the incomparable actor with a perfect sense of theatre.

DR. THOMAS JONES (1870-1955)
Lloyd George

A DAUGHTER OF THE SEA

We put out from La Palice in the evening, after some happy hours ashore, enjoying the unfamiliar scenery, and buying curios to take home to our loved ones. We had had a good shaking in crossing the Channel, but had we known it, that was only like the murmur of a distant sea in comparison with what we were now to experience. It was so quiet in the harbour that we deluded ourselves that the storm would have abated before we had ventured out, but the elements had only been gathering their forces together, and when the ship left the shelter of the land, the old Bay of Biscay rushed to meet us like a warrior to the fray.

The Captain shouted from the bridge, "Clear decks—all passengers to go below!" But I felt my heart full of rebellion. I was unwilling to miss one of the Creator's most impressive sights. With great difficulty I managed to reach the captain, and for five anxious minutes I pleaded my case with him, soberly but earnestly. I wished to see the storm as well as feel it. "There is but one safe way," said the kindly skipper, "you will have to be lashed to one of the masts with a strong rope." I was prepared to agree to any such condition in order to have my wish, and therefore, after I had been lapped in a sailor's oilskin, so as to keep dry, I was securely lashed to the mast, while the officers and sailors smiled compassionately at my madness. But the old captain well understood. He was Irish, and the Celtic dreams had not faded from his heart.

The storm increased, and as if it were that the winds and the angry waves were not enough, the thunder and lightning came to swell the chorus, the mountainous waves washed over the frail vessel, the lightning flashed on the boiling blue-white foam making a rainbow of the sea, and then darkness, sky and sea each for the more sombre, and in that awesome blackness the thunder was heard roaring and reverberating as if it came from the depths of the dark abyss, until all the timbers of the old ship were bruised and trembling. Then came the forked lightning, time and again to dart and weave like fiery serpents through the rigging. But the sight reached its highest sublimity in the couriers of fire striding the waves from peak to peak as if they were caressing the crests of the blue-white brine. And for the life of me I could not but admire the old ship for her splendid battling through it all. Strange and terrible are the Creator's forces; yes, but strange and terrible too are the devices of man, who is created in His image; and never before had I seen and felt how close is the link between them.

I experienced four hours of sheer ecstasy which have left their impression on my whole life. Blessed is he who has undergone a similar experience. But while my soul was feasting on this magnificence, my poor body was paralysed by cold and fatigue. The old skipper treated me very tenderly, and he also had the grace to keep silent. His warm Irish nature understood that speech was impossible after such depth of feeling, and that my great need now was rest, and I did have rest in all its sweetness. I was later told that I had slept round the clock, and when I awoke and looked through the port-hole, the sun was smiling cheerfully; the green banks of Portugal were slowly coming into sight, and O! the world was lovely indeed that morning. It had never been so lovely, and I was beginning life anew.

ELUNED MORGAN (1870-1938)
Gwymon y môr
translated from the Welsh by
D. M. LLOYD

THE CHAIRING OF THE BARD

Hedd Wyn, "the Hero of the Black Chair of Birkenhead," a winner of the chief bardic prize at the Eisteddfod of 1917, was killed, a victim to the war, six weeks before the award was announced. Commenting on his death; "The Welsh Outlook" said: "He died at 29, and Wales has lost in him one of her best poets." His home was at Trawsfynydd, in Merioneth.

Mute in an alien soil he lies;
The close-clenched hands move not at all,
And muffled in earth's heavy pall
The heavy, unawakening eyes.

Lived is the life, the course is run,
Complete the little destined round,
The broken limbs laid underground,
And all their joys and journeys done.

In tender light the moon again
  Trawsfynydd's lonely moorland steeps;
  He only unremembering sleeps
By the dark trench that saw him slain.

Trawsfynydd! whose gray mountain side,
  Whose lichened stones and bracken sere
  In peaceful days his heart held dear,—
But far, far hence thy lover died!

Ah, friends, let not that lovely moon
  Make you forget our poet lad;
  Sorrow itself is doubly sad
That mourns a life cut short so soon.

Sad from his books the poet to call
  And into war's rough work to thrust;
  Sad was the sentence "Dust to dust,"
And sad in alien lands to fall.

And oh! to leave his work undone,
  To leave the woods, the laughing rills,
  The meads, the dales, the heath-clad hills,
And all the glories of the sun!

The mystic Chair, expectant, dumb,
  Seems in its dark funereal state
  With arms outstretched for him to wait
Who comes not now, and will not come.

R. WILLIAMS PARRY (1884-   )
translated from the Welsh by
SIR H. IDRIS BELL

[A. W. Hutton

THE MENAI STRAITS

[R. Cecil Hughes

MAWDDACH ESTUARY AND CADER IDRIS

[R. Cecil Hughes

ABERGLASLYN PASS

WAR EPITAPH

Naval Instructor Tom Elwyn Jones, B.Sc.,
H.M.S. Defence

The shy, warm-hearted, long must he abide
  Far from our kenning in his ocean grave.
Cold and uncomforted the death he died,
  Whelmed in the sea-flood 'neath the wandering wave.

Ah, strange, unmoving multitude who sleep
  With the sea tangle o'er their sightless eyes!
In the fish-haunted spaces of the deep,
  On beds of pearl our light of learning lies.

R. WILLIAMS PARRY (1884-   )
translated from the Welsh by
SIR H. IDRIS BELL

OLD AGE

Tonight I could describe to you not so much the things that happened when young Twm of Llain Wen and I were boys in school, but the very smell of the old school and of those damp old books in the cupboard by the door. Only this afternoon I could hear Twm's teeth gnashing as he fought with the master thirty-two years ago. And I felt the touch of my teacher's velvet bodice on my cheek as she marked my sums. Somehow or other thirty-two years of my life have vanished into thin air and Twm and I are in school together, two young cubs in our twelfth year. Tonight, Twm lies in his grave, a man of forty-four. His mother is still alive, an old lady of eighty-eight, living with her daughter Gwen in the old house, Llain Wen . . .

As I looked at her sitting there, an old old woman,

my mind went back to the time when I used to call at Llain Wen for Twm on the way to school. She was then a round red-cheeked apple-dumpling of a woman, moving briskly about the house. . . . I thought of that hard-working mother, and of this old woman sitting by the fire with folded hands.

I think she still wore the same clothes. I couldn't remember ever seeing her without her white cap under her black straw hat. And it wasn't a goffered cap like the one Betsan Ifan wore when I was a boy, but a frilled cap, with a little round black hat turned down, its brim bound with velvet and a feather round the crown. I never saw her wearing any other, and I never once saw her without it in the house. She wore a homespun petticoat, a flannel bodice, and a blue and white apron; on her feet a pair of clogs with shiny clasps. "The same kind of clothes," I said to myself, but a different face and a different pair of arms. These weren't the arms I used to see long ago kneading a panful of dough until it heaved like a bog under her hands. There was little of her face to be seen, for she tied the strings of her cap under her chin, and that little was crinkled like mud after rain. Her hands yellow and mottled like damp-stained wallpaper, a drop of water in the corner of her eye. She shook her head all the time, sometimes up and down, sometimes sideways. . . .

KATE ROBERTS (1891-)
Old Age
translated from the Welsh by
DR. L. WYN GRIFFITH

SISTERS

When Meri Ifans was twenty she married, and her life after that was very like many other women's lives—work, rearing children, occasionally quarrelling within the four walls of her own home. John Ifans, her husband, was miserly, quiet, entertaining; for the most part, agreeing with you on every point. He neither smoked nor drank nor swore, although he kept sheep and ponies. Meri was a clean, tidy person, mistress of every branch of housewifery. They had nine children, and Meri's house was as clean when the ninth was born as it had been when the first child came. The trace of her tough, strong arms was everywhere in her home. There was not a reeve in the wall-paper with which she had covered the walls. Along the floors brightness succeeded to brightness in a direct line, to the farthest corner. The sweet smell of her dairy was enough to bring you from your bed when you were laid low in sickness. Her butter was firm in August, and its taste as good a month after making as on the first day, for the pressure of her powerful arms on the 'thin' saucer drove every drop of water from it. An odour of cleanliness, a scent not unlike the scent of summer, or of apples beginning to dry, pervaded the cupboards and drawers where she stored her clothes and linen. The clothes lay in the cupboards like books piled one on the other, their back to view, in neat rows. Such a 'grain' was there on her clean linen, that you would almost imagine you still felt the heat of the iron, if you pressed it to your cheek weeks after it had been ironed. In short, one look at Meri Ifans's home was enough to convince that housework was akin to poetry and not a wearying and a drudgery. . . .

KATE ROBERTS (1891-)
Sisters
translated from the Welsh by
WALTER DOWDING

QUITE EARLY ONE MORNING

. . . Oh, the town was waking now. And I heard distinctly, insistent over the slow speaking sea, the voices of the town blown up to me. Thus some of the voices of a cliff-perched town at the far end of Wales moved out of sleep and darkness into the newborn, ancient and ageless morning, moved and were lost.

And the voices said:

I am Miss May Hughes the Cosy, a lonely lady,
waiting in her house by the nasty sea,
Waiting for her husband and her pretty baby
to come home at last wherever they may be.

I am Captain Tiny Evans, my ship was the "Casper,"
and Mrs. Tiny Evans has been dead for many a year.
"Poor Captain Tiny, all alone," the neighbours whisper,
but I like it all alone and I *hated* her.

Clara Teify-Jenkins, "Madame" they call me,
an old contralto with her dressing gown on,
And I sit at the window and I sing to the sea
for the sea doesn't notice that my voice has gone.

The Reverend Frogmore Williams making morning tea,
very weak tea, too, you mustn't waste a leaf;
Every morning making tea in my house by the sea
I am troubled by one thing only, and that's—Belief.

Open the curtains, light the fire, what's a servant for.
I am Mrs. Ogmore-Pritchard and I want another snooze.
Dust the china. Feed the canary. Sweep the drawing-room floor.
And before you let the sun in, mind he wipes his shoes.

I am only Mr. Griffiths, very shortsighted, B.A. . . . Aber.
As soon as I've finished my egg I must shuffle off to school.
O patron saint of teachers, teach me to keep order,
And *forget* those words on the blackboard: "Griffiths Bat is a fool."

Do you hear that whistling? It's me. I'm Phoebe,
The maid at the King's Head. And I'm whistling like a bird.
Somebody's spilt a tin of pepper in the tea.
There's twenty for breakfast. And I'm not going to say a word.

I can see the Atlantic from my bed where I always lie
night and day, night and day, eating my bread and slops.
A quiet cripple staring at the sea and the sky,
I shall lie here till the sky goes out and the sea stops.

DYLAN THOMAS (1914-53)

Humour, Romance and Sentiment

SEITHENYN

"Prince Seithenyn," said Elphin, "I have visited you on a subject of deep moment. Reports have been brought to me, that the embankment, which has been so long intrusted to your care, is in a state of dangerous decay."

"Decay," said Seithenyn, "is one thing, and danger is another. Every thing that is old must decay. That the embankment is old, I am free to confess; that it is somewhat rotten in parts, I will not altogether deny; that it is any the worse for that, I do most sturdily gainsay. It does its business well: it works well: it keeps out the water from the land, and it lets in the wine upon the High Commission of Embankment. Cupbearer, fill. Our ancestors were wiser than we: they built it in their wisdom; and, if we should be so rash as to try to mend it, we should only mar it."

"The stonework," said Teithrin, "is sapped and mined: the piles are rotten, broken, and dislocated: the floodgates and sluices are leaky and creaky."

"That is the beauty of it," said Seithenyn. "Some parts of it are rotten, and some parts of it are sound."

"It is well," said Elphin, "that some parts are sound: it were better that all were so."

"So I have heard some people say before," said Seithenyn; "perverse people, blind to venerable antiquity: that very unamiable sort of people, who are in the habit of indulging their reason. But I say, the parts that are rotten give elasticity to those that are sound: they give them elasticity, elasticity, elasticity. If it were all sound, it would break by its own obstinate stiffness: the soundness is checked by the rottenness, and the stiffness is balanced by the elasticity. There is nothing so dangerous as innovation. See the waves in the equinoctial storms, dashing and clashing, roaring and pouring, spattering and battering, rattling and battling against it. I would not be so presumptious as to say, I could build anything that would stand against them half an hour; and here this immortal old work, which God forbid the finger of modern mason should bring into jeopardy, this immortal work has stood for centuries, and will stand for centuries more, if we let well alone. It is well: it works well: let well alone. Cupbearer, fill. It was half rotten when I was born, and that is a conclusive reason why it should be three parts rotten when I die."

THOMAS LOVE PEACOCK (1785-1866)
The Misfortunes of Elphin

AN EARLY SABBATARIAN

It is recorded in the Triads that "Gwrgi Garwlwyd killed a male and female of the Cymry daily, and devoured them; and, on the Saturday, he killed two of each, that he might not kill on the Sunday." This can only be a type of some sanctimonious hero, who made a cloak of piety for oppressing the poor.

THOMAS LOVE PEACOCK (1785-1866)
The Misfortunes of Elphin

PROFESSIONAL JEALOUSY

It is worthy of observation that there lived in the neighbourhood of this City of Legions in our time, a Welshman named Melerius, who . . . acquired the knowledge of future and occult events. . . . If the evil spirits oppressed him too much, the Gospel of St. John was placed on his bosom, when, like birds, they immediately vanished; but when that book was removed, and the History of the Britons, by Geoffrey Arthur (i.e. Geoffrey of Monmouth) was substituted in its place, they instantly reappeared in greater numbers, and remained a longer time than usual on his body and on the book.

GIRALDUS CAMBRENSIS (1147-*c.* 1220)
The Itinerary through Wales
translated from the Latin by
SIR RICHARD COLT HOARE

MY PURSE, GRAMERCY FOR THIS!

My velvet purse, my priest, my coffer of gold, my means of grace, my dear saviour, my prophet, thou art my companion, we speak the same tongue. There is no better, more-freely giving saviour under heaven than thou, my nest of gold. Nor any better discharger of debts to the foreigner: my purse, gramercy for this!

I have owned horses, I have been respected; jewels, weapons, sacred relics, brilliant gems, heavy rings of gold, chains, nine heaps of brooches, fashionable clothes —all these have I possessed; a very wise man am I in my country, and I intend to continue in this way of life. My kindred are numerous in Emlyn: my purse, gramercy for this!

I have learnt a piece of Solomon's book, and the seven liberal arts, and things of high repute. I have learnt how to recognise the achievements of Paradise—a comforting teaching of ecclesiastical enlightenment. The people will tell how I learnt to practise brave feats of arms, how to conquer in battle. I have learnt to excel in the bardic metres: my purse, gramercy for this!

Many a prosperous family claims kinship with me—nine times are they more numerous than my real kin:

I have a surfeit of them, but it is all for a purpose. I know I shall have dealings with all sorts of people, with never a lack of bosom friends. All wayfarers, all who are in need, every vagabond minstrel, all who struggle against adversity, every one with a most civil tongue, will seek my aid: my purse, gramercy for this!

When wealth is great, says the sibyl, Gwenddydd, all is well with us every day; we enjoy drink, and the world's best food, and every condition in which men delight. With a complimentary name I shall be mentioned, and with a graceful turn of phrase, in the song of the true favourite of the muse. I shall be highly honoured in every market-place, and shall have a high seat in every feast in my country; and be received with lavish respect: my purse, gramercy for this!

Should I be caught in flagrant theft, and taken to account, and have to face an enquiry or a trial, I know that I should be exonerated. There are forty who would, without any persuasion, perjure themselves three Sundays in succession in my interest; and the officials are all with me—they would be most considerate in their interrogation. Thou art my servant, my golden one: my purse, gramercy for this!

Maidens have poured their love on me; I could have all the favours I sought. Love-messengers have reached me from as far as lower Conway. I could have a million, and more if I wanted. Not for my life am I permitted to leave a tavern in my own time—I am grasped by my arm and led towards the mead. I know why I am respected, a bestower of largesse: my purse, gramercy for this!

It is for my gold, I know it, that I shall find the whole world sweet and kind. I shall be received by the whole of Wales, never neglected; I shall have all her houses, her castles, and lands. I shall be loved in Paradise; God will receive my whole body, a sober thought! My name shall live, my soul shall find rest in heaven; the indulgence of Popes can be got, and the satisfaction of every warring enemy.

My purse, gramercy for this!

attributed to SIR PHYLIP EMLYN (15th century)
translated from the Welsh by
D. M. LLOYD

PISTOL EATS THE LEEK

GOWER: Nay, that's right; but why wear you your leek today? Saint Davy's day is past.

FLUELLEN: There is occasions and causes why and wherefore in all things: I will tell you, asse my friend, Captain Gower:—the rascally, scald, peggarly, lousy, pragging knave, Pistol,—which you and yourself, and all the 'orld, know to be no petter than a fellow, look you now, of no merits,—he is come to me, and prings me pread and salt yesterday, look you, and pid me eat my leek: it was in a place where I could not preed no contention with him; but I will be so pold as to wear it in my cap till I see him once again, and then I will tell him a little piece of my desires.

GOWER: Why, here he comes, swelling like a turkeycock.

FLUELLEN: 'Tis no matter for his swellings nor his turkeycocks. *Enter Pistol.* Got pless you, Auncient Pistol! you scurvy, lousy knave, Got pless you!

PISTOL: Ha! art thou bedlam? dost thou thirst, base Trojan, to have me fold up Parca's fatal web? Hence! I am qualmish at the smell of leek.

FLUELLEN: I peseech you heartily, scurvy, lousy knave, at my desires, and my requests, and my petitions, to eat, look you, this leek: because, look you, you do not love it, nor your affections, and your appetites, and your disgestions does not agree with it, I would desire you to eat it.

PISTOL: Not for Cadwallader and all his goats.

FLUELLEN: There is one goat for you. (*Strikes him.*) Will you be so goot, scald knave, as eat it?

PISTOL: Base Trojan, thou shalt die.

FLUELLEN: You say very true, scald knave,—when Got's will is: I will desire you to live in the mean time, and eat your victuals: come, there is sauce for it. (*Strikes him again.*) You call'd me yesterday mountain-squire; but I will make you to-day a squire of low degree. I pray you, fall to: if you can mock a leek, you can eat a leek.

GOWER: Enough, captain: you have astonisht him.

FLUELLEN: I say, I will make him eat some part of my leek, or I will peat his pate four days.—Pite, I pray you; it is goot for your green wound and your ploody coxcomb.

PISTOL: Must I bite?

FLUELLEN: Yes, certainly, and out of doubt, and out of question, too, and ambiguities.

PISTOL: By this leek, I will most horribly revenge: I eat and eat, I swear——

FLUELLEN: Eat, I pray you: will you have some more sauce to your leek? there is not enough leek to swear by.

PISTOL: Quiet thy cudgel; thou dost see I eat.

FLUELLEN: Much goot do you, scald knave, heartily. Nay, pray you, throw none away; the skin is goot for your proken coxcomb. When you take occasions to see leeks hereafter, I pray you, mock at 'em; that is all.

PISTOL: Good.

FLUELLEN: Ay, leeks is goot:—hold you, there is a groat to heal your pate.

PISTOL: Me a groat!

FLUELLEN: Yes, verily and in truth, you shall take it;

or I have another leek in my pocket, which you shall eat.

PISTOL: I take thy groat in earnest of revenge.

FLUELLEN: If I owe you any thing, I will pay you in cudgels; you shall be a woodmonger, and buy nothing of me but cudgels. Got b' wi' you, and keep you, and heal your pate. (*Exit.*)

PISTOL: All hell shall stir for this.

GOWER: Go, go; you are a counterfeit cowardly knave. Will you mock at an ancient tradition,—begun upon an honourable respect, and worn as a memorable trophy of predeceased valour,—and dare not avouch in your deeds any of your words? I have seen you gleeking and galling at this gentleman twice or thrice. You thought, because he could not speak English in the native garb, he could not therefore handle an English cudgel: you find it otherwise; and henceforth let a Welsh correction teach you a good English condition. Fare ye well. (*Exit.*)

WILLIAM SHAKESPEARE (1564-1616)
from *King Henry the Fifth*
Act V, scene I

FLUELLEN AND GOWER

GOWER: . . . O, 'tis a gallant king!

FLUELLEN: Ay, he was porn at Monmouth, Captain Gower. What call you the town's name where Alexander the Pig was porn?

GOWER: Alexander the Great.

FLUELLEN: Why, I pray you, is not pig great? the pig, or the great, or the mighty, or the huge, or the magnanimous, are all one reckonings, save the phrase is a little variations.

GOWER: I think Alexander the Great was born in

Macedon: his father was call'd Philip of Macedon, as I take it.

FLUELLEN: I think it is in Macedon where Alexander is porn. I tell you, captain, if you look in the maps of the 'orld, I warrant you sall find, in the comparisons between Macedon and Monmouth, that the situations, look you, is both alike. There is a river in Macedon: and there is also moreover a river at Monmouth: it is called Wye at Monmouth; but it is out of my prains what is the name of the other river; but 'tis all one, 'tis alike as my fingers is to my fingers, and there is salmons in both. If you mark Alexander's life well, Harry of Monmouth's life is come after it indifferent well; for there is figures in all things. Alexander,—Got knows, and you know,—in his rages, and his furies, and his wraths, and his cholers, and his moods, and his displeasures, and his indignations, and also being a little intoxicates in his prains, did, in his ales and his angers, look you, kill his pest friend, Cleitus.

GOWER: Our king is not like him in that: he never kill'd any of his friends.

FLUELLEN: It is not well done, mark you now, to take the tales out of my mouth, ere it is made and finisht. I speak but in the figures and comparisons of it: as Alexander kill'd his friend Cleitus, being in his ales and his cups; so also Harry Monmouth, being in his right wits and his goot judgements, turn'd away the fat knight with the great-pelly doublet: he was full of jests, and gipes, and knaveries, and mocks; I have forgot his name.

GOWER: Sir John Falstaff.

FLUELLEN. That is he: I'll tell you there is goot men porn at Monmouth.

WILLIAM SHAKESPEARE (1564-1616)
from *King Henry the Fifth*
Act IV, scene 7

MR. MORGAN ON CAPTAIN WHIFFLE

His *valet de chambre* plied him with a smelling-bottle: one footman chafed his temples with Hungary-water; another sprinkled the floor with spirits of lavender; a third pushed Morgan out of the cabin, who coming to the place where I was, sat down with a demure countenance; and, according to his custom, when he received any indignity which he durst not revenge began to sing a Welch ditty. I guessed he was under some agitation of spirits, and desired to know the cause; but, instead of answering me directly, he asked, with great emotion, if I thought him a monster and a stinkard. "A monster and a stinkard!" said I, with some surprise; "did any body call you so? "—'Got is my judge,' replied he, "Captain Fifle did call me both; aye, and all the water in the Tawy will not wash it out of my remembrance. I do affirm, and avouch, and maintain, with my soul, and my pody, and my plood, look you, that I have no smells about me but such as a christian ought to have, except the effluvia of tobacco, which is a cephalic, odoriferous, aromatick herb; and he is a son of a mountain-goat who says otherwise. As for my being a monster, let that be as it is: I am as Got was pleased to create me; which, peradventure, is more than I shall aver of him who gave me that title; for I will proclaim it before the world, that he is disguised, and transfigured, and transmographied, with affectation, and whimsies; and that he is more like a papoon than one of the human race."

TOBIAS SMOLLETT (1721-71)
Roderick Random

A KNIGHT-ERRANT IN WALES

I have on the seat behind me the constitution of Mr. John Probert: a knight-errant, dubbed by the noble lord in the blue ribbon, and sent to search for revenues and adventures upon the mountains of Wales. The commission is remarkable; and the event not less so. . . .

Probert, armed and accoutred,—and paid, proceeded on his adventure;—but he was no sooner arrived on the confines of Wales, that all Wales was in arms to meet him. That nation is brave, and full of spirit. Since the invasion of King Edward, and the massacre of the bards, there never was such a tumult, and alarm, and uproar, through all the region of Prestatyn. Snowdon shook to its base; Cader Idris was loosened from its foundations. The fury of litigious war blew her horn on the mountains. The rocks poured down their goatherds, and the deep caverns vomited out their miners. Every thing above ground, and every thing under ground, were in arms.

In short, Sir, to alight from my Welsh Pegasus, and to come to level ground; the *preux* Chevalier Probert went to look for revenue, like his masters upon other occasions; and like his masters, he found rebellion. . . . The wise Britons thought it more reasonable that the poor, wasted, decrepit revenue of the principality should die a natural than a violent death. They chose that their ancient moss-grown castles should moulder into decay, under the silent touches of time, and the slow formality of an oblivious and drowsy exchequer than that they should be battered down all at once by the lively efforts of a pensioned engineer. As it is the fortune of the noble lord to whom the auspices of this campaign belonged, frequently to provoke resistance, so it is his rule and his nature to yield to that resistance in all cases whatsoever. He was true to himself on this occasion.

He submitted with spirit to the spirited remonstrances of the Welsh. Mr. Probert gave up his adventure, and keeps his pension;—and so ends "the famous history of the revenue adventures of the bold Baron North, and the good Knight Probert, upon the mountains of Venedotia."

EDMUND BURKE (1729-97)
Speeches
('*Plan of Economical Reform.*' Speech in House of Commons, Feb. 11, 1780)

TWM SHON CATTI

As I drew near I distinguished a stout burly figure of a man, seemingly about sixty, with a short pipe in his mouth.

"Ah, is it you?" said the figure in English, taking the pipe out of his mouth; "good evening; I am glad to see you." Then shaking some burning embers out of his pipe, he put it into his pocket, and trudged on beside me. . . .

"And where do you live?"

"Oh, not very far from Tregaron."

"And what kind of place is Tregaron?"

"Oh, very good place; not quite so big as London, but very good place."

"What is it famed for?" said I.

"Oh, famed for very good ham; best ham at Tregaron in all Shire Cardigan."

"Famed for anything else?"

"Oh, yes! famed for great man, clever thief, Twm Shone Catti, who was born there."

"Dear me!" said I; "when did he live?"

"Oh, long time ago, more than two hundred year."

"And what became of him?" said I; "was he hung?"

"Hung, no! only stupid thief hung. Twm Shone

Catti clever thief; died rich man, justice of the peace and mayor of Brecon."

"Very singular," said I, "that they should make a thief mayor of Brecon."

"Oh, Twm Shone Catti very different from other thieves; funny fellow, and so good natured that everybody loved him—so that they made him magistrate, not, however before he had become very rich man by marrying great lady who fell in love with him."

"Ah, ah," said I; "that's the way of the world. He became rich, so they made him a magistrate; had he remained poor they would have hung him in spite of all his fun and good-nature. Well, can't you tell me some of the things he did?"

"Oh, yes, can tell you plenty. One day in time of fair Tom Shone Catti goes into an ironmonger's shop in Llandovery. 'Master,' says he, 'I want to buy a good large iron porridge pot; please to show me some.' So the man brings out three or four big iron porridge pots, the very best he has. Tom takes up one and turns it round. 'This look very good porridge pot,' said he; 'I think it will suit me.' Then he turns it round and round again, and at last lifts it above his head and peeks into it. 'Ha, ha,' says he; 'this won't do; I see one hole here. What mean you by wanting to sell article like this to stranger?' Says the man, 'there be no hole in it.' 'But there is,' says Tom, holding it up and peeking into it again; 'I see the hole quite plain. Take it and look into it yourself.' So the man takes the pot, and having held it up and peeked in, 'as I hope to be saved,' says he, 'I can see no hole.' Says Tom, 'good man, if you put your head in, you will find that there is a hole.' So the man tries to put in his head, but having some difficulty, Tom lends him a helping hand by jamming the pot quite down over the man's face, then whisking up the other pots Tom leaves the shop, saying as he goes, 'Friend, I suppose you now see that there is a hole in the pot, otherwise how could you have got your head inside?'"

GEORGE BORROW (1803-81)
Wild Wales

JOHN PRITCHARD THE COBBLER'S SERMON ON POTATOES

TEXT "*Woe unto you, hypocrites, for ye are like unto white-washed tombs,*" *etc.*

I don't know whether you all understand this hard word hypocrite, but you all know what potato apples are. They look so green and bright and round, these potato apples, you would fancy that they are the fruit. And the potatoes are all out of sight, you see, underground. But the potato apples are not the fruit, they will all rot off, or the pigs get them; but the potatoes get out of the ground round and sound, they are the fruit. It is just the same with the hypocrites; they are flourishing enough now; they are green enough now. What does the Psalmist say? I saw the ungodly in prosperity, flourishing like a green bay tree. And the true Christian is like the potatoes, he is underground; the weight of this world is heavy on him. But the time will come, my brethren, when the hypocrite will rot away like the potato apples, and the true Christian like a healthy pink eye will rise out of the dust of this world, and shine glorious in the Kingdom of Heaven. Heaven make us potatoes every one of us.

ROBERT ROBERTS (1834-85)
The Life and Opinions of R. R., a wandering scholar . . .

WILL BRYAN AND THE CLOCK

"You know that old eight-day clock in our kitchen? Of late it has been apt to lag a bit behind time,—*a fault by the way, not entirely unknown amongst other orders of superior creatures . . .*[1] I thought all along I could cure it if I had the time, although I had never before tried to clean a clock,—but you know that I am not bad at all at trying my hand at things! Well then, when the folks went to Wrexham Fair,—*with strict injunctions that Will in the meantime should diligently apply himself to weighing and wrapping sugar, which occupation the said Will considered unworthy of his admitted abilities, and the said Will, following his more congenial inclinations, betook himself to clock-cleaning, thinking that thereby he did not waste valuable time by putting the time-keeper to rights.* But it was a bigger job than I had reckoned, I tell you; for in taking it to pieces, I had to write notes where every part came from, and to what they belonged. And after I had cleaned it all, and put butter on every cog, screw and bar,—there was no oil in the house—it was well on in the afternoon, although I did without dinner so as not to waste time, and it was high time to start putting it together again before the gaffer came home from the fair. *So far—good.* But when I betook myself to putting the old eight-day piece together, and to consult my notes,—you never saw the like: I was like Mr. Brown, the vicar; I couldn't read my own notes! But I learnt this much, that the man who goes to clean clocks, just like the preacher, should be able to do the job without notes. You never saw such a mess. But you must remember that I was *labouring under great disadvantages*, for my only tools were a jack-knife and a pair of blacksmith's tongs. I was running with sweat, lest the old 'Pilgrim's Progress' should return from the

[1]The phrases in italics are in English in the original. (*Editor.*)

fair before I had assembled the old clock somehow. I worked like a ' black,' and got it together into some sort of shape. But I had one spare wheel, and not the remotest idea where to fix it or what to do with it, so I put it in my pocket,—here it is, look," said Will, as he showed it to me.

"Well, I put the old ' eight ' back in its place, and wound it, and the first thing that ' *my nabs* ' did was to strike and strike right to the bottom. It struck thousands and thousands, and the noise was driving me dotty; the din was such that I feared the neighbours would think that the squire's daughter was getting married! After striking all it could. ' *my nabs* ' decided to stay put. As long as I pushed the pendulum the old ' eight ' kept going fairly well, but as soon as I stopped, so would the clock. To tell you the truth, I laughed till I was rolling—I couldn't stop laughing to save my life. *So here endeth a true account of the clock-cleaning. But wait a bit.*

"Soon the old couple returned from the fair, and the first thing my mother did was to look at the clock. I had tried guessing what the time of their arrival would be, and had set it pretty near the mark as I thought. But the old dame spotted that the clock had stopped, and said she, ' What's the matter on the old clock, William? ' ' Has it stopped? ' said I. ' I should think so, two hours ago,' said she, and she gave the pendulum a push. I was nearly choked, wanting to laugh. ' What —is—the—mat-ter—on—this—old—clock?" said the old dame again, and she shook it as you have seen them trying to wake a drunkard sleeping by the roadside. For an excuse to laugh, I said, ' Really, I believe, mam, that it's got a knot in the bowels, just like the squire's hunter, and that we'll have to shoot it or open it.' But at that point, in came the maid, and she split on me that I had been all day cleaning the old ' eight.' You never saw such a row! My mother went to pieces, and the gaffer saw red. I really think the old boy would have liked to leather me, but he knew he couldn't. *And Will went to his boots.* The next day they sent for Mr. Spruce, the watchmaker, to see to the old eight-day piece, but I knew he couldn't put it right, for Will had one wheel in his pocket, and Will had his revenge. '*Give it up*,' said the old 'mainspring.' But when this chap gets the back of the old folks for six hours, he is *bound* to perform miracles on the old 'eight.' Well, there you are, I've told you my 'scrape.' But, *honour bright*, is it a fact that you've been 'born again'?"

DANIEL OWEN (1836-95)
Rhys Lewis
translated from the Welsh by
D. M. LLOYD

BETI JONES'S SUPPER

But, to return to the subject of the ordinary everyday meals of the farmer's family and the various kinds of 'spoon-food' that could be made, I think this is the appropriate place in which to tell the story of the famous supper prepared by Beti Jones, y Ceunant. . . .

The story goes that Beti Jones had tired of cooking different kinds of food for her very numerous children. She had twenty-five of them, and each one demanded a different supper. This was too much and Beti Jones, her patience exhausted, resolved to teach her brood a lesson. She was a woman of character and originality, and the method she adopted to solve the supper problem was characteristic. She asked the children, beginning with the eldest and ending with the youngest, what they would like for supper.

"Robin, what will you have for supper tonight?" "Porridge," said Robin.

"Nel, what will you have?" "*Siot.*"

"Mari, what will you have?" "Posset."

"Dic, what will you have?" "Hot buttermilk and bread."

"Siân, what will you have?" "Whey."

"Twm, what will you have?" "Flummery," said Twm.

"Sionyn, what will you have?" "Cold *siot*."

"Cit, what will you have?" "Bread and milk."

"Dei, what will you have?" "Milk gruel."

"Abraham Ephraim, what will you have?" "Bread soaked in small beer."

"Hannah Deborah, what will you have?" "Oatmeal gruel."

"Jacob Henry, what will you have?" "Potatoes in buttermilk."

"Ruth Salomi, what will you have?" "*Picwsmali*" (oatcake soaked in hot buttermilk, another form of *siot*).

"Charles Edward, what will you have?" "Turkey pie" (bread, with a little butter, pepper and salt, and boiling water added).

"Humphrey Cadwaladr, what will you have?" "Junket."

"Claudia Dorothy, what will you have?" "Bread and water."

"Margaret Alice, what will you have?" "Water posset."

"Goronwy, what will you have?" "Cold buttermilk and bread."

"Arthur, what will you have?" "Caudle."

"Blodwen, what will you have?" "Broth."

"Gwladys, what will you have?" "*Brewis*."

"Rhys, what will you have?" "*Siot* posset."

"Corwena, what will you have?" "Wheat flour gruel."

"Caradoc, what will you have?" "Toast and milk."

"Llewelyn, my little one, what will you have?" "I'll have porridge, like Robin."

"Good lad," said Beti Jones, "you'll make a man yet."

"No, I'll have whey, like Siân. No, flummery, the same as Twm."

"You shall have it, my boy."

Having thus ascertained the wishes of all her children Beti Jones disappeared into the back-kitchen without making any kind of comment and without the usual scolding, which surprised the family, for it was quite out of character. However, Beti remained out of sight in the back-kitchen for a considerable time, and when she reappeared in the living kitchen it was with the baking pan in her arms. This she placed on the kitchen table, and then she began carrying in the vessels in which she had prepared the various foods demanded by her brood. When all had been collected she poured the contents into the baking pan, stirring the whole mess up with the porridge stick, a job calling for a good deal of muscular strength. This done, she spooned the resulting mess into the bowls from which the children ate, filling each bowl according to her knowledge of each child's requirements and capacity, and finally placing them along the table before her astonished offspring. There were some faint attempts at rebellion, but Beti was a resolute woman and stood over her brood, porridge stick in hand like a truncheon, until all had been eaten. That cured them of finicky fancies about their food, and the story was a standing warning to us children of a later generation.

HUGH EVANS (1854-1934)
The Gorse Glen
translation from the Welsh by
E. MORGAN HUMPHREYS

ANTICHRIST, OR THE REUNION OF CHRISTENDOM: AN ODE

"*A Bill which has shocked the conscience of every Christian community in Europe.*" *Mr. F. E. Smith, on the Welsh Disestablishment Bill.*

Are they clinging to their crosses,
F. E. Smith,
Where the Breton boat-fleet tosses,
Are they, Smith?
Do they, fasting, trembling, bleeding,
Wait the news from this our city?
Groaning, "That's the Second Reading!"
Hissing "There is still Committee!"
If the voice of Cecil falters,
If McKenna's point has pith,
Do they tremble for their altars?
Do they, Smith?

Russian peasants round their pope
Huddled, Smith,
Hear about it all, I hope,
Don't they, Smith?
In the mountain hamlets clothing
Peaks beyond Caucasian pales,
Where Establishment means nothing
And they never heard of Wales,
Do they read it all in Hansard
With a crib to read it with—
"Welsh Tithes: Dr. Clifford answered,"
Really, Smith?

In the lands where Christians were,
F. E. Smith,—
In the little lands laid bare,
Smith, O Smith!

Where the Turkish bands are busy,
And the Tory name is blessed
Since they hailed the Cross of Dizzy
On the banners from the West!
Men don't think it half so hard if
Islam burns their kin and kith,
Since a curate lives in Cardiff
Saved by Smith.

It would greatly, I must own,
Soothe me, Smith!
If you left this theme alone,
Holy Smith!
For your legal cause or civil
You fight well and get your fee;
To your God or dream or devil
You will answer, not to me.
Talk about the pews and steeples
And the Cash that goes therewith!
But the souls of Christian peoples . . .
Chuck it, Smith.

GILBERT KEITH CHESTERTON (1874-1936)

PRIDE OF LINEAGE

Robin Iachwr, the greatest antiquary of our countrey, being at Gwedir with my grandfather, and going one day to a *Chwareufa gampau*, where the countrey was assembled at a place called Gardd-y-Velin in the parish of Llanrwst, asked whether he would command him any service thither. Nothing, said my grandfather, haveing a nosegay in his hand by chance, but deliver this nosegay to the best gentleman thou seest in the company, upon the credit of thy skill; who delivered the same with protestation of his charge in the presence of all the company to Llywelyn ap David, Rhys Llywelyn ap David's father. I cannot however get his pedigree in any certaintie, to joyne them to ours: the reason is, that poverty soone forgets whence it be descended, for it is an ancient received saying, that there is noe poverty but is descended of nobilitie, nor noe nobilitie but is descended of beggerie. . . .

Yet a great temporall blessing it is, and a greate heart's ease to a man to find that he is well descended, and a great griefe it is for upstarts and gentlemen of the first head to looke backe unto their descents being base, in such sort, as I have knowne many such hate gentlemen in their hearts, for noe other cause, but that they were gentlemen.

SIR JOHN WYNNE (1553-1626)
The History of the Gwedir Family.

PERTHIR AND WERNDEE

Mr. Lorimer pointed out to me a window remarkable for a curious anecdote, relating to the contest for precedence, between the rival houses of Perthîr and Werndee, which though less bloody, was not less obstinate, than that between the houses of York and Lancaster. Mr. Proger, dining with a friend at Monmouth, proposed riding to Werndee in the evening, but his friend objecting, because it was late and likely to rain, Mr. Proger replied, "With regard to the lateness of the hour, we shall have moonlight, and should it happen to rain, Perthîr is not far from the road, and my cousin Powell will, I am very sure, give us a night's lodging." They accordingly mounted their horses, but being soon overtaken by a violent shower, rode to Perthîr, and found all the family retired to rest. Mr. Proger, however, calling to his cousin, Mr. Powell, opened the window, and looking out, asked, "In the name of wonder, what means all this noise? Who is there?" "It is only I, your cousin Proger of Werndee, who am come to your hospitable door for shelter from the inclemency of the weather, and hope you will be so kind as to give me and my friend a lodging." "What, is it you, cousin Proger? You and your friend shall be instantly admitted, but upon one condition, that you will allow, and never hereafter dispute, that I am the head of the family." "What did you say?" returned Mr. Proger. "Why, I say, if you expect to pass the night in my house, you must allow that I am the head of the family." "No sir, I would never admit that; were it to rain swords and daggers, I would ride this night to Werndee, rather than lower the consequence of my family. Come up, Bald, come up." "Stop a minute, cousin Proger, have you not often confessed that the first earl of Pembroke (of the name of Herbert) was the youngest son of Perthîr, and will you set yourself above the earls of Pembroke?" "True, I must give place to the earl of Pembroke, because he is a peer of the realm; but still, though a peer, he is of the youngest branch of my family, being descended from the fourth son of Werndee, who was your ancestor, and settled at Perthîr, whereas I am descended from the eldest son. Indeed my cousin Jones of Llanarth is of an older branch than you, and yet he never disputes that I am the head of the family." "Why, cousin Proger, I have nothing more to say, so good night to you." "Stop a minute, Mr. Powell," said the stranger, "You see how it pours, do admit me at least; I will not dispute with you about your families." "Pray sir, what is your name, and where do you come from?" "My name is . . . and I come from the county of . . ." "A Saxon of course; it would be very curious indeed sir, should I dispute with a Saxon about families; no sir, you must suffer for the obstinacy of your friend, and so a pleasant ride to you both."

WILLIAM COXE (1747-1828)
An Historical Tour in Monmouthshire (1801)

A BRAGGADOCHIO WELSHMAN

Is the oyster that the pearle is in, for a man may be pickt out of him. He hath the abilities of the mind in *potentia*, and *actu* nothing but boldnesse. His clothes are in fashion before his body: and hee accounts boldnesse the chiefest vertue; above all men hee loves an herald, and speaks pedegrees naturally. He accounts none well descended, that call him not cousin; and preferres Owen Glendower before any of the nine worthies. The first note of his familiarity is the confession of his valour; and so he prevents quarels. He voucheth Welch, a pure and unconquered language, and courts ladies with the story of their chronicle. To conclude, he is precious in his owne conceit, and upon S. Davies day without comparison.

SIR THOMAS OVERBURY (1581-1613)
Characters

THE NOBLE HEAD

And Bendigeid Vran commanded them that they should cut off his head. "And take you my head," said he, "and bear it even unto the White Mount, in London, and bury it there, with the face towards France. And a long time will you be upon the road. In Harlech you will be feasting seven years, the birds of Rhiannon singing unto you the while. And all that time the head will be to you as pleasant company as it ever was when on my body. And at Gwales in Penvro you will be fourscore years, and you may remain there, and the head with you uncorrupted, until you open the door that looks towards Aber Henvelen, and towards Cornwall. And after you have opened that door, there you may no longer tarry, set forth then to London to bury the head, and go straightforward."

So they cut off his head, and these seven went forward therewith. And Branwen was the eighth with them, and they came to land at Aber Alaw, in Talebolyon, and they sat down to rest. And Branwen looked towards Ireland and towards the Island of the Mighty, to see if she could descry them. "Alas," said she, "woe is me that I was ever born; two islands have been destroyed because of me!" Then she uttered a loud groan, and there broke her heart. And they made her a four-sided grave, and buried her upon the banks of the Alaw. . . .

Then they went to Harlech, and there stopped to rest, and they provided meat and liquor, and sat down to eat and drink. And there came three birds, and began singing unto them a certain song, and all the songs they had ever heard were unpleasant compared thereto; and the birds seemed to them to be at a great distance from them over the sea, yet they appeared as distinct as if they were close by, and at this repast they continued seven years.

And at the close of the seventh year they went forth to Gwales in Penvro. And there they found a fair and regal spot overlooking the ocean; and a spacious hall was therein. And they went into the hall, and two of its doors were open, but the third door was closed, that which looked towards Cornwall. "See, yonder," said Manawyddan, "is the door that we may not open." And that night they regaled themselves and were joyful. And of all they had seen of food laid before them, and of all they had heard of, they remembered nothing; neither of that, nor of any sorrow whatsoever. And there they remained fourscore years, unconscious of ever having spent a time more joyous and mirthful. And they were not more weary than when first they came, neither did they, any of them, know the time they had been there. And it was not more irksome to them having the head with them, than if Bendigeidfran had been with them himself. And because of these fourscore years, it was called "the Entertaining of the noble Head." . . .

One day said Heilyn the son of Gwynn, "Evil betide me, if I do not open the door to know if that is true which is said concerning it." So he opened the door and looked towards Cornwall and Aber Henfelen. And when they had looked, they were as conscious of all the evils they had ever sustained, and of all the friends and companions they had lost, and of all the misery that had befallen them, as if all had happened in that very spot; and especially of the fate of their lord. And because of their perturbation they could not rest, but journeyed forth with the head towards London. And they buried the head in the White Mount, and when it was buried, this was the third goodly concealment; and it was the third ill-fated disclosure when it was disinterred, inasmuch as no invasion from across the sea came to this island while the head was in that concealment.

And thus is the story related of those who journeyed over from Ireland.

The Mabinogion (*Branwen*)
translated from the Welsh by
LADY CHARLOTTE GUEST

BIRDS OF RHIANNON

Come again this evening, birds of Rhiannon,
Sing us a song from o'er the blue wave,
The smiles on our faces will reveal our hearts' gladness
After long grief and affliction grave.

All is not well in Wales or in Erin,
And after long pillage they both lie bare;

Their people are leaderless, their steps uncertain,
No poet's song to reveal their despair.

Raise the dead with your soul-stirring music,
Give hope to the living in their transient day,
Weave a tune from our glorious story,
A hymn, or an air, or harmonious lay.

Come again this evening, birds of Rhiannon,
Sing us a song from o'er the blue wave,
The smiles on our faces will reveal our hearts' gladness
After long grief and affliction grave.

D. GWENALLT JONES (1899-)
Ysgubau'r Awen
translated from the Welsh by
D. M. LLOYD

BLODEUWEDD

And then once upon a time he (Lleu Llaw Gyffes) went to Caer Dathyl to visit Math son of Mathonwy. The day he went to Caer Dathyl, she (Blodeuwedd, his wife) was stirring about the court. And she heard the blast of a horn, and after the blast of the horn, lo, a spent stag going by, and dogs and huntsmen after it, and after the dogs and the huntsmen a troop of men on foot coming. "Send a lad," said she, "to learn what the company is." The lad went and asked who they were. "This is Gronw Bebyr, he who is lord of Penllyn," said they. And that the lad told her.

He went after the stag, and on Cynfael river he overtook the stag and slew it. And what with slaying the stag and baiting his dogs, he was busied till the night closed in on him. And as the day declined and night was drawing near, he came past the gate of the court. "Faith," said she, "we shall be ill-spoken of by the chieftain for letting him go at this hour to another domain, if we do not ask him in." "Faith, lady," said they, "it is only right to ask him in." Then messengers went to meet him and ask him in. And then he accepted the invitation gladly and came to the court, and she came herself to meet him, to make him welcome, and to give him greeting. "Lady," said he, "God repay thee thy welcome."

They changed their garb and went to sit down. Blodeuwedd looked on him, and the moment she looked there was no part of her that was not filled with love of him. And he too gazed on her, and the same thought came to him as had come to her. He might not conceal that he loved her, and he told her so. She knew great joy at heart, and their talk that night was of the affection and love they had conceived one for the other. Nor did they delay longer than that night ere they embraced each other. And that night they slept together.

And on the morrow he sought to depart. "Faith," said she, "thou wilt not go from me to-night." That night too they were together. And that night they took counsel how they might stay together. "There is no counsel for thee," said he, "save one: to seek to learn from him how his death may come about, and that under pretence of loving care for him."

On the morrow he sought to depart. "Faith, I do not counsel thee to go from me today." "Faith, since thou dost counsel it, I will not go," said he. "Yet I say there is danger that the chieftain whose court it is may return." "Aye," said she, "to-morrow I will give thee leave to depart."

On the morrow he sought to depart and she did not prevent him. "Now," said he "remember what I told thee, and speak closely with him, and that under pretence of importunity of love of him, and draw from him what way his death might come about."

And that night he came home. They spent the day in

[T. Ifor Rees

NANTGWYNANT

[R. Cecil Hughes

BALA LAKE

[*The British Travel and Holidays Association*

IN HENRY VAUGHAN'S COUNTRY: THE VALE OF USK

talk and song and carousal. And that night they went to sleep together, and he spoke to her, and a second time, but meantime not one word did he get from her. "What has befallen thee?" he asked; "and art thou well?" "I am thinking," said she, "that which thou wouldst not think concerning me. That is," said she, "I am troubled about thy death, if thou wert to go sooner than I." "Ah," said he, "God repay thee for thy loving care. But unless God slay me, it is not easy to slay me," said he. "Wilt thou then, for God's sake and for mine, tell me how thou might be slain? For my memory is a surer safeguard than thine." "I will, gladly," said he. "It is not easy," said he, "to slay me with a blow; and one must needs be a year making the spear wherewith I should be smitten, without making anything of it save when folk were at Mass on Sunday." "Is that certain?" said she. "Certain, faith," said he. "I cannot be slain within a house," said he, "nor can I outside. I cannot be slain on horseback, nor can I a-foot." "Why," said she, "in what manner then couldst thou be slain?" "I will tell thee," said he. "By making a bath for me on a river bank, and making a vaulted frame over the tub, and thatching it well and snugly too thereafter, and bringing a he-goat," said he, "and setting it beside the tub, and myself placing one foot on the back of the he-goat and the other on the edge of the tub. Whoever should smite me when so, he would bring about my death." "Why," she replied, "I thank God for that. That can be avoided easily."

The Mabinogion (*Math son of Mathonwy*)
translated from the Welsh by
GWYN JONES *and* THOMAS JONES

PRINCE MADOC'S FAREWELL

Why lingers my gaze, where the last hues of day
  On the hills of my country in loveliness sleep?
Too fair is the sight for a wanderer whose way
  Lies far o'er the measureless worlds of the deep;
Fall, shadows of twilight, and veil the green shore,
That the heart of the mighty may waver no more.

Why rise on my thoughts, ye free songs of the land,
  Where the harp's lofty soul on each wild wind is borne?
Be hush'd, be forgotten! for ne'er shall the hand
  Of the minstrel with melody greet my return.
No! no! let your echoes still float on the breeze,
And my heart shall be strong for the conquest of seas.

'Tis not for the land of my sires to give birth
  Unto bosoms to shrink when their trial is nigh.
Away! we will bear over ocean and earth
  A name and a spirit that never shall die;
My course to the winds, to the stars I resign,
But my soul's quenchless fire, oh! my country, is thine.

(MRS.) FELICIA DOROTHEA HEMANS (1793-1835)

I HATE IT

I am sprung from the princes of Wales and from the barons of the Marches, and when I see injustice in either race, I hate it.

GIRALDUS CAMBRENSIS (1147-*c.* 1220)
translated from the Latin by
SIR RICHARD COLT HOARE

GOOD WILL

I took no count in the world of such things,
as I had Good Will for my shield:
For what can strike so fiercely that Good Will cannot resist it?
What is so hard that Good Will makes it not easy?
What is so exalted that Good Will may not reach it?
What is so deserving that Good Will cannot merit it?
Good Will is Love, Truth, the Author of all Arts, the Key to
all Treasure, saith Demosthenes.
To conclude, There is nothing so high in heaven above,
or so far down in the depths of the earth,
nothing so hidden in the deep centre of art,
or in the mysteries of nature,
that Good Will may not surround it, open it, expound it,
and reveal it.

ROWLAND VAUGHAN (*c.* 1590-1667)
Dedicatory letter to Yr Ymarfer o Dduwioldeb
translated from the Welsh by
D. M. LLOYD

EPIGRAMS

MARS, MORS. WAR, DEATH

War bringeth Dearth, Dearth Death to Men on Earth;
War therefore's worse than either Death or Dearth.
Our Troubles War begins, Death finisheth,
In War small distance is 'twixt Dearth and Death.

OF ALEXANDER

One World, one Alexander not confin'd:
O than the world, immenser was his mind.
To this one World, one Man was not compleat:
Great Alexander, but the World more great.

OF ONE CALLED DAVIS

From London Davisses thou bragg'st Descent,
And dost dissent from British Orient.
Ignoble thou, a noble Stock and pure
Disclaim'st, and claim'st from Parents more obscure:
Thou with thy native soyle dost well agree,
For thou of it, and it's asham'd of thee.

JOHN OWEN, the Epigrammatist (*c.* 1560-1622)
translated from the Latin by
THOMAS HARVEY

CARPE DIEM

Cambric white your yellow hair
Shall be that day, maiden fair;
Your cheeks no more bright as gold,
Wrinkled neck and features old;
You will be a withered crone,
And I decrepit and alone.
Mirror soon the truth will show—
Skin's lustre gone, and youth's glow.
No voice or harp will thrill you then,
You will miss the love of men:
Love, strange maid, make love today,
Your bright hue has but short stay.

attributed to DAFYDD AP GWILYM (*c.* 1325-*c.* 1385)
translated from the Welsh by
D. M. LLOYD

CAPEL HEBRON

In Capel Hebron the choirs are singing,
And Martha and Jane and Hywel and Emrys
Are lost in the rapture of anthem and chorus
And the walls of the chapel are shaking with song,
And wave after wave of music crashes
Over the maddened multitude.
Chorus of Handel, mighty and glorious,
Rolls and reverberates again and again,
Tearing the barriers and bastions asunder,
Shaking the heart and the depths of the soul.
O spirit of music and wonder and passion
Flood with thy rapture our derelict valleys,
And give unto men the motion to action,
The impulse to build what is worthy of man.

IDRIS DAVIES (1905- 53)

HISTORICAL TRADITION OF KING BRUTUS

To William Camden

Books may be burn'd, and Monuments may lie
Demolished, thy works and mine may die:
But a Tradition National, alive
While is that Nation, will in force survive.

JOHN OWEN, the Epigrammatist (*c.* 1560-1622)
translated from the Latin by
THOMAS HARVEY

A PATRIOT'S VISION

Every well-informed person must have beheld with indignation the truth of the observation of Campbell and other political writers—that in their manufactures,

"The Welsh have the labour, and strangers the profit." This begets an anxiety in every generous mind, that the present race should rouse from their lethargy, and make use of the advantages which the all-bountiful hand of Nature has so profusely strewed before them. They may have their vallies as so many forests of waving corn, judiciously intermixed with pastures, covered with herds of lowing kine: they may have their hills whitened with improved breeds of sheep, to enable them to increase their manufacture in a threefold degree: they may make their mountains verdant with evergreen plantations variegated with the autumnal russet of the deciduous oak, that valuable component in Britain's bulwark, while their bowels are pregnant with the oars of various metals: they have perennial streams issuing in every direction: and to crown the whole, the ocean offers its service, to waft their exports abroad, to return them the profits of barter, at many safe and commodious harbours; and to supply them with fish, along a line of two hundred miles of beautifully variegated shores.

GWALLTER MECHAIN (WALTER DAVIES, 1761-1849)
Agriculture of North Wales, 1810

TO MY MOTHERLAND

Dear motherland, forgive me, if too long
I hold the halting tribute of my song;
Letting my wayward fancy idly roam
Far, far from thee, my early home.
There are some things too near,
Too infinitely dear
For speech; the old ancestral hearth,
The hills, the vales that saw our birth,
Are hallowed deep within the reverent breast:
And who of these keeps silence, he is best.

Yet would not I appear,
Who have known many a brighter land and sea
Since first my boyish footsteps went from thee,
The less to hold thee dear;
Or lose in newer beauties the immense
First love for thee, O birth-land, which fulfils
My inmost heart and soul,—
Love for thy smiling and sequestered vales,
Love for thy winding streams which sparkling roll
Through thy rich fields, dear Wales,
From long perspectives of thy folded hills.

Ay! these are sacred, all;
I cannot sing of them, too near they are.
What if from out thy dark yews, gazing far,
I sat and sang, Llangunnor! of the vale
Through which fair Towy winds her lingering fall,
Gliding by Dynevor's wood-crowned steep,
And, alternating swift with deep,
By park and tower a living thing
Of loveliness meandering;
And traced her flowing onward still,
By Grongar dear to rhyme, or Dryslwyn's castled hill,
Till the fresh upward tides prevail,
Which stay her stream and bring the sea-borne sail,
And the broad river rolls majestic down
Beneath the gray walls of my native town.

Would not my fancy quickly stray
To thee, sea-girt St. David's, far away,
A minster on the deep; or, further still,
To you, grand mountains, which the stranger knows:
Eryri throned amid the clouds and snows,
The dark lakes, the wild passes of the north;
Or Cader, a stern sentinel looking forth
Over the boisterous main; or thee, dear Isle
Not lovely, yet which canst my thought beguile—

Mona, from whose fresh wind-swept pastures came
My grandsire, bard and patriot, like in name
Whose verse his countrymen still love to sing
At bidding-feast or rustic junketing? . . .

I may not sing of you,
Or tell my love—others there are who will,
Who haply bear not yet a love so true
As that my soul doth fill—
If to applaud it lead, or gain, or fame;
Better than this it were to bear the pain
Which comes to higher spirits when they know
They fire in other souls no answering glow;
Love those who love me not again,
And leave my country naught, not even a name.

SIR LEWIS MORRIS (1833-1907)

THE SOUL OF A NATION

But Wales has a soul, a soul which is her own. And she can lose it. Education may thrive, religion may increase its hold, freedom may be won, the poor may arise from the dust and become powerful, the wealthy may be strong and flourish like the green bay, and the nation's soul may weaken and fade. The nation may lose itself in the empire, and be a dead member and not a living one, her voice never more to be heard. And if that calamity were to come about, Wales would be without a soul, and the world would be the poorer. When the next upsurge of freedom and religion would take place, Wales would not be there to hold up the banner; her voice would have been silenced. . . .

May Wales succeed in every possible way. Equality and freedom will come; a University and a Hospital Service; and many a dream will be fulfilled. But let us not lose sight of the nation's soul, lest among much fine building and enthusiastic committee-work it vanish from sight. May it be fostered in the schools and the various colleges of the University. But the hearth is its cradle. The spirit of Wales is born in the mountain farmhouse, in the cottage by the brook, in the coal-miner's home. And if it be not fostered the Welsh nation will become merely derivative and second rate, an imitator of something inferior to her own true life. If she guards her soul, she has it in herself to make her contribution among the leaders of the world. In a delicate love of country, and in steadfast faith, may our aim be no less.

SIR OWEN M. EDWARDS (1858-1920)
Er Mwyn Cymru
translated from the Welsh by
D. M. LLOYD

AVALLON

Far over the wave lies a land of delight
Where grief lingers not, nor time's grey blight;
Men know no pain on that peerless shore,
Caressed by the breezes that play evermore:
Every heart is gay, and life is a song
In Avallon's isle all the day long.

A blissful land filled with dreams of old
That calmed our fears through ages untold;
Hopes and desires are treasured there,
And the fruits of our travail grow rich and rare;
There shame does not sear, and faith is strong,
And no hearts made weak by an ancient wrong.

On that island's shore burns the pure flame
Of the muse that oft to our poets came

With words of fire that men might arise
From the dust to a nobler enterprize.
Unwearied by age, or by grief and care,
The breath of the nation's life is there.

T. GWYNN JONES (1871-1949)
translated from the Welsh by
D. M. LLOYD

WALES

Sometimes I feel an impulse
To quit my native land,—
A land that loathes her burden
And will not make a stand;
A ready prey to raucous guile,
Wasting her substance all the while,—

And fly to sun-drenched islands
In the blue Southern Sea
Where prodigals with merry hearts
Live long and carelessly;
And join the dance in a green grove
To sweet guitars arousing love;

Where truth and right and duty
Are not the helpless prey
Of subtle words we would unlearn
In fear day by day;
Slogans, hysteria, come not there,
Nor weary hopes of a day more fair.

Men live in pure enjoyment
Of the simple things of life,
The sinister grip eluding
Of commercial greed and strife,
No currying favour or renown
By dragging their own country down.

Ah no! I can no other
Than stand here, come what may,
True to the land that bore me
Though sad her plight to-day;
With all her faults, my Wales has grown
Into the marrow of my bone.

And with the few who love her
Through every strain and shock,
Dreading no boorish insult,
Scorning the knaves who mock,
I call on our nation's youth
To come to terms with her ancient truth.

And when the supercilious
Uprooted, upstart crew
Maintain it is but folly
That moves our loyal few,–
Then come what may, I'll stand or fall
With the little band that gives her all.

E. PROSSER RHYS (1901-45)
translated from the Welsh by
D. M. LLOYD

A VINEYARD PLACED IN MY CARE

EMRYS: My lord Garmon,
Thou too wert a leader of armies yonder in Gaul
Ere thou wert captured by the love of God and brought to a city of saints;
And I today would be taught by thee.
GARMON : What foe fearest thou?
EMRYS: Last night, Vortigern's couriers came with cruel tidings:
On the banks of the Dee two hosts today have descended,

From the east the Saxon, and the Pictish fleet from the north.
They wait till the swamps are dried by the winds of spring,
And at Easter they hasten towards Powys.

GARMON: What would'st thou of me?

EMRYS: God's nobleman, hearken,
A vineyard was set by a man on a sunlit hill,
He hedged her, and planted within her the noblest vines,
He enclosed her strongly, and built a tower in her midst,
And to his son he gave her, a goodly heritage,
That his name might be known among men from age to age.
But a herd of swine have broken into the vineyard,
Have trampled the fence, and root and devour the vines;
Is it not well for the son to stand in the breach
And to call his friends to his aid,
That the breach may be closed and the heritage made secure?
Garmon, Garmon,
A vineyard placed in my care is Wales, my country,
To deliver unto my children
And my children's children
Intact, an eternal heritage:
And behold, the swine rush on her to rend her.
Now will I call on my friends,
Scholars and simple folk,
'Take your place by my side in the breach
That the age-old splendour be kept for ages to come.'
And this, my lord, is the vineyard of your Beloved too;
From Llan Fair to Llan Fair, a land where the Faith is established.
Wilt thou not come to lead my host to Powys?

GARMON: In the name of the Lord of Hosts,
I come, O King.
THE HOST: Halelujah! Salve.
Germanus will lead the Britons,
Germanus will lead the Britons,
And Wales for Christ.

SAUNDERS LEWIS (1893-)
from *Buchedd Garmon*
translated from the Welsh by D. M. LLOYD

I'R HEN IAITH A'I CHANEUON
(*To the Old Tongue and its songs*)

When I am listening to the sweet, tuneful airs of my country,
sung by fresh and young Welsh voices that love them,
in the language so strong and beautiful,
that has grown out of the ageless mountains
and the deep, dark valleys,
I am fulfilled as I am in no otherwise fulfilled.

Then am I caught up into a realm of natural being,
and am one with my fathers,
and with them that shall come after me,
and with those who yet, in these no unregenerate days,
do speak that speech of wondrous beauty
that our fathers wrought.

WALTER DOWDING (1897-)

WALES

Martyrs' dust through countless ages
And the saints lie in thy breast,
Thou didst give them breath and being,
Thou didst call them to thy rest.

On thy roads are seen the footprints
  Made by angels from above,
And the Holy Ghost has settled
  In thy branches like a dove.

Bards have heard in winds and breezes
  Sighs of sacrificial pain,
Deep within thy darkest forests
  The Rood Tree doth still remain.

His Resurrection was thy springtime,
  Thy summer was His triumph green,
And in the winter of thy mountains
  Tabernacles have been seen.

Providential dews and raindrops
  On thy fields of oat and corn,
And his Glory on the harness
Of thy horses in the morn.

Thy ships have sped o'er many waters,
  Laden with a precious prize,
Their sails have borne across the oceans
  Calvary's richest merchandise.

For Himself thy God has chosen
  Thee to love Him evermore,
And His Covenant is written
  On the lintel of thy door.

Thy saints are clothed in morning radiance,
  They love thee, thy joy and pride,—
Like a mother-bird thou callest,
  Warm beneath thy wing they hide.

D. GWENALLT JONES (1899-   )
translated from the Welsh by D. M. LLOYD

AFFINITY

To know who I am for me is a feat
In lush lowland fields, away from peat.

The red in my blood has for centuries known
That all soil is not like the soil where I've grown.

But I know who I am, by hill and heath,
By crag,—and rushes and a lake beneath.

T. H. PARRY-WILLIAMS (1887-)
translated from the Welsh by
D. M. LLOYD

LAME ANTS

In the old Welsh legends there is a story of a man who was given a series of what appeared to be impossible tasks to perform ere he could reach the desires of his heart. Amongst other things he had to do was to recover every grain of seed that had been sown in a large field, and bring it all in without one missing by sunset. He came to an ant-hill and won all the hearts and enlisted the sympathies of the industrious little people. They spread over the field and before sundown the seed was all in except one grain, and as the sun was setting over the western skies a lame ant hobbled along with that grain also. Some of us have youth and vigour and suppleness of limb; some of us are crippled with years or infirmities, and we are at best but lame ants. But we can all limp along with some share of our country's burden, and thus help her in this terrible hour to win the desire of her heart.

DAVID LLOYD GEORGE (1863-1945)
Recruiting Speech at Bangor, 1915

LIFE

This leaf now sear and a prey to the wind,
Its fate draws a tear:
It is old—born only this year![1]

*   *   *   *   *

If the tongue only spoke all that the mind knows, there wouldn't be any neighbours.

from the *Red Book of Hergest* (*c.* 1400)
translated from the Welsh by
D. M. LLOYD

APPOINTMENT OF A JUDGE

If it is the King's wish to appoint as court judge a person uninitiated and untrained in law, that person should remain in the court with the King, questioning and listening to judges during their visits from the country to the King's court, acquainting himself with the laws, and customs, and procedures, and the King's authorised rulings, and, above all, the Three Columns of Law, and the values of all domesticated animals, and of the wild beasts with which men are concerned, and listening to plaintiffs and defendants in disputations, and to be in the presence of judges when they give their verdicts, and to hear their deliberations, and to be attentive when they refer matters to the King because they are in doubt and desire his clarification. Let him spend a whole year in this manner. Then the King's

[1]This poem dates probably from the ninth century.

chaplain should take him to the church, together with the twelve leading officers of the court, to hear Mass, and after the Mass, and an offering having been made by each one present, may the chaplain cause him to swear on the relics, and the altar, and the consecrated elements on the altar, that he will never knowingly give false judgement by yielding to any entreaty or bribe, and neither from the love nor the hatred of any person. Afterwards, let the whole party return to the King, and declare what has been performed. Then it is right that the King should give him office if he is satisfied with him, and place him in a seat worthy of him. Symbolic gifts should then be given him: a ' throwboard ' from the King, and a gold ring from the Queen, and never should he give these away or sell them.

No one is entitled to be a judge unless trained in this manner, or well versed in law, and sworn in this way never in his life to render false justice.

From the ancient Welsh Laws, according to the Book of Blegywryd, who is reputed to have been a jurist in the court of the 10th-century King Hywel the Good. The earliest manuscripts date from the 12th century
translated from the Welsh by
D. M. LLOYD

ADVICE FOR THE WELSH

Having hitherto so partially and elaborately spoken in favour of the English, and being equally connected by birth with each nation, justice demands that we should argue on both sides; let us therefore, at the close of our work, turn our attention towards the Welsh, and briefly, but effectually, instruct them in the art of resistance. If the Welsh were more commonly accustomed to the Gallic mode of arming, and depended more on steady fighting than on their agility; if their princes were unanimous and inseparable in their defence;

or rather, if they had only one prince, and that a good one; this nation, situated in so powerful, strong, and inaccessible a country, could hardly ever be completely overcome. If, therefore, they would be inseparable, they would become insuperable, being assisted by these three circumstances; a country well defended by nature, a people both contented and accustomed to live upon little, a community whose nobles as well as privates are instructed in the use of arms; and especially as the English fight for power, the Welsh for liberty; the one to procure gain, the other to avoid loss; the English hirelings for money, the Welsh patriots for their country. The English, I say, fight in order to expel the natural inhabitants from the island, and secure to themselves the possession of the whole; but the Welsh maintain the conflict, that they, who have so long enjoyed the sovereignty of the whole kingdom, may at least find a hiding place in the worst corner of it, amongst woods and marshes; and, banished, as it were, for their offences, may there in a state of poverty, for a limited time, perform penance for the excesses they committed in the days of their prosperity. For the perpetual remembrance of their former greatness, the recollection of their Trojan descent, and the high and continued majesty of the kingdom of Britain, may draw forth many a latent spark of animosity, and encourage the daring spirit of rebellion. Hence during the military expedition which king Henry II made in our days against South Wales, an old Welshman at Pencadair, who had faithfully adhered to him, being desired to give his opinion about the royal army, and whether he thought that of the rebels would make resistance, and what would be the final event of this war, replied, "This nation, O king, may now, as in former times, be harassed, and in a great measure weakened and destroyed by your and other powers, and it will often prevail by its laudable exertions; but it can never be totally subdued through the wrath of man, unless the wrath of God shall concur. Nor do I think, that any other nation than this of Wales, or any other language, whatever may hereafter come to pass, shall, in the day of severe examination before the Supreme Judge, answer for this corner of the earth."

GIRALDUS CAMBRENSIS (1147-*c.* 1220)
The Description of Wales
translated from the Latin by
SIR RICHARD COLT HOARE

PENILLION SINGING

Besides the single songs, there were songs in dialogue, approaching very nearly to the character of dramatic poetry; and penillion, or unconnected stanzas, sung in series by different singers, the stanzas being complete in themselves, simple as Greek epigrams, and presenting in succession moral precepts, pictures of natural scenery, images of war or of festival, the lamentations of absence or captivity, and the complaints or triumphs of love. This penillion-singing long survived among the Welsh peasantry almost every other vestige of bardic customs, and may still be heard among them on the few occasions on which rack-renting, tax-collecting, common-enclosing, methodist-preaching, and similar developments of the light of the age, have left them either the means or inclination of making merry.

THOMAS LOVE PEACOCK (1785-1866)
The Misfortunes of Elphin

PENILLION

Hardd yw Conwy, hardd yw Nefyn,
Hardd yw brigau coedydd Mostyn,
Harddaf lle'r wy'n allu 'nabod
Yn y byd yw dyffryn Meifod.

(Conway is fair, Nevin is fair, the tips of the Mostyn trees are fair, the fairest place I can ever know in the world is Meivod Valley.)

Cleddwch fi, pan fyddwyf farw,
Yn y coed dan ddail y derw;
Chwi gewch weled llanc penfelyn
Ar fy medd yn canu'r delyn.

(Bury me, when I am dead, in the trees under the oak leaves; you shall see a yellow-haired youth on my grave playing the harp.)

Mae dwy galon yn fy mynwes,
Un yn oer a'r llall yn gynnes;
Un yn gynnes am ei charu,
A'r llall yn oer rhag ofn ei cholli.

(There are two hearts in my bosom, one is cold and the other warm; one is warm through love of her, and the other is cold through fear of losing her.)

A WELSH HARPER

While thus from theme to theme the Historian passed,
The words he uttered, and the scene that lay
Before our eyes, awakened in my mind
Vivid remembrance of those long-past hours;
When, in the hollow of some shadowy vale,
(What time the splendour of the setting sun

Lay beautiful on Snowdon's sovereign brow,
On Cader Idris, or huge Penmaenmawr)
A wandering Youth, I listened with delight
To pastoral melody or warlike air,
Drawn from the chords of the ancient British harp
By some accomplished Master, while he sate
Amid the quiet of the green recess,
And there did inexhaustibly dispense
An interchange of soft or solemn tunes,
Tender or blithe; now, as the varying mood
Of his own spirit urged,—now as a voice
From youth or maiden, or some honoured chief
Of his compatriot villagers (that hung
Around him, drinking in the impassioned notes
Of the time-hallowed minstrelsy) required
For their heart's ease or pleasure.

WILLIAM WORDSWORTH (1770-1850)
The Excursion

AT THE EISTEDDFOD

The close-ranked faces rise,
With their watching, eager eyes,
And the banners and the mottoes blaze above:
And without, on either hand,
The eternal mountains stand,
And the salt sea river ebbs and flows again,
And through the thin-drawn bridge the wandering
winds complain.

Here is the Congress met,
The bardic senate set,
And young hearts flutter at the voice of fate;
All the fair August day

Song echoes, harpers play,
And on the unaccustomed ear the strange
Penillion rise and fall through change and counter-
change.

Oh Mona, land of song!
Oh mother of Wales! how long
From thy dear shores an exile have I been!
Still from thy lonely plains,
Ascend the old sweet strains,
And at the mine, or plough, or humble home,
The dreaming peasant hears diviner music come.

This innocent, peaceful strife,
This struggle to fuller life,
Is still the one delight of Cymric souls—
Swell, blended rhythms! still
The gay pavilions fill.
Soar, oh young voices, resonant and fair;
Still let the sheathed sword gleam above the bardic
chair.

* * * * *

The Menai ebbs and flows,
And the song-tide wanes and goes,
And the singers and the harp-players are dumb;
The eternal mountains rise
Like the cloud upon the skies,
And my heart is full of joy for the songs that are still,
The deep sea and the soaring hills, and the steadfast
Omnipotent Will.

SIR LEWIS MORRIS (1833-1907)

A HUNTING SCENE

Pwyll, Prince of Dyved was lord of the seven Cantrevs of Dyved; and once upon a time he was at Narberth his chief palace, and he was minded to go and hunt and the part of his dominions in which it pleased him to hunt was Glyn Cuch. So he set forth from Narberth that night, and went as far as Llwyn Diarwya. And that night he tarried there, and early on the morrow he rose and came to Glyn Cuch, when he let loose the dogs in the wood, and sounded the horn, and began the chase. And as he followed the dogs, he lost his companions; and whilst he listened to the hounds, he heard the cry of other hounds, a cry different from that of his own, and coming in the opposite direction.

And he beheld a glade in the wood forming a level plain, and as his dogs came to the edge of the glade, he saw a stag before the other dogs. And lo, as it reached the middle of the glade, the dogs that followed the stag overtook it and brought it down. Then looked he at the colour of the dogs, staying not to look at the stag, and of all the hounds that he had seen in the world, he had never seen any that were like unto these. For their hair was of a brilliant shining white, and their ears were red; and as the whiteness of their bodies shone, so did the redness of their ears glisten. And he came towards the dogs, and drove away those that had brought down the stag, and set his own dogs upon it.

And as he was setting on his dogs he saw a horseman coming towards him upon a large light-grey steed, with a hunting horn round his neck, and clad in garments of grey woollen in the fashion of a hunting garb.

The Mabinogion (*Pwyll Prince of Dyved*)
translated from the Welsh by
LADY CHARLOTTE GUEST

THE GAME OF KNAPPAN

But being drawn to speak of the exercise of the body, I cannot overpass a game used in one part of this shire among the Welshmen, both rare to hear, troublesome to describe, and painful to practise, yet for the rarity thereof, I crave pardon to trouble you, and though somewhat long, yet as brief as I may. This game is called *Knappan*, and not unfittly, as shall be shewed, the game is thought to be of great antiquity, and is as followeth. . . .

I will let you know that this *Knappan* happeneth and falleth out to be by two meanes, the one is a settled or standing *Knappan*, the day and place being known and yearly observed. Of these *Knappan* days in Penbrokshire there were wont to be five in number . . . And at these days and places were these games wont yearly to be exercised without any matchmaking or appointment, and therefore I call these standing *Knappans*. Other the like plays would oftentimes be by making of match between two gentlemen . . . which most commonly fall out to be the greatest plays, for in these matches the gentlemen would divide the parishes, hundreds or shires between them, and then would each labour to bring the greatest number, and would therein entreat all his friends and kinsmen in every parish to come and bring his parish wholly with him, by which means great number would most usually meet, and therefore against these matches there would also resort to the place divers victuallers with meat, drink and wine of all sorts, also merchants, mercers, and pedlers would provide stalls, and booths, to shew and utter their wares, and for these causes, some to play, some to eat and drink, some to buy, and some to sell, and others to be seen (you know what kind I mean) great multitudes of people would resort beside the players. . . .

Their matches are commonly made without stint of number, but as they happen to come . . . The companies being come together, about one or two of the clock, afternoon, beginneth the play, in this sort, after a cry made, both parties draw together into some plain, all first stripped bare, saving a light pair of breeches, bare headed, bare bodied, bare leggs and feet, their clothes being laid together in great heaps under the charge of certain keepers appointed for the purpose, for if he leave but his shirt on his back, in the fury of the game it is most commonly torn to pieces, and I have also seen some long lock gallants trimly trimmed at this game, not by polling, but by pulling their hair and beards . . .

The foote companie thus meeting, there is a round ball prepared of a reasonable quantity, so as a man may hold it in his hands and no more. This ball is of some massy wood, as box, yew, crab, or holly tree, and should be boiled in tallow for to make it slippery and hard to be holden. This ball is called *Knappan*, and is by one of the companie hurled bolt upright to the air, and at the fall, he that catcheth it hurleth it towards the country he playeth for, for goal or appointed place there is none; neither needeth any, for the play is not given over until the *Knappan* be so far carried that there is no hope to return it back that night. . . . The *Knappan* being once cast forth, you shall see the same tossed backward and forward, by hurling throws in strange sort, for in three or four throws you shall see the whole body of the game removed half a mile or more, and in this sort it is a strange sight to see a thousand or fifteen hundred naked men to concur together in a cluster in following the *Knappan* as the same is hurled backward and forward. There is beside the corps or main body of the play, certain scouts or fore-runners whose charge is always to keep before the *Knappan* which way soever it pass, these always be of the adverse part, between the other party and home, lest by surreption the *Knappan* should be snatched by a borderer of the game, and so carried away, by foot or horse. To those scouts you shall all day hear the body of the main play cry with loud voices continually, *Cadw ôl!* (Keep the back!), that is look well to their backs, as though their chief care lay in that point, as it doth indeed. If the *Knappan* happen to come to the hands of a lusty hurler, he throweth the same in a wonderful sort towards his Country, further than any man would judge the strength of the arm were able. If it happen to the hands of a good footman he presently singleth himself, and runneth and breaketh out of the body of the game into some plain ground in the swiftest sort he can, which being perceived, all the company followeth, where the good footmanship of all the company is plainly discerned, being a comfortable sight to see five or six hundred good footmen to follow in chase a mile or two as grayhounds after a hare. You shall see some gain in running upon his precedents, some forced to come behind those that were once foremost, which greatly delighteth the beholders, and forceth them to follow likewise to see the pleasure of the chase. Thus the one seeketh to win honour by his footmanship until he be overtaken by a better runner, or encountered by one of the scouts, which will not fail to meet with him, and when he seeth himself near surprised, or that his breath or legs faile him, he hurleth the ball forward towards his Country, with a great violence, and perchance it lighteth to some of his fellows, who carrieth the same as far again; which notwithstanding is not given over as long as the main body is anything near at hand. And when the ball happeneth to one of the contrary part it cometh back again as fast, and in this sort you shall in an open field see two thousand naked people follow this ball backward and forward, east, west, north, and south, so that a stranger that casually should see such a multitude so ranging naked, would think them distracted. It is strange to behold with what eagerness this play is followed, for in the fury of the chase they respect neither hedge, ditch, pale, or wall, hill, dale, bushes, river or rocke, or any other passable impediment, but all seemeth plain unto them. Wherein also they shew such agility in running, such activity in leaping, such strength and skilful deliverance in hurling, such boldness in assaulting, such stoutness in resisting, such policy in inventing, such skill in preventing, as taking them out of their game, they are not able to perform or invent half the prowess or devices shewed in the same, a thing much noted of men of judgement.

The horsemen have monstrous cudgels of three foot and a half long, as big as the party is well able to wield, and he that thinketh himself well horsed maketh means to his friends of the footmen to have the *Knappan* delivered him, which being gotten, he putteth spurs and away as fast as the legs will carry; after him runneth the rest of the horsemen, and if they can overtake him, he summoneth a delivery of the *Knappan*, which should be thrice by law of the game. But now they scarce give it once till he strike; and if he hold the *Knappan* it is lawful for the assailant to beate him with his cudgel till he deliver it. The best of foot troops also will follow the horse, who are so well enseymed (*i.e.* 'trained') by the often exercise of the game, as that when the horsemen miss to fetch up the *Knappan*, the foot will oftentimes recover the same, and will in heat of chase, follow the *Knappan* two or three miles, till the horse be spent, and will bring back the *Knappan* when it is out of sight and past hope. . . .

You shall see gamesters return home from this play with broken heads, black faces, bruised bodies, and lame legs, yet laughing and merrily jesting at their harms, telling their adversaries how he brake his head, to another that he strake him on the face, and how he repaid the same to him again, and all this in good mirth, without grudge or hatred. And if any be in arrerages to the other they score it up till the next play, and in the meantime will continue loving friends. . . .

GEORGE OWEN, OF HENLLYS (1552-1613)
The Description of Pembrokshire

GRAVEYARD FLOWERS

There is a large, widely-branching yew-tree in the churchyard, not at all decayed, which girts eighteen feet six inches. This was its true description in 1803. I saw it in 1806, not indeed decayed, but stripped of its venerable arms, and left a bare trunk, divested of all its grandeur. The graves, in this receptacle of the dead, are planted with flowers, such as pinks, carnations, sweet-williams, gilliflowers, and all the variety that the pious attentions of the relations can procure. Some of them are made fragrant with thyme, hyssop, southern-wood, rosemary, and other aromatic productions. This is a very common practice in Glamorganshire; and it is a maxim never to plant any flowers or herbs on graves, but such as are sweet-scented.

BENJAMIN HEATH MALKIN (1769-1842)
The Scenery . . . of South Wales

BY THE SEA

Ar lan y môr mae carreg wastad,
Lle bûm yn siarad gair â'm cariad;
O amgylch hon mae'r teim yn tyfu,
Ac ambell sbrigyn o rosmari.

By the sea there is a flat stone,
Where I have been speaking a word to my beloved;
Around it grows the thyme,
And a few sprigs of rosemary.

TRADITIONAL

LIME-WASHED COTTAGES

Another circumstance which adds to the respectable appearance of the cottages is the universal practice of whitening them, which gives a peculiar neatness and gaiety to the villages, though their uniform glare is perhaps a little too dazzling for the eye. This has been the custom of the country from very remote ages, and is extended even to the barns and stables, to the walls of yards and gardens. It is noticed and praised in the most ancient Welsh poems, and certainly evinces a very early sensibility to the arts and decencies of life. Indeed an attention to such external appearances has at all times been favoured by the circumstances of a country abounding with lime, coal to burn it, and excellent stone for building.

BENJAMIN HEATH MALKIN (1769-1842)
The Scenery . . . of South Wales

HOSPITALITY AND REFINEMENT

Busy commerce, and what is styled refined manners, are the banes of genuine hospitality. In Wales, most families, until of late, were inclined to support their indigent relations, to avoid the opprobium that any of their kindred had their names entered in the parish books. At length, by our connections with the English, we borrowed their manners, changed our spirit of hospitality for modern refinement; and our poor, like those of our neighbours, were relieved entirely from the general assessments; which in many places, have advanced in a twentyfold rate within the memory of men now living. The Welsh acknowledge kindred, and formerly considered themselves bound by the ties of nature to support their indigent relations, to the *ninth* degree (*nawved ach*).

GWALLTER MECHAIN (WALTER DAVIES, 1761-1849)
Agriculture of North Wales, 1810

LOCAL MANNERS

There are many circumstances of local manners, totally differing from the habits and character of their fellow islanders, which cannot fail to strike the most superficial observer. An uncommon vivacity, both of tone and gesture, meeting half way the saturnine demeanour of the English and the caricatured vehemence of the French, with a uniformity and peculiarity of dress, gives in a great degree a foreign air to every concourse of the country people. The dress in Glamorganshire is not so strongly marked as in most other counties, except that the women universally adopt the man's hat: but they wear it with a very good grace, and are remarkably neat in their attire, as well as comely in their persons, and graceful in their carriage. This cleanliness and decency in dress, as well as in general habits, under whatever depression of poverty they may labour, is a genuine characteristic of true civilization. It has already been mentioned, that dancing is a favourite amusement with them; and they practise it with a skill almost exclusively their own. There are few in the condition of servants, who cannot dance well; and the gentry not infrequently introduce their domestics into the set, on occasions of festivity, when numbers add to the zest, without detracting from the decorum of their recreation.

BENJAMIN HEATH MALKIN (1769-1842)
The Scenery . . . of South Wales

A DOMESTIC SCENE

I am tempted to tell another little story. It illustrates so well the atmosphere of our happy home. I was home on a visit, and, I believe, a professor at St Andrews at the time. I was sitting in the kitchen, the only living-room, chatting with my mother, when my father came in. He had been out, taking his usual evening walk after his day's work, along the quiet country road, and in the dark. "I think," he said to my mother as he was sitting down, "I think I have caught two lovers." "No!" cried my mother as full of excited interest as if she were a young woman, "who were they, Elias?" "I'll not tell you," he replied, "for you will not believe me." She begged, and of course, he gave in, bidding me observe that my mother would refuse to believe him. "It was Robert Davies, the tailor," he said, "and Mrs. Roberts, the widow who lives at the chapel house."

Robert Davies was a serious-minded elder, about sixty-five years old and a widower. "Don't talk nonsense!" cried my mother, rejecting his tale just as he had foretold. "Well," said he at length, when she persisted in her unbelief, "I'll tell you what I saw, and you can judge for yourself. As I was passing the door of Mrs. Roberts's house, it was opened and a flood of light poured out. Robert Davies walked in, and I saw him quite plainly. He had a ham under his arm. I lingered about, and in about a quarter of an hour or twenty minutes Robert Davies came out, *without the ham.*" "Well! well!" cried my mother, her scepticism completely overcome by the evidence of the "*ham,*" which was evidently, for her as for my father, conclusive proof of marital intentions, if not also of the tender passion. I thought the whole scene between my father and my mother one of the most humorous I had ever witnessed, and felt I had discovered a new use for hams!

SIR HENRY JONES (1852-1922)
Old Memories

THOMAS BARTLEY ON DOMESTIC ECONOMY

One day, while discussing with his wife Barbara the advantages of rearing a pig, Thomas Bartley said—

"You hear some folks say that rearing a pig is the most foolish thing under the sun. But I have always remarked that they are lazy folks, and feckless who say so, folks with no idea of management. Why, only yesterday, old Betty William it was who asked me,—'Thomas Bartley,' says she, 'do you think that rearing a pig is a paying proposition?' And says I to her—'If everyone paid as well as the pig, we would all rub along nicely, Betty. Never did I see a pig that didn't pay, but I *have* seen womenfolk who never pay at all.' She owes me a florin for patching a pair of shoes, Lord knows how long; I saw my chance to have a thrust at the old girl, and never did you see a quicker change in the conversation. But between you and me,—in the strict sense of the word, I don't think that rearing a pig does *pay*, that is if you were to count up everything, and set a price on all your labour. It certainly does not pay for folks who are too stuck up—no offence, mind—to fetch a truss of straw and clean out the sty, and it does not pay for a man without sufficient conscience to feed it properly—for a pig, you know, like any other creature, must have proper food before it will thrive. But I do say this—and I will say it to my dying day—that for a

[*A. W. Hutton*

SOUTH STACK LIGHTHOUSE, HOLYHEAD

[*Valentine*

THE GREEN "BRIDGE," PEMBROKESHIRE

[*R. Cecil Hughes*

RIVER WYE, NEAR RHAYADER

poor man—for a man who lives by his day's work—that he can do nothing better than keep a pig, and particularly if he has growing near his home some wild carrot and nettle—excellent food for a pig. The way I look at it—keeping a pig is uncommonly like the savings-bank. You would never say, in the strict sense, that the savings-bank *pays*—for man alive, what is two and a half? It's not worth a man's taking his bit of brass there—if it's for the interest. And yet nobody in his senses would deny that it is a good thing to put money in the savings-bank. To my way of thinking—and for a common working man I have reared as many pigs as anyone in the country—a pig pays better than the savings-bank. For this is how it is: Think of a man bent on living carefully, and putting his money in the savings-bank. Very good. Say that he saves a bob a week. Right. But some weeks the man is in a 'pinch'—he loses a day's work—or he is tempted to buy something he doesn't need, and the savings bank is given a miss, and you would be surprised the difference it makes at the end of the year. But if the man only had a pig and a conscience in the matter of feeding it, he would simply have to look around for food, even though he might have to go short himself.

"And I'll tell you another thing—a man doesn't like to take trifles to the bank, and if he tries to keep them at home to grow into a decent sum, there will always be a snag that will make him dig into them. Didn't you hear tell of old Ned Jones trying to save money at home? No? Ned decided to give up the 'bacy and to save money without telling his wife, like. His pay was twelve shillings, and Ned had his hide-out under the bed-posts. He had been at it for fifteen weeks, and had saved—so he thought—seven and sixpence—half a crown under each of three of the bed-posts. But one day, after coming home from work, Ned suspected that his wife had been cleaning the room—a thing she did once a year, you know, and when he saw his chance, Ned slunk into the room to see if his money was safe. He put his shoulder under the bed—I heard him tell the story myself—and up went one post. 'Curse it,' said Ned, 'one half-crown gone.' He went to the second post: another had disappeared, and so had the third, and Ned never saw a trace of any of them. The wife was glad enough of them, I bet. There was a bit of a row, as you may well imagine, and they tell me they have never been quite the same to each other since, and that Ned now smokes more than ever. It is very hard for a poor man to save money at home.

"Half a more, where was I? Oh yes—a man doesn't like, somehow, to carry trifling sums to the bank, for by seeing him go there often, people start saying he is worth his thousands, and everyone pesters him for the loan of money, and if he gets stuck himself he gets no sympathy. But if a man keeps a pig, he always finds a bit of food for him three times a day, hardly missing it, and bit by bit the pig comes to something in the end, you know! They tell me that's how the Paddies manage to live, and that they would rather do without home-rule than a pigsty, and I can well believe it. But it has struck me that the poor are now rearing fewer pigs than in the old days, especially in the towns. And they tell me that it is not because they are coming up in the world, but because they are not allowed to by the Local Board, and because American bacon is getting so cheap. To my way of thinking, the greatest curses that ever came to this land are the Local Board and the American bacon. The Local Board is stopping the people in the towns keeping a pig, and that is why the poor, today, never think of growing potatoes in a field. For what is the good of growing potatoes if they can't keep a pig? And there they are, all the year round, without provisions, and running to the shop for a penn'orth of American bacon and a penn'orth of potatoes—unlike the old folks with two hogsheads of potatoes in the garden, and a pig hanging from the roof. It is beyond me how the poor manage to live in these towns. And they tell me that they have a pretty lean look. And it's all because of the Local Board. I know of nothing like the Local Board to breed laziness. In the old days a man after coming home from work, and having a wash, and his tea, would take a turn to the potato field to do a bit of weeding, or digging, or he would clean a bit around the pig. But now it's the pubs. And you never hear any more of a 'potato crop supper.' And all because of the Local Board! I never heard the like! What are you saying—to keep fevers away? Nonsense! They tell you that if the pig-sty is within five yards of the house, the fevers are bound to come, but if it is five yards and two inches away, the people are safe! Did you ever hear such rubbish? I admit that there is now less smallpox than there used to be, but small thanks to the Local Board for what is the work of the good Lord in His mercy—and the vaccination! Do you know, I wouldn't like to have to answer for the Local Board for all the rice in China. They are in for a reckoning some day. But thank goodness, they can't touch me!"

DANIEL OWEN (1836-95)
Enoc Huws
translated from the Welsh by
D. M. LLOYD

'KNOCKERS' IN MINES

People that know very little of arts or sciences or of the powers of Nature . . . will laugh at us Cardiganshire miners that maintain the being of knockers in mines—a kind of good natured impalpable people but to be seen and heard, and who seem to us to work in the mines . . . However this is, I must speak well of these knockers, for they have actually stood my very good friends, whether they are aerial beings called spirits, or whether they are people made of matter, not to be felt by our gross bodies, as air and fire the like. Before the discovery of Esgair y Mwyn mine, these little people (as we call them here) worked hard there day and night, and there are abundance of honest sober people that have heard them; (although there are some people amongst us who have no notion of them or of mines either), but after the discovery of the great ore, they were heard no more. When I began to work at Llwynllwyd they worked so fresh there for a considerable time that they even frightened some young workmen out of the work. This was when we were driving levels and before we had got any ore, but when we came to the ore then they gave over and I heard no more talk of them. Our old miners are no more concerned at hearing them blasting, boring holes, landing leads, than if they were some of their own people, and a single miner will stay in the work in the dead of the night without any man near him and never think of any fear or harm that they will do him, for they have a notion the knockers are of their own tribe and profession and are a harmless people who mean well. Three or four miners together shall hear them sometimes, but if the miners stop to take notice of them the knockers will also stop; but let the miners go on at their own work,—suppose it is boring—the knockers will also go on as brisk as can be in landing, blasting or beating down the loose. And they are always heard at a little distance from them, before they come to ore. These are odd assertions, but they are certainly facts, though we cannot and do not pretend to account for them.

LEWIS MORRIS (1700-65)
Morris Letters

THE FAIRIES IN WALES

In former times, more than at present, there were frequent appearances of the Fairies in Wales. . . . Abundance of people saw them, and heard their musick, which everyone said was low and pleasant, but none could ever learn the tune. Heard their talking like that of many talking together, but the words seldom heard. But to those who did hear they seemed to dispute much about future events, and about what they were to do; whence it came to a proverb in the parish concerning disagreeing persons: *Ni chytunant hwy mwy na bendithy mamau*, i.e. they will no more agree than the fairies.

They appeared diverse ways, but their most frequent way of appearing was like dancing companies with musick, and in the form of funerals. When they appeared like dancing companies, they were desirous to entice persons into their company, and some were drawn among them and remained among them some time; usually a whole year, as did Edmund William Rees, a man whom I well knew, and was a neighbour, who came back at the year's end, and looked very bad. But either they were not able to give much account of themselves or they durst not give it, only said they had been dancing, and that the time was short. . . . It was the general opinion in times past, when these things were more frequent, that the fairies knew whatever was spoken in the air without the houses, not so much what was spoken in the houses. I suppose they chiefly knew what was spoken in the air at night. It was also said that they rather appeared to an uneven number of persons to one, three, five, etc. And oftener to men than to women. Thomas William Edmund of Havodavel, an honest pious man, who often saw them, declared, that they appeared with one bigger than the rest going before them in the company.

But very often appeared in the form of a funeral before the death of many persons, with a bier, and a black cloth, in the midst of a company about it, on every side, before and after it. The instances of this were so numerous, that it is plain, and past all dispute that they infallibly foreknew the time of man's death. . . . We have a constant proof of this in the Corpse Candles, whose appearance is an infallible sign that Death will follow, and they never fail going the way that the Corpse will go to be buried, be the way ever so unlikely that it should go through. But to give some instances in Aberystruth Parish:

It was told me that Mr. Howel Prosser, Curate of Aberystruth, seeing a funeral going down the Church lane late in the evening towards the Church, imagined it was the body of a man from the upper end of the parish towards Breconshire, whom he heard before was sick, and thought was now dead and going to be buried. He put on his Band in order to go to perform the burial office, and hastened to go to meet the burial. When he came to it, he saw a people he did not know, of which he took no notice, as they came from the borders of Breconshire. But putting his hand to the bier to help carry the corpse, in a moment all vanished, and to his very great surprize and astonishment, there was nothing in his hand but the skull of a dead horse. . . .

But the following is a more certain instance:

Isaac William Thomas, who lived not far from thence, being at one time at Havodavel, and seeing, as it appeared to him, a Funeral coming down the mountain, as it were to go towards Aberbeeg, or Lanhithel Church. He stood in a field by a wall which was between him and the highway leading to Aberbeeg. When the funeral, which came close to the side of the wall, was come just over against him, he reached his hand and took off the black vail which was over the bier and carried it home with him. It was made of some exceeding fine stuff, so that when folded it was a very little substance, and very light. He told this to several. I knew the man myself, and in my youthful days conversed with him several times. I wish I had spoken with him after this had happened, and had asked many particular questions about it, to have more particular knowledge of this extraordinary supernatural affair . . . but the opportunity for this, in this world, as many others of this nature is lost for ever. But the light of Eternity will shew Myriads of Myriads of things which we cannot know here, nor are fit to know; and which we shall there certainly and infallibly know, without error, as they are, and no otherwise.

EDMUND JONES (1702-93)
. . . *The Parish of Aberystruth*

THE KYHIRRAETH

The judicious Joshua Coslet— who lived on that side the river Towy which runs through the middle of Caermarthenshire, where the *Kyhirraeth* is often heard, gave me the following remarkable account of it:—

That it is a doleful disagreeable sound heard before the deaths of many, and most apt to be heard before foul weather: the voice resembles the groaning of sick persons who are to die; heard at first at a distance, then comes nearer, and the last near at hand; so that it is a three-fold warning of death,—the king of terrors. It begins strong and louder than a sick man can make, the second cry is lower, but not less doleful, rather more so; the third yet lower and soft, like the groaning of a sick man, almost spent and dying; so that a person well remembering the voice, and coming to the sick man's bed who is to die, shall hear his groans exactly alike, which is an amazing evidence of the spirit's foreknowledge. Sometimes when it cries very loud it bears a resemblance of one crying who is troubled with a stitch. If it meets any hindrance in the way it seems to groan louder. It is, or hath been very common in the three commots of Ynys Cennin.

EDMUND JONES (1702-93)
Apparitions . . . in Wales

METHODISM AND SUPERSTITION

Grandfather, then, was in great good humour over his thatching. Cadwaladr and Tom were spinning straw ropes, and Jack and we boys assisting. The stories of last night were referred to, and re-discussed in all sorts of ways. Tom Roberts looked at them in the Methodist aspect, Jack in the jocular, Cadwaladr in the cynical view, but all believed in them without reserve. One might expect Tom, at least, to be sceptical from his Methodist and Radical leanings, but it was far otherwise: he was of all by far the most credulous. Neither did his Methodist training tend to check superstition in him; it rather enhanced it. Methodist books of that date swarmed with marvels; supernatural appearances, warnings, singing in the air, sudden judgements on rulers and persecutors; God's miracles and the devil's miracles abounded everywhere. The *Lives of the Saints* is not more full of such wonders than the *Mirror of the Times*, the Methodist Church History. And for people who read the Old Testament histories so much, what more natural than to expect miracles everywhere? The witch Esther had her parallel in the witch of Endor: the magic of Ellis was the legitimate successor of that of Egypt. Scepticism on these subjects is more prevalent now, but thirty years ago it was rare indeed in the Welsh *cwms*. To disbelieve supernaturalism was then thought utter infidelity; it was flying in the face of Providence—an obstinate hardening of the mind against all evidence.

ROBERT ROBERTS (1834-85)
The Life and Opinions of R. R., a wandering scholar . . .

AT THE GATE

Thereupon we turned our faces from the great city of Perdition, and went up to the other little city. In going along, I could see at the upper end of the streets many turning half-way from the temptations of the gates of Perdition and seeking for the gate of Life; but whether it was that they failed to find it, or grew tired upon the way, I could not see that any went through, except one sorrowful faced man, who ran forward resolutely, while thousands on each side of him were calling him fool, some scoffing him, others threatening him, and his friends laying hold upon him, and entreating him not to take a step by which he would lose the whole world at once. "I only lose," said he, "a very small portion of it, and if I should lose the whole, pray what loss is it? For what is there in the world so desirable, unless a man should desire deceit, and violence, and misery, and wretchedness, giddiness and distraction? Contentment and tranquillity," said he, "constitute the happiness of man; but in your city there are no such things to be found. Because who is there here content with his station? Higher, higher! is what everyone endeavours to be in the street of Pride. Give, give us a little more, says everyone in the street of Lucre. Sweet, sweet, pray give me some more of it, is the cry of everyone in the street of Pleasure.

"And as for tranquillity, where is it? and who obtains it? If you be a great man, flattery and envy are killing you. If you be poor, everyone is trampling upon and despising you. After having become an inventor, if you exalt your head and seek for praise, you will be called a boaster and a coxcomb. If you lead a godly life and resort to the Church and the altar, you will be called a hypocrite. If you do not, then you are an infidel or a heretic. If you be merry, you will be called a buffoon. If you are silent, you will be called a morose wretch. If you follow honesty, you are nothing but a simple fool. If you go neat, you are proud; if not, a swine. If you are smooth speaking, then you are false, or a trifler without meaning. If you are rough, you are an arrogant, disagreeable devil. Behold the world that you magnify!" said he; "pray take my share of it."

ELLIS WYNNE (1671-1734)
Visions of the Sleeping Bard (*Bardd Cwsc*)
translated from the Welsh by
GEORGE BORROW

ARRANT THIEVES

I marvelled that he should speak of the Princes, and of the proudest among these gentry, as arrant thieves. "Pray, my Lord," I asked, "how is it you say that these noble gentlemen are worse thieves than the highwaymen?"

"Thou art easily deceived," said he. "Is not the knave who goes about the world, sword in hand and followed by his ravagers, killing and burning and stealing states from their rightful owners, and who afterwards expects to be hailed as a conqueror, is he not worse than a petty thief who takes a purse on the highway? What is the tailor who steals a piece of cloth, beside the great man who, out of the mountain, steals the half of a parish? As against the one, ought not the other to be called an arrant thief? The other stole only scraps, whereas he has taken from the poor man the food of his beast and so his own living and that of his weak ones. What is the stealing of a handful of flour at the mill to the storing of a hundred bushels to rot so that later one bushel may be sold for the price of four? What is the half-clad soldier, who takes thy clothes at the point of the sword, to the lawyer who steals thy whole estate from thee with a goose-quill, so that thou have neither right nor remedy against him? And what is a cut-purse, who steals five pounds, to the dice-loader who robs thee of five score pounds in the third part of a night? And what is a swopper who would deceive thee in some decrepit old hack to the apothecary who cheats thee of thy money and thy life with some useless drug? What are all these thieves, compared with that great queen of thieves who robs them all of these goods and of their hearts and souls at the end of the fair?"

ELLIS WYNNE (1671-1734)
Visions of the Sleeping Bard (*Bardd Cwsc*)
translated from the Welsh by
T. GWYNN JONES

FIRST PRINCIPLE OF SOCIETY

My first task was to make arrangements to supersede the evil conditions with which the population was surrounded, by good conditions. And as soon as society can be made to think rationally on a true foundation, to replace inferior by superior conditions will be found to be the task which society has to learn, and in good earnest to commence in practice. In fact, this is the great lesson which mankind has now to acquire and to put into execution over the world. For, with the certainty of a law of nature,—as are the circumstances or conditions with which man is surrounded through life, so must he become. Surround him with evil circumstances or conditions,—and his thoughts and conduct must become evil; while when surrounded through life with good conditions only, his thoughts and conduct must be good. The problem for man now to solve, therefore is—"What are evil, and what are good conditions?" And "How are the evil to be superseded by the good, in peace, beneficially for all, and with universal consent?" And when the first principle on which society should be based shall be understood and consistently applied to practice, the problem will be easily solved and carried into execution.

ROBERT OWEN (1771-1858)
The Life of Robert Owen by himself

A SENSE OF VALUES

"There are men who are ever groping for the God of truth, and who know what it is to lose nights of sleep in a keen and arduous struggle for the light. They know well what it is to be sorely wounded by doubts and unbelief, and yet they do not give up the quest for the healing balm. I call these men the sons of God, although there are some among them whose names are not entered on the roll of any Fellowship. As you know, I hold in deep respect a number of church members who are sincere, high-principled, godly, and zealous according to their lights for church-discipline. But it appears strange to me that they can only distinguish one group of sins. Are Robert Lewis and Williams the coalman the only transgressors? Can you explain why Williams has been disciplined many times, while John Lloyd has never once been repremanded? As far as I know, no one doubts poor William's harmlessness—his besetting weakness is that he forgets that his head can't stand the effects of more than two glasses of beer, and that he is liable, after exceeding the mark, to fall on his back, or on his side, and that no one would care to defend his being in that posture. But why is there no rule calling a man to account for miserliness and greed? . . . 'That thou doest, do quickly,' said Jesus to Judas, and Judas obeyed. But there are people who fail to rise to Judas's standards. Every day they sell their Master for thirty pieces of silver—they do so calmly and with leisurely calculation, without any hurry, and with no sign, the more's the pity, that they will soon hang themselves, and go to their own place. And yet it appears that there is no disciplinary rule against such execrable specimens of humanity."

DANIEL OWEN (1836-95)
Rhys Lewis
translated from the Welsh by
D. M. LLOYD

PURITANISM AND RURAL WALES

The prevailing type of manhood in rural Wales is more austere than of old, is more coloured by Puritanism. But there is the same hospitality and neighbourliness and tenderness for the poor. Giraldus Cambrensis in 1194 wrote that "Welshmen break the first piece of every loaf for the poor." This year—seven hundred years later—the Inspector of the Local Government Board admits that despite all pressure, Welsh Guardians of the Poor have an almost unconquerable aversion to the pulling of the poor up by the roots from the country-side and heaping them together in a town workhouse. Those who aver that Puritanism has soured the Welsh temperament know little of the merriment, the sly humour and the quick-wittedness of social converse on Welsh hearths. It is true that it has given a more serious purpose to their activities. *Glân Meddwdod Mwyn* and *Codiad yr Ehedydd* have a wider sway than ever as national airs, but the great hymn-tunes with their solemn cadences and their associations with the spiritual and the Unseen have far the strongest hold upon the

Welsh people. Their response to leadership and to appeals on behalf of various modes of religious and social work, of educational movements and of the revival of political nationality is so willing, unselfish and generous that no reformer need despair.

THOMAS E. ELLIS (1859-99)
Speeches and addresses

SUNDAY

O day most calm, most bright,
  The fruit of this, the next world's bud,
Th' indorsement of supreme delight,
  Writ by a friend, and with his blood;
The couch of time, care's balm and bay,
The week were dark but for thy light:
  Thy torch doth show the way.

The other days and thou
  Make up one man, whose face thou art,
Knocking at heaven with thy brow.
  The worky-days are the back-part;
The burden of the week lies there
Making the whole to stoop and bow
  Till thy release appeare.

Man had straight forward gone
  To endlesse death; but thou dost pull
And turn us round to look on one
  Whom, if we were not very dull,
We could not chose but look on still;
Since there is no place so alone
  The which he doth not fill.

Sundays the pillars are
  On which heav'ns palace arched lies:
The other days fill up the spare
  And hollow rooms with vanities.
They are the fruitfull beds and borders
In God's rich garden; that is bare
  Which parts their ranks and orders.

The Sundays of man's life,
  Thredded together on time's string,
Make bracelets to adorn the wife
  Of the eternal glorious King.
On Sunday heaven's gate stands ope,
Blessings are plentifull and rife,
  More plentifull than hope.

This day my Saviour rose,
  And did inclose this light for his;
That, as each beast his manger knows,
  Man might not of his fodder misse.
Christ hath took in this piece of ground,
And made a garden there for those
  Who want herbs for their wound.

The rest of our Creation
  Our great Redeemer did remove
With the same shake which at his passion
  Did th' earth and all things with it move.
As Samson bore the doores away,
Christ's hands, though nail'd, wrought our salvation
  And did unhinge that day.

The brightnesse of that day
  We sullied by our foul offence;
Wherefore that robe we cast away,
  Having a new at his expence

Whose drops of bloud paid the full price
That was requir'd to make us gay,
And fit for Paradise.

Thou art a day of mirth;
And where the week-dayes trail on ground,
Thy flight is higher, as thy birth.
O let me take thee at the bound,
Leaping with thee from sev'n to sev'n,
Till that we both, being toss'd from earth,
Flie hand in hand to heav'n.

GEORGE HERBERT (1593-1633)
The Temple

SEEMING PIETY

Saying which, he snatched me up into the roodloft of a church in Wales, when the people were at service. There we beheld some whispering one to the other, some laughing, some staring at comely women, others scanning their neighbour's clothing from head to heel, some pushing their way and showing their teeth in claiming their station, some napping, others much occupied with their devotions, many of those but feigning.

"Thou hast not yet seen," said the Angel, "no, not even among unbelievers, such open shamelessness as this, but unhappily, so it is the corruption of the best is the worst corruption of all."

Then they went to communion, seeming all to have much reverence for the altar. Yet, through my friend's glass, I beheld one here and there, along with the bread, taking into his body the semblance of a mastiff, another a mole, another an eagle, another a swine, another a winged serpent, and a few, oh, how few, receiving a ray of shining light with the bread and the wine.

"See there," said he, "a Roundhead, who is to be made sheriff, and as the law demands communion at Church before the taking of office, he has come here so as not to lose it, and although there are here some who are glad to see him, there has yet been no joy amongst us because of his conversion, for unhappily he has been converted only for a season; and so thou mayst see that Hypocrisy is over bold in coming to the altar, in the presence of Emmanuel who may not be deceived. Yet, however great she may be in the City of Doom, even she has no power in the City of Emmanuel on the upper side of these ramparts."

ELLIS WYNNE (1671-1734)
Visions of the Sleeping Bard (*Bardd Cwsc*)
translated from the Welsh by
T. GWYNN JONES

SABBATH LABOUR

It would take a very great deal to persuade him to work on the Sabbath, and he would not expect his labours to be blessed if he did. But he saw no harm in spending many hours every Sabbath, standing with his pipe in his mouth watching the pig eating, and calculating when it would be ready for the knife, how much it would weigh, and after slaughter whether he would make black pudding or brawn, whether it would pay to keep or to sell the offal, to whom among his neighbours he was under obligation to send a piece of spare-rib and so on. Thomas did not think there was any harm in spending the Sabbath discussing such matters with Barbara; but he would not be induced, even by the offer of a large sum of money, to put on his leather apron for one single hour on the Lord's Day.

DANIEL OWEN (1836-95)
Rhys Lewis
translated from the Welsh by D. M. LLOYD

WILL BRYAN ON THE 'FELLOWSHIP'

Their surprise was no less when I informed them that Bob's case, and mine, and Bryan's, was to be 'brought before' the Fellowship that night. Beck, being 'Church,' had only a hazy notion what was meant by 'Fellowship,' and 'bringing before' the Fellowship, until Bryan offered him the following explanation. Will had a remarkable gift for giving the gist of what he was superbly confident that he understood, and this is how he explained to Beck the nature and purpose of the Fellowship:—

"It's like this," said he, "the Fellowship is a lot of good people thinking that they are bad, and meeting together every Tuesday evening to find fault with themselves."

"I don't follow," said Beck.

"Well," said Will, "look at it like this: You know old Mrs. Peters, and you know Rhys's mother,—and it is not because Rhys is present that I mention her—but everybody knows that they are two good-living and godly women. Well, they go to the Fellowship; Abel Hughes goes to them, and asks them what they have to say. They say they are very wicked, and guilty of ever so many shortcomings, and Mrs. Peters is often in tears as she says so. Then, Abel tells them they are not so evil as they think, and gives them counsel, and repeats lots of verses of Scripture, and then he goes to someone else, who in his turn says the same sort of thing, and they keep it up until half past eight when we all go home."

"There's nothing like that in Church," said Beck. "We never hold a Fellowship and I never heard anyone there running himself down."

"That's the difference between 'Church' and 'chapel,'" said Will. "You Churchpeople think yourselves good when you are bad, and the chapel people think themselves bad when they are good."

DANIEL OWEN (1836-95)
Rhys Lewis
translated from the Welsh by
D. M. LLOYD

Poems, Songs, Ballads

DINOGAD'S SMOCK

Dinogad's smock is checked, is checked;
Of marten skin it is made—
Tweet, tweet, twee-twee-twee!
Let us sing! let the eight servants sing!
When your dad a-hunting would go,
Spear on his shoulder, club in his hand,
Two nimble dogs he would call—
Giff! Gaff! catch! catch! bring! bring!
In coracle, fish he would kill
As a lion kills his prey.
When your dad to the mountain would go
He would bring back a roe-buck, a wild pig, a stag,
A speckled grouse from the mountain,
A fish from Derwent waterfall.
What your dad could reach with his spear,
Wild pig, and weasel, and fox,
Must be superwinged to escape!

ANONYMOUS (? 7th century)
The Book of Aneirin
translated from the Welsh by
D. M. LLOYD

THE 'ENGLYNION' OF THE GRAVES

The graves made moist by the rain:
Men of whose deeds I had nought to complain,
Here Kerwid and Kyfrid and Kaw have lain.

Grave of Tedai, father of song
By the hill of Aren lying long;
By the wave's ebb and flow
Dylan in Llan Beuno lies below.

In Aber Gwenoli
The grave of Pryderi;
Where the waves strike the land,
In Carrog, tall Gwallog lies by the sea-strand.

The son of Osfran in Camlan lies
After many a brave enterprise;
Bedevere's grave in Allt Tryvan's rise.

After trappings of purple and splendour and gold,
And warhorses swift and tall of old,
In Llan Heledd, now, Owain lies cold.

By his home in Dyved now in earth lies Alun,
In war he proved his worth,
Son of Meigen, bright was the day of his birth!

The long graves on Gwanas hill,
To tell us now, who has the skill,
How came they there, for good or ill?

Skilful-handed Lleu under the wave of the sea
By his kin lies his grave;
A man was he, his rights to none he gave.

Far from turmoil and dread,
The sod of Machavwy is spread
Over the long pale hands of Beiddog the Red.

A whelp in a lonely pack lets wail,
Yonder over the exile's grave lies their trail,
Kynddylig, son of Corknud, underneath lies pale.

Whose grave? Tall Brwyno lies here tonight;
Well stood he his ground, maintaining his right,
And where he stood, his warriors were never in flight.

Who lies in the grave in the grove yonder?
Though his foes were many, he valiantly strove,
A bull in battle, may he find mercy Above!

from the *Black Book of Carmarthen*
(*a 12th-13th century manuscript*)
translated from the Welsh by
D. M. LLOYD

LOVE AND WAR

Early rising sun, summer quickly coming;
Birds sing sweet; gloriously fine weather;
Splendid my deeds am I, fearless in battle;
I am a lion facing the host, sweeping is my fury.
I spent a night closely guarding the border
By the murmuring river-fords of Dygen Freiddyn.
Very green the untrodden grass, how sparkling the water!
The nightingale sings loudly her wonted song.
Seagulls play on the water as on a bed,
Brilliant their feathers, a gossiping company.
Far away are my thoughts in May,
Drawn by my love for a young Caerwys maiden. . . .
But in generous Owain's cause, the destroyer of our bondage,
The English tremble at the stroke of my blade.

Bright my sword, flashingly borne by a brave one,
Brilliant is the gold on my shield.
Before the turbulence of waters how warm is the day;
The sweet song of birds is the trilling of a poem.
My mind is eager for a far-away countryside

Today as I penetrate into the land by Vyrnwy's banks.
Very white are the apple twigs, clustered with flowers,
Proud the coats of the trees.
Everyone's mind strays towards his love:
I love a Caerwys maid, graceful and comely,
How I hate to be away from her. . . .
But although my Llywy is fair as the snow on the trees,
In the fight by the ramparts I poured out blood. . . .

GWALCHMAI (12th century)
translated from the Welsh by
D. M. LLOYD

MY CHOICE

My choice is a maid, wondrous slender and fair,
Beautiful and tall in her purple-hued cloak;
And my choice sensation to watch the womanly one
While she barely whispers becoming wisdom;
And my chosen lot to companion the maid,
And privy be to her charm and her boon.
My choice is a lady of the beauty of the wave,
Shrewd in thy land, and whose Welsh is refined.
My choice art thou; how reckest thou me?
Why wilt thou not tell, who in silence art sweet?
I have chosen a maid, and no regret have I,
It is proper to choose a choice lady and fair.

PRINCE HYWEL AB OWAIN GWYNEDD (*d.* 1170)
translated from the Welsh by
J. LLOYD-JONES

THE HIRLAS POEM

A shout was raised, with the first break of day,
defiance vain, sent by the enemy;
our men were red-speared, after heavy toil,
and o'er the walls of Maelor camp, death stared.

And I sent men, in daring deeds unmatched,
and fearless, to the test of blood-red blades,—
let him, who anger a brave man, beware,
for from such anger, woe is wont to come.

May that, which makes me silent, leave me now,—
cup-bearer, for our drinking, bring the horn,
marked with long streaks of blue, and ringed with gold,
which soothes the pangs of longing, and whose flow
is foaming like the crest of the ninth wave.

Cup-bearer, fill the horn full joyously,
and give to Rhys in this court of largesse,
the court of Owain of the golden gifts,
the stay of thousands, called the open door'd.
Bring a full draught of bragget to the hand
of Gwgan, for the honour of his deeds;
scions of Gronwy both, mighty in war,
like nimble whelps, in action without ruth,
who merit boon in every bitter test;
men in attack, worthiest, a mighty help,
shepherds of Havren, proud when there is heard
the sound of mead-horns, great and bountiful.

And for Kynvelyn, do thou fill the horn,
an honourable guerdon of bright mead;
and yet another year if thou wouldst live,
bear not his portion hence, meet were it not;

also to Gruffudd of the crimson lance,
bring thou the wine, sparkling within the glass,—
the dragon of Arwystli, border-ward,
who starts not war, who is by war not startled,
sternest in stand, affliction in pursuit;
warriors are they who went for glory forth,
fellows in feast and fight, like Edwyn's folk;
their mead they won, like Belyn's men of old,
deservedly they drink, if any may! . . .

Fill thou the horn, for now I think again
of how our folk defended there our lands—
Selyv the fearless, rampart of Gwygyr he
with eagle-heart, who anger him, beware!
and Madawc's only son, Tudor, the brave,
like wolves were they, like lightning among twigs,
a noble pair, in purpose lion-like,
two sons of Ynyr, fierce in might are they,
whose ranks are rapid in the day of strife,
a band unswerved, feat of undaunted ones;
gashing like lions, grim in the thrusting of men,
lusting for action, with red ashen shafts,
fierce as an eagle caught in the rushing tide,
their shields all torn, in purpose, one are they;
like loud-voiced winds above the blue sea strand,
like the wild rage of storied Talgarth's waves. . . .

Out of the silver vessel, do thou fill
an honourable pledge, with reverence,—
on Gwestun field, a marvel I beheld,
Goronwy's feats would match a hundred men!
warriors of one intent together wrought,
battle-resisting, men of eager souls;
with enemies, he, the exalted leader, met,—
their lord was slain, the sea-side fort was burnt,
and they a Mwynfawr forth from prison brought,—
Meurig the son of Gruffudd, of fame foretold;

each warrior foamed with sweat when they returned,
and hill and valley bathed in sunlight lay! . . .

Cup-bearer, pour thou out the sweet, strained mead,
for those, quick-speared, and toil-worn in the fight,
pour out of proud, gold-circled drinking horns.
What toils are borne by men, to win reward,
for which the price they pay is their own souls,
there is but God who knows, or who can tell.

A man who pays no tribute, takes no oath,
who never will be found against the right,
Daniel, dragon of might, how true is he!
Cup-bearer, flattered many a time are they
whom death ne'er flatters, shall they not be praised?

Cup-bearer, bring the cordial to us all,
by the great bright fire's light and torches' gleam;
cup-bearer, thou sawest wrath at Llidwm field,
the men I honour, honoured they shall be!
cup-bearer, thou didst see the shattered mail
there, around Owain of the far-famed shield,
when Cawres by untold exertion fell,
and furious looting, ever to be sung.

Though parted now, apart we shall not be,
may we be unto Paradise received,
may we be welcomed by the King of Kings,
where the security of truth is seen!

PRINCE OWAIN CYFEILIOG (*c.* 1130-97)
translated from the Welsh by
T. GWYNN JONES

A LAMENT

Where run the white rolling waves,
Where meets the sea the mighty river,
In cruel tombs at Aberconwy
God has caused their dire concealment from us,
The red-speared warriors, their nation's illustrious sons.

DAFYDD BENFRAS (13th century)
translated from the Welsh by
J. LLOYD-JONES

WINTER-TIME

It is winter-time, very grey is the ocean,
Perched are the sea-birds, the brine is raging,
Eryri now wears a cold mantle of frost,
High runs the white billow on Enlli's blest shore.
Greater and greater grows my anguish through misery,
My mind is afflicted, bereft of my lords. . . .

BLEDDYN FARDD (13th century)
translated from the Welsh by
J. LLOYD-JONES

THE MIST

O ho! thou villain mist, O ho!
What plea hast thou to plague me so?
I scarcely know a scurril name,
But dearly thou deserv'st the same;
Thou exhalation from the deep
Unknown, where ugly spirits keep!
Thou smoke from hellish stews uphurl'd
To mock and mortify the world!
Thou spider-web of giant race,
Spun out and spread through airy space!
Avaunt, thou filthy, clammy thing,

Of sorry rain the source and spring!
Moist blanket dripping misery down,
Loathed alike by land and town!
Thou watery monster, wan to see,
Intruding 'twixt the sun and me,
To rob me of my blessed right,
To turn my day to dismal night.
Parent of thieves and patron best,
They brave pursuit within thy breast!
Mostly from thee its merciless snow
Grim January doth glean, I trow.
Pass off with speed, thou prowler pale,
Holding along o'er hill and dale,
Spilling a noxious spittle round,
Spoiling the fairies' sporting ground!
Move off to hell, mysterious haze;
Wherein deceitful meteors blaze;
Thou wild of vapour, vast, o'ergrown,
Huge as the ocean of unknown.

attributed to DAFYDD AP GWILYM (*c.* 1325-*c.* 85)
translated from the Welsh by
GEORGE BORROW

THE GROVE OF BROOM

O'er Dyved's hills there was a veil
In ancient days—(so runs the tale);
And such a canopy to me
This court, among the woods, shall be;
Where she, my heart adores, shall reign,
The princess of the fair domain.
To her, and to her poet's eyes,
This arbour seems a paradise;
Its every branch is deftly strung
With twigs and foliage lithe and young,
And when May comes upon the trees

To paint her verdant liveries,
Gold on each thread-like sprig will glow,
To honour her who reigns below.
Green is that arbour to behold,
And on its withes thick showers of gold!
Joy to the poet and the maid,
Whose paradise is yonder shade!
Oh! flowers of noblest splendour, these
Are summer's frost-work on the trees!
A field the lovers now possess,
With saffron o'er its verdure rolled,
A house of passing loveliness,
A fabric of Arabia's gold—
Bright golden tissue, glorious tent,
Of him who rules the firmament,
With roof of various colours blent!
An angel, mid the woods of May,
Embroidered it with radiance gay—
That gossamer with gold bedight—
Those fires of God—those gems of light!
'Tis sweet those magic bowers to find,
With the fair vineyards intertwined;
Amid the woods their jewels rise,
Like gleam of starlight o'er the skies—
Like golden bullion, glorious prize!
How sweet the flowers that deck that floor,
In one unbroken glory blended—
Those glittering branches hovering o'er—
Veil by an angel's hand extended.
Oh! if my love will come, her bard
Will, with his care, her footsteps guard,
There, where no stranger dares to pry,
Beneath yon Broom's green canopy!

attributed to DAFYDD AP GWILYM (*c.* 1325-*c.* 85)
translated from the Welsh by
ARTHUR JAMES JOHNES (MAELOG)

THE POET AND THE FRIAR

It's a pity the maiden who holds her court
In the green bush hears no report
Of my quarrel today on her account
With the mouse-coloured friar, which here I recount:
To confess my sins, with pious intent,
As everyone should, to the brother I went.
I informed him then, if well I recall,
That I was a poet, as is known to you all,
And had doted long on a maiden fair,
Of milk-white skin, and jet-black hair;
And from my fair slayer, ne'er a reward,—
Encouragement nil, in deed or word.
Yet I constantly loved her for years and years,
With aching heart and bitter tears.
Throughout all Wales I spread her fame
Though her cold indifference remained the same.
So much had this maiden turned my head
That my heart was set on sharing her bed.
   At this the friar did interpose,
And offered advice which here I disclose:
"To a maiden fair as the foaming wave,
Of paper-white skin, your love you gave—
In the world to come for your soul's good
Desist from loving flesh and blood.
Forget your cowyths, things vain and idle,
Tell your beads, and your passions bridle;
Not for cowyth or englyn,[1] though well they scan,
Did God redeem the soul of man.
Your minstrel songs are void of truth,

[1]*Englyn* and *cywydd* are two very popular metrical patterns in Welsh, and both have the intricate system of sound correspondences known as *cynghanedd*. It was Dafydd ap Gwilym's genius that made the *cywydd* the most popular of all metrical forms in Wales for over two centuries.

Foolish and vain, and wicked, forsooth,
Enticing men and women to evil,
Leading them on to the ways of the devil;
The praise of the body fares not well,
It drags the spirit down to hell."
  I answered the brother, I did not quail,
And countered each word of his dismal tale:
"God is not cruel as old men say,
He will not damn us, though others may,
For the love we bear towards woman or maid.
Is it not true as is often said
That three things are loved throughout the earth,
A maid, and sunshine, and good health?
The fairest flower, save God alone,
In Heaven is the Maiden next His Throne.
Save only three, all the human race
Are born of woman, in every place,—
Small wonder then that women are woo'd,
As men all over the world have proved.
From Heaven delight to man has come,
And of all sadness, hell is the home.
We are all made glad by the power of song,
The old, the young, the weak, and the strong.
As seemly it is for me to sing
As for you to preach, you gloomy thing,
And for me to wander my own sweet way
As for you to beg from day to day.
Are not the hymns and sequences sweet
In metre and rhyme and numbered feet?
And the Psalter of David, Prophet and King,
Is a poem to God that his children sing.
God studies our diet with loving care,
Our food and relish is a varied fare.
A time is appointed for drink and food,
And time for singing the praises of God;
Time to preach and for sin to grieve,

And time harmonious songs to weave.
A song is sung in every feast
To delight fair maidens and every guest,
And then in Church a *pater* we hear
That to Paradise we may draw near.
A sage of old was heard to tell,
When with his friends he caroused right well,
'A merry face, his house is full,'
Ill bodes it when long faces we pull.'
Some may delight in sanctity,
Others in mirth and jollity.
A cowyth is well sung by few,
The *pater* is known the whole world through;
Why then, holy brother, you must be wrong
To say that the biggest sin is song.
If the day ever dawns that men are fain
To sing their prayers to a harpist's strain,
And enjoy it as much as a Gwynedd lass
Loves a jovial tune,—if this comes to pass,
No cowyth will ever be Dafydd's delight,
His prayers he will sing by day and by night;
But a shame on Dafydd, if he dare essay
A prayer for a cowyth ere comes that day!"

DAFYDD AP GWILYM (*c.* 1325-*c.* 85)
translated from the Welsh by
D. M. LLOYD

TO THE GULL

Bird that dwellest in the spray,
White as yon moon's calm array,
Dust thy beauty ne'er may stain,
Sunbeam-gauntlet of the main!
Soaring with aërial motion
On the surges of the ocean.

[P. B. Abery

PONT-AR-ELAN, NEAR PLYNLIMON

[R. Cecil Hughes

NANT-Y-STALWYN FARMSTEAD AND TOWY STREAM

[*Reece Winstone*

SWALLOW FALLS, BETWS-Y-COED

Bird of lofty pinion, fed
On the fishes of the sea,
Wilt thou not disdain or dread
Hence to learn a rhapsody—
Rhymes of praise to her whose dart
Ever rankles in my heart?
Wilt thou (lily of the sea!)
Draw near, hand-in-hand with me,
To the beateous maiden's home;
(Nun that dwellest in the foam!)
With thy glossy figure climb
Round her castle's walls sublime.
Soon the girl of virgin hue,
On those tow'rs will meet thy view.
Tell her ev'ry rapt'rous word
Thou of her from me hast heard:
Court her glance—be polished—wise,
When on thee she turns her eyes:
Say her poet loves her more
Than bard ever lov'd before;
That a maid so pure and bright
By Taliesin ne'er was sung,
Nor wild Myrddin's flatt'ring tongue.
Sea-gull, if she meets thy sight,
Tell her that I must resign
Life, if she will not be mine:—
With unequalled pangs I pine!

DAFYDD AP GWILYM (*c.* 1325-*c.* 85)
translated from the Welsh by
ARTHUR JAMES JOHNES (MAELOG)

EPIGRAMS

TO PONTICUS

Thou ask'st what years thou hast? I answer None:
For what thou had'st, thou hast not: they be gone.

OF CONTROVERSIES

Divines contend, and yet is their contest
Under the Judge: O would it there might rest:
Divines contend, and of the Judge complain:
O would that all the strife did there remain.
Or that in us there was such strife of Love,
As Love of strife in ev'ry Sphere doth move.

OF FAITH AND CHARITY

As Trees first planted are e're fruit they bear,
So where are vertues faith must first appear;
Life lives by Faith, not without Love: as poor
Do live in hope, yet labour more and more.
Faith's first, Love's chief; for 'tis a vertue great
God to believe, to love God's more compleat.

THE FLESH AND SPIRIT

God made man's Body first, and when created,
He with a living Soul it animated.
Hence the dull Body, doth, I think, deny
T' obey the Soul; pleads Seniority.

SHEEP AND GOATS

The Goats climb Rocks, and Promontories steep,
The lower Ground depasture flocks of Sheep:
'Tis so now, but it will not still be so,
The Sheep on high, the Goats below shall go.

WE ARE DUST AND ASHES

Let none, though clad with Earth, of Heaven despair;
Nor any, though a Shadow, thin as Air:
Dust is our Flesh, Christs Body's of like clod:
Our Soul's a shadow, shadow yet of God.

JOHN OWEN, the Epigrammatist (*c.* 1560-1622)
translated from the Latin by
THOMAS HARVEY

ELEGY OVER A TOMB

Must I then see, alas! eternal night
  Sitting upon those fairest eyes,
And closing all those beams, which once did rise
  So radiant and bright,
That light and heat in them to us did prove
  Knowledge and Love?

Oh, if you did delight no more to stay
  Upon this low and earthly stage,
But rather chose an endless heritage,
  Tell us at least, we pray,
Where all the beauties that those ashes ow'd
  Are now bestow'd?

Doth the Sun now his light with yours renew?
  Have Waves the curling of your hair?
Did you restore unto the Sky and Air,
  The red, and white, and blew?
Have you vouchsaf'd to flowers since your death
  That sweetest breath?

Had not Heav'ns Lights else in their houses slept,
  Or to some private life retir'd?
Must not the Sky and Air have else conspir'd,

And in their Regions wept?
Must not each flower else the earth could breed
Have been a weed?

But thus enrich'd may we not yield some cause
Why they themselves lament no more?
That must have chang'd the course they held before,
And broke their proper Laws,
Had not your beauties giv'n this second birth
To Heaven and Earth?

Tell us, for Oracles must still ascend,
For those that crave them at your tomb:
Tell us, where are those beauties now become,
And what they now intend:
Tell us, alas, that cannot tell our grief,
Or hope relief.

LORD HERBERT OF CHERBURY (1583-1648)

THE WORLD

Love built a stately house; where *Fortune* came,
And spinning phansies, she was heard to say,
That her fine cobwebs did support the frame,
Whereas they were supported by the same:
But *Wisdome* quickly swept them all away.

Then *Pleasure* came, who liking not the fashion,
Began to make *Balcónes*, *Terraces*,
Till she had weakened all by alteration:
But rev'rend *laws*, and many a *proclamation*
Reformed all at a length with menaces.

Then enter'd *Sinne*, and with that Sycamore,
Whose leaves first sheltred man from drought and dew,

Working and winding slily evermore,
The inward walls and Sommers cleft and tore:
But *Grace* shor'd these, and cut that as it grew.

Then *Sinne* combin'd with *Death* in a firm band
To raze the building to the very floore:
Which they effected, none could them withstand,
But *Love* and *Grace* took *Glorie* by the hand,
And built a braver *Palace* than before.

GEORGE HERBERT (1593-1633)
The Temple

PEACE

My Soul, there is a Countrie
  Far beyond the stars,
Where stands a winged sentrie
  All skilfull in the wars,
There above noise, and danger
  Sweet peace sits crown'd with smiles,
And one born in a Manger
  Commands the Beauteous files,
He is thy gracious friend,
  And (O my Soul awake!)
Did in pure love descend
  To die here for thy sake;
If thou canst get but thither,
  There growes the flowre of peace,
The Rose that cannot wither,
  Thy fortresse, and thy ease;
Leave then thy foolish ranges;
  For none can thee secure,
But one, who never changes,
  Thy God, thy life, thy Cure.

HENRY VAUGHAN, the Silurist (1622-95)
Silex Scintillans

IN PRAISE OF A GIRL

Slip of loveliness, slim, seemly,
freshly fashioned, modest maiden, star serene,
Sage and queenly, gracious, granting heart;
paragon, look upon
this grave song, growing sign
that I pine, my constant moon.
No beauty clear, so dear I'll hold
not till I'm old, foam of the sea,
loveliest lily of the land,
soft of hand, white-breasted, brisk, bright, flower-
crested;
who'd not be charmed whose blood is warmed?
Moon of my nature, it was you
I viewed in my desire
because your brow is like the snow,
able, notable, gifted, gay, flawless,
laughing, skilful, peerless pearl of girls!

If from all lands girls came in bands
and from a tree one could see
that sweet society of all liveliest ones,
the paragons of town and country,
dazzling, shapely, stately, fair, I declare.
Moon of Wales, your loveliness prevails.
Your praise and glory, peerless girl,
now impel me to applaud
your sweet looks, your subtle tongue,
dawn-sweet dearest, purest, prettiest, many-beautied,
unpolluted and reputed spotless rose;
there's none to make comparison,
wave sparkling in the darkling,
with your parabling of sweet peace,

piece of goodness, fond enchantress, blithsome dove,
lucent, laughing, blameless slip of love. . . .

HUW MORUS (1622-1709)
translated from the Welsh by
GWYN WILLIAMS

THE MINER'S BALLAD

I am a jovial miner,
I wander up and down,
I have no settled station
In country or in town,
  Then a mining we will go.

I work in Pluto's regions
Where riches are in store,
And when I spend my gettings
I go and dig for more.

When soldiers run from cannon
To live another day,
We live in smoke of powder
And never run away.

When merchants lose their substance
By tempests or by floods
We feel no change of weather
But safely land our goods.

When criminals at Tyburn
Of ropes do stand in fear,
We hang in ropes so often
We fear no Tyburn here.

Tho' nobles drive in chariots
They often run in debt,
We drive upon a level
And seldom overset.

When death in silent trenches
Imprisons Lords and Kings,
We in our graves live merry
And laugh at all his stings.

Some pick the nations' pockets
As others did before,
But we maintain their credit
By picking rocks and ore.

With odd conceits and whimsies
Some do their fortunes sink,
Our whimsies raise us money,
And money raises drink.

Your sailors when a-sinking
Have many a trembling heart,
We sink to live in plenty,
Then call ye t' other quart.

They talk of peace in palaces,
I'm sure there's no such thing;
Then who hath most contentment—
A miner or a king?
  Then a-mining we will go,

LEWIS MORRIS (1700-65)

THE BARD

"Ruin seize thee, ruthless King!
Confusion on thy banners wait,
Tho' fanned by Conquest's crimson wing
They mock the air with idle state.
Helm, nor Hauberk's twisted mail,
Nor even thy virtues, Tyrant, shall avail
To save thy secret soul from nightly fears,
From Cambria's curse, from Cambria's tears!"
Such were the sounds, that o'er the crested pride
Of the first Edward scatter'd wild dismay,
As down the steep of Snowdon's shaggy side
He wound with toilsome march his long array.
Stout Glo'ster stood aghast in speechless trance:
To arms! cried Mortimer, and couch'd his quivering
lance.

On a rock, whose haughty brow
Frowns o'er old Conway's foaming flood,
Robed in the sable garb of woe,
With haggard eyes the Poet stood;
(Loose his beard, and hoary hair
Streamed, like a meteor, to the troubled air.)
And with a Master's hand, and Prophet's fire
Struck the deep sorrows of his lyre.
"Hark, how each giant-oak, and desert cave,
Sighs to the torrent's aweful voice beneath!
O'er thee, oh King! their hundred arms they wave,
Revenge, on thee in hoarser murmurs breath;
Vocal no more, since Cambria's fatal day,
To high-born Hoel's harp, or soft Llewellyn's lay.

"Cold is Cadwallo's tongue,
That hush'd the stormy main:
Brave Urien sleeps upon his craggy bed:

Mountains, ye mourn in vain
Modred, whose magic song
Made huge Plinlimon bow his cloud-top'd head.
On dreary Arvon's shore they lie,
Smear'd with gore, and ghastly pale:
Far, far aloof th' affrighted ravens sail;
The famished Eagle screams, and passes by.
Dear lost companions of my tuneful art,
Dear, as the light that visits these sad eyes,
Dear, as the ruddy drops that warm my heart,
Ye died amidst your dying country's cries—
No more I weep. They do not sleep.
On yonder cliffs, a griesly band,
  I see them sit, they linger yet,
Avengers of their native land:
With me in dreadful harmony they join,
And weave with bloody hands the tissue of thy line."

"Weave the warp, and weave the woof,
The winding-sheet of Edward's race.
Give ample room, and verge enough
The characters of hell to trace.
Mark the year, and mark the night,
When Severn shall re-echo with affright
The shrieks of death, thro' Berkley's roofs that ring,
Shrieks of an agonizing King!
She-Wolf of France, with unrelenting fangs,
That tear'st the bowels of thy mangled Mate,
From thee be born, who o'er thy country hangs
The scourge of Heaven. What Terrors round him wait!
Amazement in his van, with Flight combined,
And sorrow's faded form, and solitude behind.

"Mighty Victor, mighty Lord,
Low on his funeral couch he lies!
No pitying heart, no eye, afford
A tear to grace his obsequies.

Is the sable Warrior fled?
Thy son is gone. He rests among the dead.
The Swarm, that in thy noon-tide beam were born?
Gone to salute the rising Morn.
Fair laughs the Morn, and soft the Zephyr blows,
While proudly riding o'er the azure realm
In gallant trim the gilded Vessel goes;
Youth on the prow, and Pleasure at the helm;
Regardless of the sweeping Whirlwind's sway,
That, hush'd in grim repose, expects his evening prey.

"Fill high the sparkling bowl,
The rich repast prepare,
Reft of a crown, he yet may share the feast:
Close by the regal chair
Fell Thirst and Famine scowl
A baleful smile upon their baffled Guest.
Heard ye the din of battle bray,
Lance to lance, and horse to horse?
Long years of havock urge their destined course,
And thro' the kindred squadrons mow their way.
Ye Towers of Julius, London's lasting shame,
With many a foul and midnight murther fed,
Revere his Consort's faith, his Father's fame,
And spare the meek Usurper's holy head.
Above, below, the rose of snow,
Twined with her blushing foe, we spread:
The bristled Boar in infant-gore
Wallows beneath the thorny shade.
Now, Brothers, bending o'er th' accursed loom,
Stamp we our vengeance deep, and ratify his doom.

"Edward, lo! to sudden fate
(Weave we the woof. The thread is spun)
Half of thy heart we consecrate.
(The web is wove. The work is done.)"
Stay, oh stay! nor thus forlorn

Leave me unbless'd, unpitied, here to mourn:
In yon bright track, that fires the western skies,
They melt, they vanish from my eyes.
But oh! what solemn scenes on Snowdon's height
Descending slow their glitt'ring skirts unroll?
Visions of glory, spare my aching sight,
Ye unborn Ages, crowd not on my soul!
No more our long-lost Arthur we bewail.
All-hail, ye genuine Kings, Britannia's Issue, hail!

"Girt with many a Baron bold
Sublime their starry fronts they rear;
And gorgeous Dames, and Statesmen old
In bearded majesty, appear.
In the midst a Form divine!
Her eye proclaims her of the Briton-line;
Her lyon-port, her awe-commanding face,
Attemper'd sweet to virgin-grace.
What strings symphonious tremble in the air,
What strains of vocal transport round her play!
Hear from the grave, great Taliesin, hear;
They breathe a soul to animate thy clay.
Bright Rapture calls, and soaring, as she sings,
Waves in the eye of Heav'n her many-coloured wings.

"The verse adorn again
Fierce War, and faithful Love,
And Truth severe, by fairy Fiction drest.
In buskined measures move
Pale Grief, and pleasing Pain.
With Horrour, Tyrant of the throbbing breast,
A voice, as of the Cherub-Choir,
Gales from blooming Eden bear;
And distant warblings lessen on my ear,
That lost in long futurity expire.
Fond impious man, think'st thou, yon sanguine cloud,
Rais'd by thy breath, has quenched the Orb of day?

Tomorrow he repairs the golden flood,
And warms the nations with redoubled ray.
Enough for me: With joy I see
The different doom our Fates assign.
Be thine Despair, and scept'red Care,
To triumph, and to die, are mine."
He spoke, and headlong from the mountain's height
Deep in the roaring tide he plunged to endless night.

THOMAS GRAY (1716-71)

THE WAR-SONG OF DINAS VAWR

The mountain sheep are sweeter,
But the valley sheep are fatter;
We therefore deemed it meeter
To carry off the latter.
We made an expedition;
We met a host and quelled it;
We forced a strong position,
And killed the men who held it.

On Dyfed's richest valley,
Where herds of kine were brousing,
We made a mighty sally
To furnish our carousing.
Fierce warriors rushed to meet us;
We met them, and o'erthrew them:
They struggled hard to beat us;
But we conquered them, and slew them.

As we drove our prize at leisure,
The king marched forth to catch us:
His rage surpassed all measure,
But his people could not match us.

He fled to his hall-pillars;
And, ere our force we led off,
Some sacked his house and cellars,
While others cut his head off.

We there, in strife bewildering,
Spilt blood enough to swim in:
We orphaned many children,
And widowed many women.
The eagles and the ravens
We glutted with our foemen;
The heroes and the cravens,
The spearmen and the bowmen.

We brought away from battle,
And much their land bemoaned them,
Two thousand head of cattle,
And the head of him who owned them:
Ednyfed, king of Dyfed,
His head was borne before us;
His wine and beasts supplied our feasts,
And his overthrow, our chorus.

THOMAS LOVE PEACOCK (1785-1866)
The Misfortunes of Elphin

THE LADY OF SHALOTT

Part One

On either side the river lie
Long fields of barley and of rye,
That clothe the wold and meet the sky;
And thro' the field the road runs by
    To many-tower'd Camelot;

And up and down the people go,
Gazing where the lilies blow
Round an island there below,
The island of Shalott.

Willows whiten, aspens quiver,
Little breezes dusk and shiver
Thro' the wave that runs for ever
By the island in the river
Flowing down to Camelot.
Four gray walls, and four gray towers,
Overlook a space of flowers,
And the silent isle imbowers
The Lady of Shalott.

By the margin, willow-veil'd,
Slide the heavy barges trail'd
By slow horses; and unhail'd
The shallop flitteth silken-sail'd
Skimming down to Camelot:
But who hath seen her wave her hand?
Or at the casement seen her stand?
Or is she known in all the land,
The Lady of Shalott?

Only reapers, reaping early
In among the bearded barley,
Hear a song that echoes cheerly
From the river winding clearly,
Down to tower'd Camelot:
And by the moon the reaper weary,
Piling sheaves in uplands airy,
Listening, whispers "'Tis the fairy
Lady of Shalott."

Part Two

There she weaves by night and day
A magic web with colours gay.
She has heard a whisper say,
A curse is on her if she stay
    To look down to Camelot.
She knows not what the curse may be,
And so she weaveth steadily,
And little other care hath she,
    The Lady of Shalott.

And moving thro' a mirror clear
That hangs before her all the year,
Shadows of the world appear.
There she sees the highway near
    Winding down to Camelot:
There the river eddy whirls,
And there the surly village-churls,
And the red cloaks of market girls,
    Pass onward from Shalott.

Sometimes a troop of damsels glad,
An abbot on an ambling pad,
Sometimes a curly shepherd-lad,
Or long-hair'd page in crimson clad,
    Goes by to tower'd Camelot;
And sometimes thro' the mirror blue
The knights come riding two and two:
She hath no loyal knight and true,
    The Lady of Shalott.

But in her web she still delights
To weave the mirror's magic sights,
For often thro' the silent nights
A funeral, with plumes and lights,
    And music, went to Camelot:

Or when the moon was overhead,
Came two young lovers lately wed;
"I am half-sick of shadows," said
The Lady of Shalott.

Part Three

A bow-shot from her bower-eaves,
He rode between the barley-sheaves,
The sun came dazzling thro' the leaves,
And flamed upon the brazen greaves,
Of bold Sir Lancelot.
A red-cross knight for ever kneel'd
To a lady in his shield,
That sparkled on the yellow field,
Beside remote Shalott.

The gemmy bridle glitter'd free,
Like to some branch of stars we see
Hung in the golden Galaxy.
The bridle bells rang merrily
As he rode down to Camelot:
And from his blazon'd baldric slung
A mighty silver bugle hung,
And as he rode his armour rung,
Beside remote Shalott.

All in the blue unclouded weather
Thick-jewell'd shone the saddle-leather,
The helmet and the helmet-feather
Burn'd like one burning flame together,
As he rode down to Camelot.
As often thro' the purple night,
Below the starry clusters bright,
Some bearded meteor, trailing light,
Moves over still Shalott.

His broad clear brow in sunlight glow'd,
On burnish'd hooves his war-horse trode;
From underneath his helmet flow'd
His coal-black curls as on he rode,
As he rode down to Camelot.
From the bank and from the river
He flash'd into the crystal mirror,
"Tirra lirra," by the river
Sang Sir Lancelot.

She left the web, she left the loom,
She made three paces thro' the room,
She saw the water-lily bloom,
She saw the helmet and the plume,
She look'd down to Camelot.
Out flew the web, and floated wide;
The mirror crack'd from side to side:
"The curse is come upon me," cried
The Lady of Shalott.

Part Four

In the stormy east-wind straining,
The pale yellow woods were waning,
The broad stream in his banks complaining,
Heavily the low sky raining
Over tower'd Camelot;
Down she came and found a boat
Beneath a willow left afloat,
And round about the prow she wrote
The Lady of Shalott.

And down the river's dim expanse—
Like some bold seër in a trance,
Seeing all his own mischance—
With a glassy countenance
Did she look to Camelot.

And at the closing of the day
She loosed the chain, and down she lay;
The broad stream bore her far away,
The Lady of Shalott.

Lying, robed in snowy white
That loosely flew to left and right—
The leaves upon her falling light—
Thro' the noises of the night
She floated down to Camelot:
And as the boat-head wound along
The willowy hills and fields among,
They heard her singing her last song,
The Lady of Shalott.

Heard a carol, mournful, holy,
Chanted loudly, chanted lowly,
Till her blood was frozen slowly,
And her eyes were darken'd wholly,
Turn'd to tower'd Camelot.
For ere she reach'd upon the tide
The first house by the water-side,
Singing in her song she died,
The Lady of Shalott.

Under tower and balcony,
By garden-wall and gallery,
A gleaming shape she floated by,
Dead-pale between the houses high,
Silent into Camelot.
Out upon the wharfs they came
Knight and burgher, lord and dame,
And round the prow they read her name,
The Lady of Shalott.

Who is this? and what is here?
And in the lighted palace near
Died the sound of royal cheer;
And they cross'd themselves for fear,
    All the knights at Camelot:
But Lancelot mused a little space;
He said, "She has a lovely face;
God in his mercy lend her grace,
    The Lady of Shalott."

ALFRED, LORD TENNYSON (1809-92)

A LOVE SONG

Didst thou love me still but a little, Menna,
    Thou'ldst come as of yore
Past the sedgy banks and the weed-strewn reaches
    To the windy shore.
The pale sea-holly is sick for thy coming
    When I come alone,
And I—ah me!—but what shall I answer,
    My own, my own!

Out there on the river young lovers are rowing,
    As we two of yore,
With hands enwoven, and merry laughter
    As oar strikes oar.
Each, each has a mate—the sailor, the seamew—
    But I am alone;
O joy wouldst thou come to my boat and my bosom,
    My own, my own!

EIFION WYN (ELISEUS WILLIAMS, 1867-1926)
translated from the Welsh by
SIR H. IDRIS BELL

DAYS THAT HAVE BEEN

Can I forget the sweet days that have been,
  When poetry first began to warm my blood;
When from the hills of Gwent I saw the earth
  Burned into two by Severn's silver flood:

When I would go alone at night to see
  The moonlight, like a big white butterfly,
Dreaming on that old castle near Caerleon,
  While at its side the Usk went softly by:

When I would stare at lovely clouds in Heaven,
  Or watch them when reported by deep streams;
When feeling pressed like thunder, but would not
  Break into that grand music of my dreams?

Can I forget the sweet days that have been,
  The villages so green I have been in;
Llantarnam, Magor, Malpas and Llanwern,
  Liswery, old Caerleon, and Alteryn?

Can I forget the banks of Malpas Brook,
  Or Ebbw's voice in such a wild delight,
As on he dashed with pebbles in his throat,
  Gurgling towards the sea with all his might?

Ah, when I see a leafy village now,
  I sigh and ask it for Llantarnam's green;
I ask each river where is Ebbw's voice—
  In memory of the sweet days that have been.

W. H. DAVIES (1871-1940)

THE RETURN

Not for a moment can earth's clamour break
The silence of the heavens; though untold
The voices here below can never shake
The trackless unscarred heights that all enfold;
Nor can the factions rife of mortal man
Impair the quietness, nor aught avail
To deviate those orbs a single span
That spin a silence where all sound must fail.
  And as our living, all our days and nights
From our frail birthcry to our last death groan,
Is but a ripple faint, or shadows' flights
Across the cool sheen of the great Alone,
When we perforce slink from our foolish game
We creep but to the stillness whence we came.

T. H. PARRY-WILLIAMS (1887-   )
translated from the Welsh by
D. M. LLOYD

SNOWDROPS

I heard no trumpet sounding
Through winter's sombre tomb,
Nor noise of angels rolling
Grim headstones; in my room
I slept as deeply unconcerned
As Pilate, when there died,
After his base betrayal,
The One they crucified:
But spring's gay resurrection
Stirred all the country-side.
For when I woke at daybreak
And looked towards the moor,

Behold, a thousand snowdrops
Were crowding at my door . . .
"All in their gleaming raiment,
White as the crested wave,
And glorious like their Master
New-risen from the grave."

CYNAN (A. E. JONES, 1895-)
translated from the Welsh by
A. G. PRYS-JONES

FERN HILL

Now as I was young and easy under the apple boughs
About the lilting house and happy as the grass was green,
The night above the dingle starry,
Time let me hail and climb
Golden in the heydays of his eyes,
And honoured among wagons I was prince of the apple towns
And once below a time I lordly had the trees and leaves
Trail with daisies and barley
Down the rivers of the windfall light.

And as I was green and carefree, famous among the barns
About the happy yard and singing as the farm was home,
In the sun that is young once only,
Time let me play and be
Golden in the mercy of his means,
And green and golden I was huntsman and herdsman, the calves
Sang to my horn, the foxes on the hills barked clear and cold,
And the sabbath rang slowly
In the pebbles of the holy streams.

All the sun long it was running, it was lovely, the hay
Fields high as the house, the tunes from the chimneys,
    it was air
        And playing, lovely and watery
            And fire green as grass.
        And nightly under the simple stars
As I rode to sleep the owls were bearing the farm away,
All the moon long I heard, blessed among stables, the
    nightjars
        Flying with the ricks, and the horses
            Flashing into the dark.

And then to awake, and the farm, like a wanderer white
With the dew, come back, the cock on his shoulder; it
    was all
        Shining, it was Adam and maiden,
            The sky gathered again
        And the sun grew round that very day.
So it must have been after the birth of the simple light
In the first, spinning place, the spellbound horses walking
    warm
        Out of the whinnying green stable
            On to the fields of praise.

And honoured among foxes and pheasants by the gay
    house
Under the new made clouds and happy as the heart was
    long,
        In the sun born over and over,
            I ran my heedless ways,
        My wishes raced through the house high hay
And nothing I cared, at my sky blue trades, that time
    allows
In all his tuneful turning so few and such morning
    songs
        Before the children green and golden
            Follow him out of grace.

Nothing I cared, in the lamb white days, that time
would take me
Up to the swallow thronged loft by the shadow of my
hand,
In the moon that is always rising,
Nor that riding to sleep
I should hear him fly with the high fields
And wake to the farm forever fled from the childless
land.
Oh as I was young and easy in the mercy of his means,
Time held me green and dying
Though I sang in my chains like the sea.

DYLAN THOMAS (1914-53)
Deaths and Entrances

REMEMBRANCE

One blissful moment as the sun is setting,
A mellow moment ere the night comes on,
To bring to mind things which are long forgotten,
Now lost in dust of eras that are gone.

Now like the foam breaking on lonely beaches,
Or the wind's song and no one there to hear,
I know they call on us in vain to listen,—
The old forgotten things men loved so dear.

Things wrought through cunning skill in early ages,
Neat little dwellings and resplendent halls,
And well-told stories that are lost for ever,
And olden gods on whom no suppliant calls.

The little words of languages once living,
Lively was then their sound on lips of men,
And pleasing to the ear in children's prattle,
But now, no tongue will fashion them again.

O countless generations of earth's children,
Of dreams divine, and fragile godlikeness,
Is there but stillness for the hearts that quickened,
That knew delight and knew grief's bitterness?

Often when evening falls and I am lonely
I long once more to bring you all to mind,
Pray, is there no-one treasures and holds dear
The old forgotten things of humankind?

WALDO WILLIAMS (1904-)
translated from the Welsh by
D. M. LLOYD

Religious and Philosophical

THE FIRST WORD I WILL SAY

The first word I will say
When I arise at break of day:
'The Cross of Christ be my array.'

My Lord's livery I will wear this morning,
Hark! One sneeze my ears hear!
That's not my God, I will not fear.

Rich in that Robe I can endure;
No portent will I trust one hour:
He who made me will grant me power.

ANONYMOUS
from the *Black Book of Carmarthen*
(12-13th century manuscript)
translated from the Welsh by
D. M. LLOYD

A PIOUS POEM

Because my raiment and my joy are alike worn out
With the sin I have known,
May God not prepare for me a day of suffering;
May God in his wrath and his exasperation not prepare
a day of suffering for man (in the world to come):
Heaven's wretches are wretches on earth.
Let an earthly sinner plead with God,
And let him rise at midnight.
Offenders of Christ, do not sleep!
Let not any man's son sleep to the grief of the Son of
God,

And let him awaken at dawn.
He shall have heaven and mercy;
He shall have mercy who remembers God and does not scorn him, and heaven the night of his death.
If any man's son dies not at peace with God for the sin he has done,
It is not well for him that a soul entered his flesh.
But evil ones do not praise God as protection against a day of woe,
For the fool thinks not that he will die.

ELAETH
from the *Black Book of Carmarthen*
(12th-13th century manuscript)
translated from the Welsh by
D. M. LLOYD

ON CHRISTIANS, MERCY WILL FALL

I sought of bishop and priest and judges
From the west to the east:
'For the good of the soul what course is best?'

Paternoster, 'beati,' and the holy creed
Who chants is well served in his soul's hour of need,
Till Domesday protected in word and deed.

Carve out a way and to it, hold,
And fashion peace, which is richer than gold:
Mercy will never die or grow old.

Give food to the hungry, and the naked clothe,
And sing your devotions with suppliant lip,
You'll escape the grip of the demons you loathe.

The vain have a craving, the idle no less,
To miss the way and to go to excess;
Impure is the grain they winnow and press.

Oversleep, wild feasting and excess of mead,
And unrestrained passion given its head—
Sweet things—but bitter in the Day of Dread.

Betraying one's lord and false swearing for lands,
For the kind with hardness of heart uncaring,
That Day, all these will mean ill-faring.

From midnight devotions and lauds sung at dawn,
And on saints if we call,
On Christians, mercy will fall.

ANONYMOUS
from the *Black Book of Carmarthen*
(12th-13th century manuscript)
translated from the Welsh by
D. M. LLOYD

EPIGRAMS

GOD'S WORD

Men few things see, God all things sees foresees:
Hence men speak often, God but once decrees.

THE HOLY SPIRIT

As Doves to whitest Houses soonest come,
So th' Holy God makes cleanest Hearts his home.

TO PREACHERS

The Cock (the Mornings Herald) claps his wings,
To rouze himself before he Crows or Sings:
Preachers should do the like, first should begin
To rouze themselves; next others raise from sin.

TO CHRIST

Anchor of Hope, Faiths Ship, Loves shoreless Sea,
Earth's Salt, Heavens Sun, the Souls sole saving Plea:
Death, by thy death is kill'd, Death dead doth lie:
Yet who would think that ever Death could die?

STILL THE SAME

One God in all the World was, is, and shall:
Why is not then the same one faith for all?
One faith, like day, the world t' enlighten, even
As one Sun's in the Sky, one God in Heaven.

JOHN OWEN, the Epigrammatist (*c.* 1560-1622)
translated from the Latin by
THOMAS HARVEY

LOVE

Love bade me welcome: yet my soul drew back,
Guiltie of dust and sinne.
But quick-ey'd Love, observing me grow slack
From my first entrance in,
Drew nearer to me, sweetly questioning,
If I lack'd any thing.

A guest, I answer'd, worthy to be here:
Love said, you shall be he.
I the unkinde, ungratefull? Ah my deare,
I cannot look on thee.
Love took my hand, and smiling did reply,
Who made the eyes but I?

Truth Lord, but I have marr'd them: let my shame
Go where it doth deserve.
And know you not, sayes Love, who bore the blame?
My deare, then I will serve.

You must sit down, sayes Love, and taste my meat:
So I did sit and eat.

GEORGE HERBERT (1593-1633)
The Temple

DISCIPLINE

Throw away thy rod,
Throw away thy wrath:
O my God,
Take the gentle path.

For my hearts desire
Unto thine is bent:
I aspire
To a full consent.

Not a word or look
I affect to own,
But by book,
And thy book alone.

Though I fail, I weep:
Though I halt in pace,
Yet I creep
To the throne of grace.

Then let wrath remove;
Love will do the deed:
For with love

Stonie hearts will bleed.
Love is swift of foot;
Love's a man of warre,
And can shoot,
And can hit from farre.

Who can scape his bow?
That which wrought on thee,
Brought thee low,
Needs must work on me.

Throw away thy rod;
Though man frailties hath,
Thou art God:
Throw away thy wrath.

GEORGE HERBERT (1593-1633)
The Temple

THE PULLEY

When God at first made man,
Having a glasse of blessings standing by,
Let us (said he) poure on him all we can.
Let the world's riches, which dispersed lie,
Contract into a span.

So strength first made a way,
Then beautie flow'd, then wisdome, honour, pleasure.
When almost all was out, God made a stay,
Perceiving that alone of all his treasure
Rest in the bottom lay.

For if I should (said he)
Bestow this jewell also on my creature,
He would adore my gifts instead of me,
And rest in Nature, not the God of Nature.
So both should losers be.

Yet let him keep the rest,
But keep them with repining restlessnesse.
Let him be rich and wearie, that at least,
If goodnesse leade him not, yet wearinesse
May tosse him to my breast.

GEORGE HERBERT (1593-1633) *The Temple*

[A. W. Hutton

LLYN IDWAL

[A. W. Hutton

MOEL SIABOD AND RIVER LLUGWY

[*R. Cecil Hughes*

TELFORD'S HIGHWAY, NOW "A5"

Looking towards Capel Curig

WHERE IS CHRIST?

Wonder then, O friends, a little at the Christ, whose name is Wonderful, and limit no more that holy One of Israel in his person, life, death, or will, as we have done; for with him we have dealt as Dalilah did with Sampson. We have tyed him with our cords, and imprisoned him in our confinements. . . . We have studied how to lock up the Sun in our poor chamber, in our opinions, judgements, and Church-fellowships, in our apprehensions of the Scriptures, creatures, and light within. We have attempted to weigh his mountains in our scales, and have baptized our self-conceited mind into the name of the ballance of the Sanctuary, thinking to drink and draught up his ocean in our earthen dishes. . . . But how monstrous a vanity is it to imagine the great Lord Christ cooped up in some closet of heaven, or of one heart, or of one form or opinion? . . .

They, poor souls, intend to set up Christ in their own private way, and to build the great mountain, that shall fill the whole earth, upon their own narrow pinacle of opinion, which building of theirs must fall, because it is not broad enough to undergo the superstructure; and the generation of undergoers have been too narrowly partial. . . . And for things called Ordinances and institutions, be not thou a mocker and scorner, as if all outwards were under thy feet (if it be so indeed, why dost thou eat, drink, sleep, marry, buy, sell, or work in the clay?) let not Satan puff up in thee a vain mind; speak not reproachfully of the outward Bible, nor give it a railing accusation. It proves a tree bearing fruit, and occasioning good thoughts in many (though ink, paper and letter be dead things.) . . .

Art thou so brutish as not to see how dark the people must have been in the history and mysterie of things, if there had never been an outward Bible seen or read among us at all? . . . But for all this, idolize no book; it is not the God that can save thee, nor the word of God that made this world; only instead of vilifying of outward things (as the manner of some is) seek after the Christ who is hid through all these: for Christ filleth the Scripture, Christ appeareth through all Creatures, Christ liveth in all Saints of all forms, Christ supporteth all beings, Christ is all spiritually, and Christ is nothing carnally, Christ is God in the Father, and Christ would become man in thee. His work and his office is reconciling and reaching to bring things distant into one, and to recapitulate all things in heaven and in earth. Therefore must the Lord from heaven become man from earth.

MORGAN LLWYD (1619-59)
Where is Christ?

THEY ARE ALL GONE INTO THE WORLD OF LIGHT!

They are all gone into the world of light!
And I alone sit lingring here;
Their very memory is fair and bright,
And my sad thoughts doth clear.

It glows and glitters in my cloudy brest
Like stars upon some gloomy grove,
Or those faint beams in which this hill is drest,
After the Sun's remove.

I see them walking in an Air of glory,
Whose light doth trample on my days:
My days, which are at best but dull and hoary,
Mere glimmering and decays.

O holy hope! and high humility,
    High as the Heavens above!
These are your walks, and you have shew'd them me
    To kindle my cold love.

Dear, beauteous death! the Jewel of the Just,
    Shining nowhere, but in the dark;
What mysteries do lie beyond thy dust;
    Could man outlook that mark!

He that hath found some fledg'd birds nest, may know
    At first sight, if the bird be flown;
But what fair Well, or Grove he sings in now,
    That is to him unknown.

And yet, as Angels in some brighter dreams
    Call to the soul, when man doth sleep:
So some strange thoughts transcend our wonted theams,
    And into glory peep.

If a star were confin'd into a Tomb
    Her captive flames must needs burn there;
But when the hand that lockt her up, gives room,
    She'll shine through all the sphære.

O Father of eternal life, and all
    Created glories under thee!
Resume thy spirit from this world of thrall
    Into true liberty.

Either disperse these mists, which blot and fill
    My perspective (still) as they pass,
Or else remove me hence unto that hill,
    Where I shall need no glass.

HENRY VAUGHAN, the Silurist (1622-95)
Silex Scintillans

THE RETREATE

Happy those early dayes! when I
Shin'd in my Angell-infancy.
Before I understood this place
Appointed for my second race,
Or taught my soul to fancy ought
But a white, Celestial thought,
When yet I had not walkt above
A mile, or two, from my first love,
And looking back (at that short space,)
Could see a glimpse of his bright-face;
When on some gilded Cloud, or flowre
My gazing soul would dwell an houre,
And in those weaker glories spy
Some shadows of eternity;
Before I taught my tongue to wound
My Conscience with a sinfull sound,
Or had the black art to dispense
A sev'rall sinne to ev'ry sense,
But felt through all this fleshly dresse
Bright shootes of everlastingnesse.
    O how I long to travell back
And tread again that ancient track!
That I might once more reach that plaine,
Where first I left my glorious traine,
From whence th' Inlightned spirit sees
That shady City of Palme trees;
But (ah!) my soul with too much stay
Is drunk, and staggers in the way.
Some men a forward motion love,
But I by backward steps would move,
And when this dust falls to the urn
In that state I came return.

HENRY VAUGHAN, the Silurist (1622-95)
Silex Scintillans

THE WORLD

I saw Eternity the other night
Like a great *Ring* of pure and endless light,
    All calm, as it was bright,
And round beneath it, Time in hours, days, years
    Driv'n by the spheres
Like a vast shadow mov'd, In which the world
    And all her train were hurl'd;
The doting Lover in his quaintest strain
    Did there Complain,
Neer him, his Lute, his fancy, and his flights,
    Wits sour delights,
With gloves, and knots the silly snares of pleasure;
    Yet his dear Treasure
All scatter'd lay, while he his eyes did pour
    Upon a flowr.

The darksome States-man, hung with weights and woe,
Like a thick midnight-fog mov'd there so slow
    He did nor stay, nor go;
Condemning thoughts (like sad Ecclipses) scowl
    Upon his soul,
And Clouds of crying witnesses without
    Pursues him with one shout.
Yet digg'd the Mole, and lest his ways be found
    Workt under ground,
Where he did Clutch his prey, but one did see
    That policie;
Churches and altars fed him, Perjuries
    Were gnats and flies,
It rain'd about him blood and tears, but he
    Drank them as free.

The fearfull miser on a heap of rust
Sate pining all his life there, did scarce trust

His own hands with the dust,
Yet would not place one peece above, but lives
In feare of theeves.
Thousands there were as frantick as himself
And hugg'd each one his pelf,
The down-right Epicure plac'd heav'n in sense
And scornd pretence
While others slipt into a wide Excesse
Said little lesse;
The weaker sort slight, triviall wares inslave
Who think them brave,
And poor, despised truth sate Counting by
Their victory.

Yet some, who all this while did weep and sing,
And sing, and weep, soar'd up into the *Ring*,
But most would use no wing.
O fools (said I), thus to prefer dark night
Before true light,
To live in grots, and caves, and hate the day
Because it shews the way,
The way which from this dead and dark abode
Leads up to God,
A way where you might tread the Sun, and be
More bright than he.
But as I did their madness so discusse
One whisper'd thus,
This Ring the Bride-groome did for none provide
But for his Bride.

1 John, Chap. 2, ver. 16, 17. All that is in the world, the lust of the flesh, the lust of the Eyes, and the pride of life, is not of the father, but is of the world.

And the world passeth away, and the lusts thereof, but he that doth the will of God abideth for ever.

HENRY VAUGHAN, the Silurist (1622-95)
Silex Scintillans

THE BEST EDUCATION

The best education is that which . . . impresses the heart most with the love of virtue, and communicates the most expanded and ardent benevolence; which gives the deepest consciousness of the fallibility of the human understanding, and preserves from that vile dogmatism so prevalent in the world; which makes men diffident and modest, attentive to evidence, capable of proportioning their assent to the degree of it, quick in discerning it, and determined to follow it; which, in short, instead of producing acute casuists, conceited pedants, or furious polemics, produces fair enquirers endowed with that heavenly wisdom described by Saint James, *which is pure, then peaceable, gentle, easy to be entreated, full of mercy and good fruits, without partiality and without hypocrisy.* An education so conducted is the only means of gaining free scope for the progress of truth; of exterminating the pitiful prejudices we indulge against one another; and of establishing peace on earth and goodwill amongst men.

DR. RICHARD PRICE (1723-91)
The Evidence for a future period of improvement in the state of mankind

AN HONEST MIND

Nothing is very important except an honest mind; nothing fundamental except righteous practise, and a sincere desire to know and to do the will of God. I wish earnestly I could be, in any degree, the means of propagating this conviction. There is nothing by which any one can better serve the essential interests of society.

DR. RICHARD PRICE (1723-91)
The Evidence for a future period of improvement in the state of mankind

I GAZE ACROSS THE DISTANT HILLS

I gaze across the distant hills,
    Thy coming to espy;
Beloved, haste, the day grows late,
    The sun sinks down the sky.

All the old loves I followed once
    Are now unfaithful found;
But a sweet sickness holds me yet
    Of love that has no bound!

Love that the sensual heart ne'er knows,
    Such power, such grace it brings,
Which sucks desire and thought away
    From all created things.

O make me faithful while I live,
    Attuned but to thy praise,
And may no pleasure born of earth
    Entice to devious ways.

All my affections now withdraw
    From objects false, impure,
To the one object which unchanged
    Shall to the last endure.

There is no station under heaven
    Where I have lust to live;
Only the mansions of God's house
    Can perfect pleasure give.

Regard is dead and lust is dead
    For the world's gilded toys;
Her ways are nought but barrenness,
    And vain are all her joys.

WILLIAM WILLIAMS OF PANTYCELYN (1717-91)
translated from the Welsh by SIR H. IDRIS BELL

LO, BETWEEN THE MYRTLES

Lo, between the myrtles standing,
One who merits well my love,
Though His worth I guess but dimly,
High all earthly things above;
Happy morning
When at last I see him clear!

Rose of Sharon, so men name Him;
White and red His cheeks adorn;
Store untold of earthly treasure
Will His merit put to scorn;
Friend of sinners,
He their pilot o'er the deep.

What can weigh with me henceforward
All the idols of the earth?
One and all I here proclaim them,
Matched with Jesus, nothing worth;
O to rest me
All my lifetime in His love!

ANN GRIFFITHS (1776-1805)
translated from the Welsh by
SIR H. IDRIS BELL

GUIDE ME, O THOU GREAT JEHOVAH

Guide me, O Thou great Jehovah,
Pilgrim through this barren land;
I am weak, but Thou art mighty;
Hold me with Thy powerful hand:
Bread of heaven,
Feed me now and evermore.

Open now the crystal fountain,
  Whence the healing stream doth flow;
Let the fiery cloudy pillar
  Lead me all my journey through:
      Strong Deliverer,
  Be Thou still my strength and shield.

When I tread the verge of Jordan,
  Bid my anxious fears subside;
Death of death, and hell's Destruction,
  Land me safe on Canaan's side.
      Songs of praises
  I will ever give to Thee.

WILLIAM WILLIAMS OF PANTYCELYN (1716-91)

A MISSIONARY HYMN

O'er those gloomy hills of darkness
  Look, my soul; be still, and gaze;
All the promises do travail
  With a glorious day of grace:
      Blessed Jubil
  Let thy glorious morning dawn.

Kingdoms wide that sit in darkness,
  Let them have the glorious light;
And from eastern coast to western
  May the morning chase the night,
      And redemption,
  Freely purchased win the day.

Lord, I long to see that morning,
  When Thy Gospel shall abound,
And Thy grace get full possession
  Of the happy promised ground;
      All the borders
  Of the great Immanuel's land.

Fly abroad, eternal gospel,
  Win and conquer, never cease;
May thy lasting wide dominions
  Multiply and still increase;
      May thy sceptre
Sway the enlightened world around.

WILLIAM WILLIAMS OF PANTYCELYN (1716-91)

RICHES AND POVERTY

(A portion of an *Interlude*)

Riches

Thus all things created, the God of all grace,
Of four prime materials, each good in its place.
The work of His hands, when completed He view'd,
And saw and pronounc'd that 'twas seemly and good.

Poverty

In the marvellous things, which to me thou hast told
The wisdom of God I most clearly behold,
And did He not also make man of the same
Materials He us'd when the world He did frame?

Riches

Creation is all, as the sages agree,
Of the elements four in man's body that be;
Water's the blood, and fire is the nature
Which prompts generation in every creature.

The earth is the flesh which with beauty is rife,
The air is the breath, without which is no life;
So man must be always accounted the same
As the substances four which exist in his frame.

And as in their creation distinction there's none
'Twixt man and the world, so the Infinite One
Unto man a clear wisdom did bounteously give
The nature of every thing to perceive.

Poverty

But one thing to me passing strange doth appear:
Since the wisdom of man is so bright and so clear,
How comes there such jarring and warring to be
In the world betwixt Riches and Poverty?

Riches

That point we'll discuss without passion or fear,
With the aim of instructing the listeners here;
And haply some few who instruction require
May profit derive like the bee from the briar.

Man as thou knowest, in his generation
Is a type of the world and of all the creation;
Difference there's none in the manner of birth
'Twixt the lowliest hinds and the lords of the earth.

The world which the same thing as man we account
In one place is sea, in another is mount;
A part of it rock, and a part of it dale—
God's wisdom has made every place to avail.

There exist precious treasures of every kind
Profoundly in earth's quiet bosom enshrin'd;
There's searching about them, and ever has been,
And by some they are found, and by some never seen.

With wonderful wisdom the Lord God on high
Has contriv'd the two lights which exist in the sky;
The sun's hot as fire, and its ray bright as gold,
But the moon's ever pale, and by nature is cold.

The sun, which resembles a huge world of fire,
Would burn up full quickly creation entire
Save the moon with it's temp'rament cool did assuage
Of its brighter companion the fury and rage.

Now I beg you the sun and the moon to behold,
The one that's so bright, and the other so cold,
And say if two things in creation there be
Better emblems of Riches and Poverty.

Poverty

In manner most brief, yet convincing and clear,
You have told the whole truth to my wond'ring ear,
And I see that 'twas God, who in all things is fair,
Has assign'd us the forms, in this world which we bear.

Riches

You know that full oft, in their course as they run,
An eclipse cometh over the moon or the sun;
Certain hills of the earth with their summits of pride
The face of the one from the other do hide.

The sun doth uplift his magnificent head,
And illumines the moon, which were otherwise dead,
Even as Wealth from its station on high,
Giveth work and provision to Poverty.

Poverty

I know, and the thought mighty sorrow instils,
The sins of the world are the terrible hills
An eclipse which do cause, or a dread obscuration,
To one or another in every vocation.

Riches

It is true that God gives unto each from his birth
Some task to perform whilst he wends upon earth,
But He gives correspondent wisdom and force
To the weight of the task, and the length of the course.
(EXIT)

Poverty

I hope there are some who 'twixt me and the youth
Have heard this discourse, whose sole aim is the truth,
Will see and acknowledge, as homeward they plod,
Each thing is arrang'd by the wisdom of God.

TWM O'R NANT (THOMAS EDWARDS, 1738-1810)
Riches and Poverty, an Interlude
translated from the Welsh by GEORGE BORROW

A WELSH SERMON

The prayer ended, the old man of benign aspect entered the pulpit, and gave out his text. I was at first too much occupied with my own thoughts to pay close attention to his discourse, but before long the charm of his manner compelled me to listen. His address was a plain homely discourse upon Our Lord's words to the Woman of Samaria; nothing could have been less ornate—it was a plain unvarnished tale. But I could see that he was a master of the art of oratory; he understood his audience and spoke to their understanding, but he possessed the rare faculty of speaking to the level of a rustic audience without becoming either puerile in simplicity or coarse in vulgarity. His language was pure, though colloquial; his voice was pleasing and flexible; he had something in his voice of the minor chant which is so sweet to Welsh ears—though he was not violent in his gestures nor loud in his tones. By a quiet discourse, a discourse so quiet as to seem strange in a Methodist pulpit, he moved his audience in a powerful manner, and at the end of his sermon, which seemed to have lasted but a few minutes, he had not excited his hearers to hysterics, but he did what was better than that—he led those worn sons of toil over hallowed ground and guided them for one brief while by the still waters "of which, if a man drink, he shall never thirst."

ROBERT ROBERTS (1834-85)
The Life and Opinions of R. R., a wandering scholar . . .

A CHRISTIAN WOMAN

"Think of your mother" said he. "Did you ever meet anyone who knew so much suffering? And yet did anyone enjoy more true happiness? Where did it spring from? From looking into herself? Not a bit of it! She had learnt to look on One who is worth looking at. I always felt that the greater her trials, the greater was her joy. Her poverty only made her mind dwell on the riches which are in Christ. . . . Don't take offence, now, but the fact is that whenever I heard that your mother was in trouble, I would laugh and say, 'Well, this is another feast for Mary Lewis!' . . . Never in my life did I see anyone who could live so completely as she could on the resources of her religion. In a way of speaking, she had no business to die when she did. She was not old, and she suffered from no disease. 'Abel,' she told me, when she went to live in Thomas Bartley's house, 'there is no reason, is there, why one who possesses all things should lean on the parish? Never will I accept one penny from the parish, and that's a fact for you.' Nor did she, as you well know. I've often thought of her. When she saw that she would soon have to depend on parish relief, it had as powerful an effect on her as the husks on the prodigal son. I can imagine her saying, 'Hold on, relieving officer! This fare is an insult to my family. I will arise and go unto my Father.' I can't help feeling that your mother chose to die in order to experience the truth of the Promise that the righteous would not be found begging his bread. . . . I don't exactly commend your mother for that. But you know, there is something in religion of the finest quality that makes one fearfully independent of this world and its things!"

DANIEL OWEN (1836-95)
Rhys Lewis
translated from the Welsh by
D. M. LLOYD

JERUSALEM

My cry is for my city
  As desert sands I plod,
Jerusalem, my homeland,
  The city of my God.
When will my eyelids open,
  When will my head find rest,
In thee, my own true city,
  Jerusalem, the blest?

Grant me the living waters,
  The bread of life I crave,
I would be with my Saviour
  Who rules that city brave.
Outside the gate I'm knocking,
  Lord, open Thou the gate;
The Temple and the Sabbath
  Be ever my estate.

While earth remains my dwelling
  I wait that morning's light,
When I shall see descending
  Jerusalem the bright;
Although the heavens glower,
  And dark the clouds may be,
I sing, and trust as ever,
  Jerusalem to see.

Though heavy be my hearing,
  And though my eyes are weak,
I hear and see in Promise
  The city that I seek:

I see the walls of Zion,
  I hear the Jubilee,
I scan the Holy City,
  Jerusalem I see.

J. CEIRIOG HUGHES (1832-87)
translated from the Welsh by
D. M. LLOYD

INTIMATIONS

We have no certainty the soul but dreams
When it arises far above this life,
Above man's journey from the cradle to the grave,
Whispering of things that words will not reveal
Though we may force them far beyond their limits
Like stars into the vast eternal space.

Has not the soul a story of its own?

A dark ebb strangely murmurs in its depths
On distant shores we cannot reach, on shores
Where Memory was lost in wrecks stupendous
Of some great world or worlds.

Are the stars above
As splendid and divine as poets sing?
Their power sublime on our responding spirit
May it not be the hold of memories dim
Of far diviner scenes, radiant of God?
The stars are in us! And all poetry
Is but the recollection of our past,
Or premonition of what we shall be.

What mortal man lives now who never feels
The sudden spin of a long forgotten world
Flashing across his path, strangely familiar,
Or brushing the tip of a long promontory
Of memories?

Our imaginings, who can
Prove or disprove they are the fragments strewn
On a deep sea, the wreck of a nobler life,
And that the soul in stupor lies, until
Restored by the ever-seeking, living breath
Of poetry? O blessed hour, when God
Appears, a Sun in Majesty above
Earth's many days, and the Holy Spirit's path
A ray of light on the world's broken tracks
Lighting the way back to those heights Divine!

ISLWYN (WILLIAM THOMAS, 1832-78)
translated from the Welsh by
D. M. LLOYD

CHURCH-MEMBERSHIP

They were ' members ' of their church, and not merely ' hearers ' or ' adherents.' And to be a ' member ' of a dissenting church meant a good deal in those days. It meant much more than partaking of the sacrament when the communion was celebrated, and the little, cheap, ordinary, earthenware sacramental cup was passed around, from lip to lip. The ' members ' were a select few, who stayed behind for more intimate spiritual communion when the mass of the congregation walked out at the end of the sermon. There was hardly one of them who could not point back to the very day of his conversion or at least to a period when the sense of sin or the fear of hell,—yielding place sometimes after many weeks of torture to a consciousness of forgiveness, a great peace and a deep joy—overwhelmed the soul. That the conversion was sincere could hardly be doubted, for nothing was to be gained at that time by pretending to be a converted dissenter and much might be lost. Conversion thus meant that those who experienced it had really felt, in some fashion or another, the power of the things of the spirit, and had from that day on dedicated themselves to religion. Their homes were sacred with the daily prayers offered in them morning and evening, and sometimes at mid-day; and their knowledge of the Bible was marvellous. They read nothing else, of course, and they read it very closely; for was not every word in it 'the word of God?' My grandfather, on my mother's side, could turn at once to any verse you might want, and tell you before-hand on what page of his own big Bible it was to be found and whether at the top, middle, or bottom.

SIR HENRY JONES (1852-1922)
Old Memories

THE TRUE AND THE GOOD

The necessities of the intelligence are thus, in the last resort, the same as those of morality and religion. The True and The Good make the same claim to systematic wholeness: that is to say, the former must make room for *all* facts and the latter for *all* values. Neither can stop short of the absolute. It is not a moral one-sidedness, however pre-eminent, that can satisfy—a justice that is not also mercy, a kindness or generosity that is not just. As a matter of fact, the virtues at their best not only hold hands, but, as Plato shows, pass into one another. Temperance will turn under our very hands into courage, courage into wisdom, and any or all of them into unselfish regard for one's neighbour and service of the State. And vices, I need hardly say, pass into and generate one another in the same way. This is inevitable. For the virtues are manifestations of the same ultimate principle, are elements within the same whole, and therefore are only by help of one another.

SIR HENRY JONES (1852-1922)
A Faith that Enquires

A FRIENDLY UNIVERSE[1]

I have somewhere compared the soul of man to a city with many gates, situated on a plain and besieged by the benevolent powers of his world. Both nature and spirit, both the world of things and the world of men are perpetually proffering their gifts to him, and in the most diverse ways. If their truth and beauty and value cannot get in by one gate, they may by another. If they cannot force a passage, panoplied in the armour of reason, they may creep in through the darkness and silence like the mist into Milton's Eden. The æsthetic sense may give them entrance. He who is slow to hear the voice of truth speaking of morality and religion, and who is callous to all reasoning may hear them in music, or recognise their appeal in colour and form. The truth I would impress is *the friendliness* of the world to man, the co-operation and final identity of the purposes of nature and spirit. The contrast is real, but it is not absolute.

SIR HENRY JONES (1852-1922)
A Faith that Enquires

[1]The author wrote these words, and delivered them in a course of Gifford Lectures at a time when he was suffering from cancer in the throat and knew that he had but a short time to live.

EPILOGUE

Still the mighty mountains stand,
Round them still the tempests roar;
Still with dawn through all the land
Sing the shepherds as of yore.
Round the foot of hill and scar
Daisies still their buds unfold;
Changed the shepherds only are
On those mighty mountains old.

Passing with the passing years
Ancient customs change and flow;
Fraught with doom of joy or tears,
Generations come and go.
Out of tears' and tempests' reach
Alun Mabon sleeps secure;—
Still lives on the ancient speech,
Still the ancient songs endure.

J. CEIRIOG HUGHES (1832-87)
translated from the Welsh by
SIR H. IDRIS BELL

NOTE ON PRONUNCIATION OF WELSH

Welsh orthography is very regular and 'phonetic.' The vowels are invariably pure (except where diphthongs are shown by the placing together of two vowels). *A*, *e*, *i*, and *o* bear approximately their Italian values, and vary only in length, for they can be either long or short. *I* and *w* can be semi-consonants, in which case they have, respectively, the values of *y* and *w* in the English words, *yoke* and *wake*. Vocalic *w* resembles *-ough* in *through*, or more nearly the French *-ou* in *sou*; *y* is sometimes 'obscure' and then resembles *u* in the English word *fur*, or when short the *o* in *ivory*; Welsh *u* and the 'clear' *y* are pronounced in South Wales like Welsh *i*, but in North Wales they are sounded further back towards the throat, with raised tongue and unrounded lips. In words of more than one syllable the accent is on the penultimate (except in many compound place-names, and in a few words where the last two syllables have been compressed into one). It should be noted, however, that the distinctiveness and purity of all unaccented vowels is fully maintained.

The following consonants are sounded very nearly as in English: *b*, *c* (always hard as in *can*), *d*, *g*, *ng* (as in *sing*), *h*, *l*, *m*, *n*, *p*, *ph* (as in *photograph*), *s*, *t*. In North Wales, however, *d* and *t* are dentals as in France and Italy, and not palatals (or alveolar, to be exact) as in English and in South Wales. The Welsh *s* is always hard, as in *sea*, never soft as in *rose*, and is more heavily stressed than in English. The aspirate is always clearly heard in correctly spoken Welsh, both in initial and medial positions, even after consonants such as in *fy mhen* (my head); but *ch*, *th*, and *rh* are single sounds, *ch* as in Scottish *loch*, *th* as in English *thick* (never as in *they*), and *rh* being an aspirated *r*, the trill and the aspiration heard simultaneously. The unaspirated *r* is always distinctly trilled and never elided as in southern English. A single *f* denotes an English *v*; the English *f* is shown in Welsh as *ff*. The Welsh *dd* always denotes the soft *th* as in English *the* or *they*. There is no English sound resembling the Welsh *ll* which is an aspirated *l*, and which can be approached by very rapidly pronouncing *tl* as if they were one sound, with a strong aspiration and unvoiced.

From the above remarks it can be seen that the very frequently occurring Welsh personal name, DAFYDD is pronounced D á v *i* th (with an open *a* as in *piano*, and the *th* as in *they*). When we also bear in mind that a purely dental *d* sounds harder than the normal English *d*, and that in some dialects there is a tendency to drop *dd* in the final position, it can well be understood that this Welsh form for *David* would strike an English ear as *Taffy*!

EDITORS

1284 Statute of Rhuddlan. Edward I's 'New Order' in Wales.

1287 Rebellion of Rhys ap Maredudd.

1301 King of England's eldest son styled Prince of Wales.

1363 Appearance in Wales of Owain Lawgoch (Ywain of Wales).

1372 Abortive expedition of Owain from Harfleur.

1378 Assassination of Owain at Mortaine-sur-Garonne.

1400 Owain Glyn Dŵr (Glendower) raises his standard.

1403 Battle of Shrewsbury.

1404 Glyn Dŵr's Council at Machynlleth. French allies land at Milford Haven.

c. 1416 Death of Owain Glyn Dŵr in hiding.

c. 1430 Owain Tudor marries Catherine, widow of Henry V.

c. 1430 Carmarthen Eisteddfod.

1456 Henry Tudor (afterwards Henry VII) born in Pembroke Castle.

1461 Mortimer's Cross. Rise of Yorkists.

1469 Banbury. Death of William Herbert, Earl of Pembroke, and many of the Welsh nobility.

1471 Tewkesbury. Jasper and Henry Tudor in exile.

1485 Bosworth Field. Henry Tudor King of England.

1523 First Caerwys Eisteddfod.

1526 Death of Sir Rhys ap Thomas.

1531 Execution of Sir Rhys ap Gruffudd.

1534 Bishop Rowland Lee President Court of the Marches.

1536 Suppression of monasteries. Act of Union.

1547 First Welsh printed books.

1567 Welsh New Testament, and first printed Welsh grammar.

1568 Second Caerwys Eisteddfod.

1588 First Welsh Bible.

1593 Execution of John Penry, Puritan martyr.

1603 Unicorn replaces dragon on Royal Arms.

1621 Welsh metrical Psalter.

1630 First edition of Welsh Bible for home reading.

1639 First Independent Church in Wales (Llanfaches).

1647 Surrender of Harlech Castle by William Owen.

1649 First Baptist Church in Wales (Ilston).

1650 Act for Propagation of the Gospel in Wales.

1674 Welsh Trust (Schools and Welsh Books).

1699 S.P.C.K. (Schools and Welsh Books).

1107 Edward Lhuyd's *Archaeologia Britannica* (Foundation of modern Welsh scholarship).

1718 Printing press on Welsh soil.

1735 Beginnings of Welsh Methodism. First Welsh periodical.

1737 Circulating schools.

1742 Welsh Calvinistic Methodist Association.

1744 First publication of hymns by Pantycelyn.

1751 Cymmrodorion Society.
1785 'Welsh method' of iron puddling—expansion of iron industry.
1792 Bardic Gorsedd on Primrose Hill, London.
1795 Earliest political pamphlets in Welsh (Radical).
1797 French landing at Fishguard.
1804 Trevithick's steam locomotive at Quaker's Yard.
1811 First Calvinistic Methodist ordinations in Wales (Break with Established Church).
1826 Telford's Menai Suspension Bridge.
1830 Abolition of Welsh Courts of Great Sessions.
1831 Merthyr riots, and hanging of Dic Penderyn.
1839 Chartist Riots. Opening of Bute Docks, Cardiff.
1843 Rebecca Riots. Hugh Owen's letter on education, and consequent increase of schools. First publication of *Yr Amserau* and *Y Cronicl* (great advance of vernacular 'Radical' press).
1847 'Treason of the Blue Books.'
1858 Llangollen Eisteddfod. (First on 'National' scale.)
1867 Welsh Colony in Patagonia.
1868 Return of 22 Welsh Liberal members, including Henry Richard, 'Apostle of Peace.'
1872 University College of Wales, Aberystwvth.
1883 University College, Cardiff.
1884 University College, Bangor.
1886 T. E. Ellis, M.P. for Merioneth.
1888 'Welsh' made a 'class subject' in schools of Wales.
1889 Welsh Intermediate Education Act. County Councils.
1890 D. Lloyd George M.P. for Caernarvon Boroughs.
1893 Charter of University of Wales.
1895 'Cymru Fydd' National Federation.
1898 South Wales Miners' Federation.
1900 Keir Hardie M.P. for Merthyr (First Labour member).
1902 Bangor Eisteddfod (Landmark of modern literary renaissance).
1907 Welsh Dept. of Board of Education. Charters of National Library of Wales and National Museum.
1911 National Health Insurance Commission (Wales).
1919 Welsh Board of Health.
1920 Disestablishment of the Church in Wales.
1920 University College, Swansea.
1922 Urdd Gobaith Cymru (Welsh League of Youth).

FIRST LINES OF POEMS

LIST OF AUTHORS

LIST OF AUTHORS

OTHER SOURCES

LIST OF TRANSLATORS